FILTHY QUEENS

A History of Beer
in Ireland

Dr Christina Wade

NINE BEAN ROWS

FILTHY QUEENS

A History of Beer
in Ireland

For George, my furry supervisor and all-round partner in crime.
I couldn't have done any of this without you.

CONTENTS

INTRODUCTION: COMMUNING WITH GHOSTS

ITS LURE WAS UNDENIABLE.

From the doors of Shamus Brady's public house, scents of butter, sugar, whiskey and beer tempted passers-by, a siren's song so strong that men were forced to take a detour home lest they catch even a small waft and have to go in.

Served 'screeching hot' to any and all who came to Brady's pub, scolteen was beer mixed with whiskey, eggs, butter, sugar and spices to create something perhaps uniquely Irish.[1] Though 'screeching hot' beer sounds like something most of us would rather avoid, for centuries heated ale was not only endured but desired. It was a popular drink served in public houses in 19th-century Ireland and was the backbone of recipes like lambswool (made from warm ale and roasted apples) and posset.

Our 'screeching hot' version comes from Isabella Travers Steward's *The Interdict*. Steward was born in Cork in 1796 and devoted much of her life to writing, creating poetry and finishing a total of five novels. But she isn't the only source for this delightful mixed drink. In *The Scenery and Antiquities of Ireland*, written around 1841 by J. Stirling Coyne and N.P. Willis, Mr Inglis recalls the virtues of the beverage served at a public house tucked away on the shores of Lough Gill in Co. Sligo, though this version also included caraway seeds. He tells readers that throngs of customers came to this lovely lakeside spot to sample cups of the stuff while taking in the spectacular view of the lough.[2]

We aren't so different from our ancestors. We love our hot whiskeys to cure all manner of colds. We drink spiced wines and ciders while taking in the lights at Christmas markets. In the Bavarian city of Regensburg, you may even be served a mulled beer. Suffice it to say we can relate to all those customers sitting on the banks of a lake more than 150 years ago with their lovely hot alcoholic drinks, admiring the scenery.

One line Steward wrote in *The Interdict* perfectly encapsulates our approach in this book: 'Thus did we hold converse with the dead, each in a chosen nook; oftimes interchanging thoughts and sympathies, quoting or reciting from a favoured author.'[3] In this passage, Steward describes a family's reading activities, each person tucking themselves away in a corner to read books written by those long since deceased. Reading aloud to each other and including those words, written centuries before, in the family's current conversations was a way to reconnect with those figures from the past. In this practice, these ancestors are not passive actors, but active participants in the discourse of the day. The words of the departed aren't irrelevant, but are alive and alight with wisdom and consequence. This will be much the same in this book. As we progress, we will speak with these spirits, learning much from their lives and even their deaths.

[3]

Beer is in many ways the perfect medium to go about this. It's often easy for us to treat the past like another planet and the people who lived there as entirely alien to us. But it's hard to do that when you see them doing exactly what you might be doing this weekend: having a beer with friends, telling stories to each other in a pub or ranting to your colleagues about how bad a specific brewery is. Much as we do now, so have people done for millennia. In this book, you'll find that, at least in terms of beer history, things aren't all that different. We make business deals over a few pints. We get married with kegs of beer. We pair our dinners with tasting samples of a variety of brews. We treasure our favourite drinks and like to argue over why they are superior.

In this book you'll find early medieval monks who wrote beer reviews so terrible any Untappd fan would feel right at home; Christmas beers brewed especially for those long, cold nights; and an 18th-century courtesan who had a delightfully wicked streak of beer snobbery. There will be beer tastings, parties, music and wakes. We'll meet thieves and murderers, saints and goddesses. We'll hear stories of kings and paupers, witches and bishops, of Irish, English and Vikings, starting in the Late Iron Age and going all the way up to the early 20th century.

And we can't forget the laws. From medieval edicts about malt quality to early modern water regulations, there are so very many rules. So. Many. Some things never change. Of course, there will be some marked differences too, notably the human sacrifice. Oh, and the zombies.

The history of beer is intimately intertwined with the history of us. We'll look at this ubiquitous brew alongside some of the biggest events in the story of Ireland, including the arrival of the Vikings, the English invasion and colonisation, the 1641 Rebellion, the Great Hunger, Daniel O'Connell and the cause of Catholic Emancipation, and more. We will barely skim the surface of these events before diving into the role of beer in them, so where I can, I recommend further reading. I've also included notes for each chapter at the end of the book.

Two brief caveats before we move on. The first is that this work will deal with some topics that could be quite upsetting. There will be mentions of murder, torture, rape, cannibalism, colonisation, slavery, human sacrifice and all manner of atrocities. Keep that in mind as we progress.

The second is that in 1922, a fire tore through the Public Records Office at the Four Courts in Dublin, destroying the building and countless historical documents. While incredible efforts have been made recently to recreate many of these lost works, the impact that this loss has had on the history of Ireland is profound.[4] Unfortunately, especially compared with many other countries, we have a dearth of records, so throughout this book, especially in the early chapters, I will be using what we *do* have. These can often be literary sources or myths, which of course might not be factual, but they can still reveal a bit about the society that made them. Each of these works is valuable for understanding beer history if we look closely enough.

As we go through the book I will try to make connections between the past to tangible places that you can visit now. Whether they are buildings that still dot the landscape or ruins of walls that once enclosed our cities, I will relate to things that you can see or maybe even touch. These might be artefacts found in our museums, things that you pass on your daily commute or maybe even something that was once buried in your town. It could even be your pint glass or what kind of beer you're drinking. And not just things, but also ideas, such as the folklore that you can still hear at your local pub or the reasons why we drink at funerals.

But before we get too far into it, let me lay out the chapters to give you a better idea of what we will explore.

Focusing on the lives of Irish saints, in Chapter 1 we investigate medieval brewing in religious communities. We look to the stories of

St Brigid, St Patrick and others to learn about the role of ale in these monastic communities. Exploring stories of miraculous brew days, bathtub beers and eternity spent drinking the stuff, we compare Ireland's brewing nuns to elsewhere in Europe to get an idea of whether Ireland was particularly unusual in this regard or perhaps following an accepted norm. And don't forget the demons!

In Chapter 2, we shift our focus from the religious to the secular, looking at early medieval Irish brewing in the lives of laypeople. Investigating myths, legal codes and the rights of kings, we tease fact from fiction to learn how important ale was to power and dominance, as well as finding out just who the worst guests in an alehouse were.

Chapter 3 marks the arrival of the Vikings, and with them their own ale rituals. We look at some of the unique traditions of these invaders as well as how medieval Scandinavian and Irish culture amalgamated after their arrival. We explore the different types of Viking ales alongside stories of human sacrifice and cannibalism. And don't forget those aforementioned zombies.

Chapter 4 heralds the English invasion and colonisation of Ireland in 1169. Like the Vikings before them, the English brought their own ale traditions with them. This chapter explores the years between the first invasion to the arrival of the Black Death and considers the impact ale had on both Irish and English lives as well as legal dramas.

In Chapter 5, we explore Ireland after the Plague, looking at how a fascination with death manifested in funeral ales and burial rituals. We take a deeper dive into what kinds of brews might have been made in English-held Ireland and how women played a central role in brewing. Importantly, we also investigate the alewife-as-witch myth to discover the truth brewing under the surface in Irish history.

Chapter 6 sees us progressing into the early modern period, where we disentangle the lives of alewives from the fictions written about them and examine why one author decided to call the brewing women of Dublin 'filthy queens'. Importantly, this chapter also considers the place of ale and beer in the 1641 Rebellion, looking at the 1641 Depositions to glean the importance brewing had not only to the military might, but also to the average person.

Exploring the state of brewing in 18th-century Ireland, Chapter 7 examines the porter wars between English and Irish breweries and how these defined the era. Examining newspaper articles, adverts and even the memoirs of Ireland's most famous courtesan, this chapter looks at how Irish porter came to be associated with patriotism, even while the industry itself fell into decline. We also consider where we might still find women brewing in this century, years after many were pushed from the trade. On this note, we also look at women brewing for their own households through recipe books and letters, even finding evidence of one woman asleep at the mash tun, so to speak.

Building on this, Chapter 8 examines the upswing of the Irish brewing industry in the 19th century and the increasing politicisation of the trade. Importantly, we also consider the 'beer gap' and why many people in Ireland were too poor to afford the beverage except on special occasions. We also learn about the huge industrial breweries that defined the nation at the end of the century and why one brewery had a copper (a vessel used in brewing) so big it could fit a house inside it. Finally, we look at the role women played in commercial breweries and where they might be found even after they were largely pushed out of the trade.

So sit back, relax and maybe even make yourself a bit of scolteen.[5] Or if that isn't quite your style, crack open an Irish stout or porter. As I've said before, fully immersing your senses in the history is a wonderful way to connect with those who are long lost to the annals of time. Drinking a beer is something people have been doing for millennia, so it's the perfect way to embrace the past and those who lived before us. It's a way to connect with the stories and people written about in these pages and to feel a kinship with them. And thus shall we go, as we commune with our ghosts in this book.

A GODDESS,
A NUN AND A
SAINT WALK INTO
A BREWERY

SHE STOLE *EVERYTHING*.

Filched, poached, nicked, swindled, purloined – whatever you want to call it, she was up to her neck in it. From swords to butter, anything of value that she could get her hands on was quickly liberated from her father's house. However, this particular penchant for the five-finger discount wasn't because she fancied herself a wealthy woman. No, much like Robin Hood and his Merry Men, she was stealing from the rich to give to the poor. But in contrast to the strict doctrine of Thou Shalt Not Steal, she had the Christian god's blessing to get up to her thieving antics. In fact, it was in many ways because of her complete disregard for property ownership that people who met her recognised her holiness.

And just who is this paragon of morality? It's none other than St Brigid herself.

As you can imagine, this did not exactly endear her to her family. In fact, her father decided that they'd had enough and tried to sell her off into slavery to a king of Leinster. But while he goes to proposition this king, *he leaves her with his very expensive, very valuable sword*. You know, to watch over while he conducts his business. Smart decision.

What happened next is obvious to even the most casual observer. In true Brigid form, she stole that sword and gave it to the nearest sick person. Interestingly, the king concludes that it is precisely because she is completely unapologetic about her thievery that she is very holy. Of course. To wit, he asks her if she would steal his wealth and cattle, to which she essentially replies 'obviously', and that she would then give it all away. The king takes this as a sign of her piety and sends her to be a nun, which is precisely what she'd wanted in the first place.[1]

It's among these stories of her religious life, deeply entwined with her miracles, that we find a relationship with that most important of beverages: ale.

A saint, a goddess and a nun walk into a brewery...

What sounds like a set-up to a dad joke is in fact the fascinating origin of a famous figure who is possibly an amalgamation of all three characters: The Nun, The Goddess and The Saint. It's fitting that our journey begins with Brigid, who personifies the melding of traditions and cultures, much like Irish beer history: a goddess who became a saint, a nun who blended with ancient traditions. Her murky origins were perhaps begged, borrowed and stolen from pagan cultures to mix with Christian traditions, producing something wholly new and uniquely Irish, much like our cultural brewing traditions would be.

Stories of our Brigid are veiled in mystery, though several folkloric origins have varying degrees of possibility. Some modern writers contend that she was originally a goddess, while others say she was always a nun. What we actually have written evidence for is very, very little. From medieval annalistic sources, we are told that she was born around 451 CE. Her death is recorded in the *Annals of Tigernach* and the *Chronicum Scotorum* in 525 CE.[2] We can't know for sure. We are told she founded the double monastery at Kildare, which translates from the Irish, *Cill Dara*, to mean Church of the Oak, and that she performed countless miracles.

To be clear, there is no scholarly consensus on whether or not Brigid even existed. We have no writings from the woman herself and we have no sources about her that were made in her lifetime.

For example, the earliest source we can identify was written by a monk in Kildare called Cogitosus in the 7th century, more than 150 years after she died, not to mention that his work might have been politically motivated.[3] Some scholars argue that this work was a response to the early medieval English church and their challenges to the monastic power in Kildare, where Brigid's religious community lay.[4] Others contend it was written because of the power struggles between the religious orders in Kildare and Armagh.[5]

Furthermore, of particular importance to us is the fact that Cogitosus' St Brigid is one of the first, if not *the* first, lives of a saint in Ireland. He didn't have any other home-grown works to base his writings on, so he essentially had to create his own genre within Irish monastic literature (though there would have been plenty of saints' lives coming from the European continent that he would most likely have been familiar with).[6]

As with any written work, the audience is key. Every author has some kind of bias, some underlying drive to even choose their topic, let alone decide how it's presented. Oral traditions that were passed down over the centuries before eventually being written down long after they originated form the backbone of many medieval studies, but we must try to disentangle the bias of the writers who finally put the stories to paper from what the original tales might have revealed. It's like a game of telephone where over the years, without strict protocols in the retellings, the original truths can get missed for all the misunderstandings, or sometimes even blatant fictions. Plus the people writing the stories, like Cogitosus, may have had real reasons for choosing to tell the story or to present the life of Brigid in a certain way.

These issues with sources and the distance in time from their subject are going to be problems throughout Irish history, one that we will revisit again and again. But we're in luck with our stories of Brigid, whether it's Cogitosus' writings or some later accounts, because in our study of beer history we don't actually need to worry so much about whether or not she was real. The stories of Brigid can tell us a lot about the people who wrote them and the communities that made up their audience. They were writing what they knew or perhaps what they saw in their own lifetimes. While the tales contained in these works may not themselves be true, they can reveal to us the truth of brewing and drinking ale in early medieval Ireland.

As for the stories about Brigid, they might tell us quite a bit about what life was like in medieval nunneries – and more to the point, what brewing might have been like there. Brigid herself often appears to have made up her own rules. In between founding monastic communities and praying, she also spent quite a bit of time defying the laws of physics. In one instance, she exploded both her own eye and two belonging to a nobleman in a fierce reply to his insolent remarks regarding her taking the veil. But making ale was her forte and she wasn't going to let a pesky little thing like science slow her down.

ಶ

In the second half of the 5th century, Brigid's newly consecrated nuns gathered together to formulate a plan – or perhaps more likely, to panic.

Brigid had decided she was going to brew some ale for Easter. However, she appears to have chosen to do this at the very last minute. You see, at this time the festivities surrounding this High Holiday were of critical importance to the newly formed and developing Christian Church, so it wasn't something to screw up.[7] This was a new move by Brigid as we are told that brewing at Easter time wasn't usual, so the nuns weren't exactly prepared. More to the point, there simply wasn't enough malt or equipment to carry out this task – or at least, that's how it appeared.

But Brigid was determined, so she turned to her divine connections for help. And so the one measure of malt was enough to supply all of the surrounding churches for at least nine days in total.[8]

But she didn't stop there.

After her first miraculous brew day, she decided that she wanted even more ale for the bishop. However, this time she decided to forgo the brewing process altogether and go straight for the miracle, turning some water she had handy into ale.[9] But this wasn't just your normal, average ale. This ale, we are told, was the best ale in the world and had an aroma like wine.[10]

What is particularly striking is that Brigid brewing and providing ale for the people around her wasn't mentioned as a remarkable task, miraculous brew day aside. It's clearly written as though her nuns would know how to brew. Brigid knew that having only one measure of malt and limited equipment for all those people was too little. The nuns knew that too, hence the panic. It was a miracle that it could be done. Indeed, the only thing that's miraculous is the amount she was able to produce and how she was able to produce it. This likely implies that at the time this story of her life was written, religious women in Ireland were brewing at monastic sites even if it wasn't normally done at Easter time.

The Easter tale isn't Brigid's only association with miraculous ale. She had a penchant for creating ale from thin air, or more accurately, water. In a lesser-known story, she turned well water into three jugs of ale to cure her ailing foster mother.[11] But perhaps the most famous tale that makes the rounds on beer blogs is the bathtub beer. This has often been misinterpreted as her turning her own bathwater into ale, but this is not quite the case. Instead, in the original version, Brigid came across some people who had contracted leprosy. They were suffering from thirst and begged her for some ale. As she wasn't carrying casks of it in her pockets, she realised she would have to make some. Luckily, she had her well-established skill set of miraculous brews and she happened to see some water nearby that had been prepared for bathing, so she blessed it, thus turning it into the miracle ale.[12]

I will conclude with one final tale before we move on. In 'Brigid's Prayer', a medieval Irish poem, our titular character says that she thinks heaven is a giant lake of beer and that she wants to watch Jesus and the rest of the 'heavenly family' drink for 'all eternity'. In other versions, she includes all the people of heaven drinking. I've got lots of questions about the logistics of this, mostly related to sanitation, though these probably aren't concerns in the afterlife. Overall, I have to say that spending perpetuity with, or in, a giant lake of ale doesn't sound too shabby. Thus, drinking ale was an important – you could even say divine – part of life in medieval Ireland, something you might want to carry on doing throughout your immortal existence.

You can still find echoes of Brigid's community. Tucked away in the middle of the Kildare town centre, behind the shops and pubs, is Kildare Cathedral, also known, of course, as St Brigid's. Originally built by the Norman Bishop Ralph of Bristol in 1223, it was allegedly made on the site that Brigid herself had used for her monastery. Over the centuries, the cathedral had fallen into ruins and needed extensive rebuilding in the 19th century, incorporating the old stone works into the new building. Within its walls you can find hints of its past, with early modern vaults and tombs.

St Brigid has become the stuff of beer legends here in Ireland, and many a modern brewer has taken notice of her connection to our favourite beverage. Kildare is also home to Two Sisters Brewing, run by Judith and Susan Boyle, fifth-generation publicans who made Brigid's Ale using local malts and honey.

It's not just in the stories of Brigid, however, that we can see evidence for brewing in religious houses. Historians like Richard Unger clearly demonstrate that brewing ale was part and parcel of religious life for both men and women throughout the European continent.[13] The Irish archaeological material also supports such a claim. All over Ireland, archaeological sites of these medieval monastic communities reveal much to us about life in those places and, importantly, about brewing. At Glendalough, these investigations have even revealed malted barley, according to the exhibition at the National Museum of Ireland– Archaeology. More than 800 cereal-drying kilns have been found and excavated in the country in the past 30 years or so, most of which date to the medieval period, specifically between the 4th and 13th centuries.[14] Some of these kilns were found directly on these monastic sites or church settlements[15] and could have played a critical role in malting barley or other grains like rye, oats or wheat for making ale.

Tracy Collins's groundbreaking work, *Female Monasticism in Medieval Ireland: An Archaeology*, provides deeper insights into what nuns might have been getting up to in their communities.[16] Collins argues that these monastic enclosures would have had things like barns, fishponds, orchards and, critically, brewhouses. Much of her evidence comes from later medieval sources, but we can extrapolate that the brewing at these places didn't suddenly begin at this time, but rather had carried on since at least the time of Cogitosus' writing. It's certainly a possibility, as we saw in the stories of St Brigid.

At the nunnery in Kilculliheen in Waterford, Collins found that a granary was once listed at the site.[17] In addition to evidence for this granary, she found a fiant regarding this nunnery that offers more conclusive clues. A fiant is a kind of warrant created by the council or deputy to the Irish chancery to make letters patent. Letters patent were legal orders, issued by the king in this instance, to grant things like pardons, rights, titles, property and the like.[18] This fiant says there were rooms for corn processing and brewing at Kilculliheen, which led Collins to naturally conclude that brewing had been taking place there.

This wasn't the only evidence that she found. Timolin, a nunnery in Co. Kildare, had extensive holdings, stretching to Wicklow, Kilkenny and even Limerick. It was here that she discovered a different kind of link between brewing and monastic communities, something that will appear later in our text with some frequency: ale as a tithe. Collins found that the tenants of Timolin, particularly those who brewed and sold their product commercially, gave one gallon of ale to the nunnery each time they made it.[19] This might not seem like a significant amount, but as we will see in Chapter 4, it could prove to be quite a burden.

Of course, it wasn't just brewing ale that was important – so was drinking it. Ale was a critical part of the diet and as such held an important place in religious life. The women and men who lived in these places brewed it for their own consumption as well as for their local communities, as Brigid's tales tell us. This continued throughout the Middle Ages. From the time Brigid existed to long after she died, monks and nuns drank ale as part of their daily diet.

Though slightly outside the scope of our current chapter, perhaps one of the most famous nuns to ever exist, Hildegarde von Bingen, wrote extensively about her experiences with ale and brewing in 12th-century Germany. From her we can learn not only that she and her fellow nuns drank ale, but that they also drank water, wine and other beverages. She writes that if a person wants to make a light meal for the evening, called a *meranda*, they can soak pieces of bread in wine, beer or water. Each has their own benefits, she writes. The version soaked in wine doesn't do much good and can make a person's insides dry out; the beer version is better, she remarks, likely because beer and bread are close cousins. But the best version is water because it's 'more healthful'.[20] Throughout her work, she recommends various times when ale, or beer, might be preferred to wine or water, and vice versa. She doesn't recommend drinking plain water when a person is suffering from psychosis; instead, she recommends consuming a potion of water and costmary alongside beer.[21] She tells readers that a person whose lungs are bad should drink beer over water or even wine.[22] She also recommends that women drink beer, or also wine, if they are struggling with prolonged periods.[23]

Von Bingen wrote a lot about the use of ale with medicine, but we will tackle that subject later on in this book. Our last bit from Hildegarde before we place her in context is that in her opinion, hops aren't much use to humans, except perhaps as a preservative for beverages because of their bitterness.[24]

You could accuse me here of doing the very thing I mentioned at the start of the chapter regarding the stories of Brigid written well after her death – namely, using much later sources to justify something so far in the past – but it's important to establish a continuity of behaviour. Brigid and her nuns, if they existed, didn't invent brewing at their community, and they also weren't the last to do so. Nuns (and monks) brewed, and drank, ale throughout the Middle Ages, and not just in Ireland, but throughout Europe.

Furthermore, we have to look at the sources that still exist. As I mentioned in the introduction, we simply don't have many sources from the medieval period here in Ireland because they were destroyed in the 1922 Four Courts fire, so sometimes we have to look elsewhere to see if similar things happened in other countries to reach meaningful conclusions based on the data that we do have – data that tells us that brewing took place in Ireland in religious communities. Before we return to those early medieval brewing days from an Irish monk's perspective, I want to share one more later medieval tale that comes from Caesarius of Heisterbach, Germany, written around 1223. While it's a different country and a different time period, it's a good example of how drinking ale wasn't limited to Ireland but was, in fact, a widespread occurrence. Plus it's a great story.

Poor Sister Euphemia had been tormented by demons ever since she was a small child. They spent years harassing her and pressuring her to marry. The demons specifically demanded that she find a rich, young, good-looking husband who would give her nice clothes and fancy food instead of taking her vows as a nun.[25]

This might not sound like a bad deal to modern readers, but Euphemia was determined to choose her own destiny and she wanted to be a nun. When she refused the infernal request to wed, she asked one demon what would happen next. Naturally, he tried to chuck her out of a window. Apparently, defenestration was a diabolical means of handling naysayers. Not to worry, though! She was saved by divine angelic intervention. But the demons continued to follow her.

One stormy night (because nothing spooky ever happens on a peaceful evening), Sister Euphemia found herself unable to sleep in her convent. As she lay awake in her bed, she suddenly saw what at first glance appeared to be her two best nun friends. They beckoned to her, calling out in the darkness that they should all go down to the cellar to drink some ale.

But Euphemia was not so easily fooled. You see, not only had they broken their rule of silence, but it was also a ridiculous hour to be suggesting to go off drinking. Euphemia knew as soon as they spoke that they were in fact hellish creatures come to tempt her into the sin of drunkenness. So she enacted that most bulletproof of safety measures, used by children and adults alike to hide from monstrous closet-dwelling beings and the creatures that live under the bed: she hid under the covers.

Unfortunately for Euphemia, her strategy was only marginally effective, as 'one of the evil spirits came near, and laid his hand upon her breast, pressing it with so much violence, that blood was driven out in great quantities through her mouth and nose'.[26] After torturing Euphemia in this manner for a bit, these demonic entities changed into great dogs, leapt out of the window and vanished into the ether from whence they came.

Besides lots of demonic entries and exits through windows, our story of Sister Euphemia tells us that brewing was an important part of life in the nunnery – that they had ale on hand to drink and that it was a part of their diet. It also hints that the brewing was conducted on site with the mention of the convent beer. We have seen that this was the case across religious settlements.

Critically, we are also introduced to the idea that drinking could be associated with demons. Ale itself might not be viewed as dangerous, but the temptation of demons and their calls for her to live a secular life of sin might push its use into evil. Ale was perhaps one of those liminal things, existing as both good and evil, depending on how you consumed it. If we dig deeper into the stories of Irish saints, we can see that this was also the view in early medieval Ireland.

The life of another Irish saint, Columban, a missionary who lived around 540–615 CE, reveals a close encounter with Satan himself. Unlike other stories in which the demons were compelling our pious characters to act in a wanton manner, here the devil was in the drink.

Columban went out among the Swabians, who at this time worshipped Wodan. He found them preparing to sacrifice their ale to this god in what he termed a 'heathen offering'. Columban was not best pleased. In fact, he was enraged by what he believed to be an abomination. He approached this cask of ale and breathed upon it. The force of his breath caused it to fall and smash to pieces, the ale running from its remains. You see, according to Columban, the devil himself was concealed in the cask, and it was through the ale that he desired to infect the worshippers with his evil and steal their very souls. We are told that the 'heathens' were amazed by Columban's actions of the day.[27]

Besides being a complete waste of perfectly good ale, this story is depressing for another reason: it represents the destruction of non-Christian beliefs under an increasingly fanatical Church. But this story is not true. It's a trope, a kind of writing meant to highlight the holiness of the saint and the wickedness of non-believers. We know this because the author, Monk Jonas, is fairly obvious in his intentions and also because he mixes up pagan ideologies, assuming that the god Wodan of the Germanic tribes is the same as the Roman god Mercury. Nonetheless, it's an interesting story that reiterates the importance of ale in broader medieval Europe.

It also illuminates another concept: that ale and drunkenness could be gateways to problematic behaviours, or in this case, the very loss of your immortal soul. It's reminiscent of Sister Euphemia and her demonic peer pressure and is yet another example of the intertwining of ale with demons, much in contrast to our miraculous brews. Ale could be saint and sinner, healer and destroyer. This dichotomy will be visible throughout Irish beer history.

On the opposite end of the spectrum, St Columban performed a miracle to increase the amount of ale that was held in a monastic community. Essentially, the cellarer – that is, the person in charge of brewing and storing beer in the community – brought up some ale but forgot to plug the vessel it was stored in before he went to see St Columban and so feared that nothing would be left upon his return. However, with a little help from the saint, 'he saw the beer (ale) had run into the jar and not the least drop had fallen outside, so that you would have believed that the jar had doubled in size'.[28]

In another tale, when Columban arrived at the monastery of Fontaines in France, he came upon 60 brothers who had only two loaves of bread and very little ale among them. When he heard this, he told them to bring these to him, whereupon Columban prayed to his God and these multiplied enough to satisfy every man in attendance with plenty of leftovers.[29]

Of course, we can't talk about Irish saints without mentioning Patrick. When St Patrick wasn't driving out all the snakes from the island, he was driving out poison from ale. In the later medieval *Betha Phatraic*, or *On the Life of Saint Patrick*, he was off visiting a king whereupon a wizard, or druid, depending on the translation, added poison to his ale. But Patrick was on to him, and he 'blessed the cruse and inverted the vessel, and the poison fell there out, and not even a little of the ale fell. Patrick afterwards drank the ale.'[30] Further, we have the saint blessing a town with an 'abundance of food and ale and prosperity in this city after us',[31] thus highlighting the importance of ale to the upkeep of the town.

That same text mentions Cruimther Mescan, who was St Patrick's brewer.[32] The name Mescan is still synonymous with good beer in Ireland, as that is the name of the Irish craft brewery that specialises in making Belgian beers. Like the case with Brigid's nuns, this suggests that brewing was being conducted at his monastic community.

Like Brigid, Patrick is linked with ale over and over again in the stories about him. In one decidedly fictional story, he travelled to Dublin on a trip of conversion for the Scandinavians living there, something that wouldn't have been possible until Patrick had been in the ground for four centuries. But like Brigid's story, it doesn't matter all that much if it's true.

It may tell us about the writer or about what the writer knew of Ireland or religious life. In this tale, the male heir apparent to the kingdom of Dublin and his sister had died on the same day. Patrick had already begun to raise people from the dead, so the king, hearing this, promised all prayers to God if Patrick would spare and revive his two offspring. Lo and behold, Patrick was able to cheat death and bring them back. From then on, offerings from the city would be made to Patrick and his successors, and among this tribute was 'of every tavern a vessel of mead or of ale'.[33]

This tribute of ale to monastic communities is critical. While this story is fictional, a toll of ale and mead given to religious groups was something that certainly existed in medieval Ireland and spanned centuries, as we saw from Collins's study at the nunnery at Timolin.

We can see that ale features prominently in the lives of early medieval Irish saints. What this tells us is that ale was perhaps ubiquitous in these circles. It was part of daily life and an important, but mundane, part of their diet. St Brigid's brewing nuns, St Columban's miraculous multiplying ales and St Patrick's brewer and his tithe in ale all serve to demonstrate the role of this beverage in medieval food culture. Irish medieval monks and nuns drank and brewed ale, much like their Continental counterparts. While these stories are not necessarily true, they can tell us what the culture of their authors was like. They reveal to us that for both the author and their readers, brewing monks and nuns weren't something absurd or ridiculous. They are presented as a matter of course and were likely accepted as such.

But not every religious community in Ireland was thrilled about the blasé consumption of ale.

Let's venture beyond the stories of saints' lives now to look at writings from Irish monks themselves. But first, I want to give you a bit of context for these men so that you can better understand why they believed what they did. Specifically, I want to disabuse you of the notion that these monasteries were tranquil communities of pacifists who spent all their time in prayer and devotion.

Many of us have heard tales of the Vikings coming over and sacking churches and monasteries. They are presented as horrific invaders desecrating the holiest places in Ireland. But the Irish were quite capable of sacking religious places themselves, and not only by secular rulers, but sometimes by other church communities. These communities went to war with each other, and everyone else for that matter.[34] Kildare sacked Tallaght in 824 CE. The vice-abbot of Kildare died fighting the Vikings at Donamase. In 760 CE, a priest killed a bishop, Echtigen, by Brigid's altar in Kildare, and henceforth no priests performed mass there in front of a bishop.[35] In 807 CE, Cork went to war with Clonfert and the King of Munster, Feidhlimidh Mac Crimthainn, who was also a Céli Dé monk who went off and plundered many abbeys ... like Kildare. These weren't just bastions of mild-mannered people contemplating the vagaries of life (well, maybe they did in between their musings on the importance of violence to the maintenance of power).

The Céli Dé monks weren't just busy engaging in warfare in their free time. They were also hard at work figuring out if they should be drinking ale.

In the 8th century, two prominent Céli Dé reformers, Máelrúain of Tallaght and Dublittir of Finglas, had much to say on this matter.[36] Tallaght and Finglas are now part of the larger urban sprawl of Dublin, but at this time they were separate religious communities, and quite prominent ones at that, referred to as 'the eyes of Ireland'.[37]

Céli Dé put an 'emphasis on individual piety' and 'a rejection of the world'.[38] But Máelrúain and Dublittir had conflicting thoughts on drinking ale. They both believed that the enjoyment of food was sinful. Keep in mind, though, that what a monk preached and the lived reality of his monastic community might be two very different things. This sounds at a minimum like wishful thinking or just pure delusion, as it was probably quite difficult to never enjoy your food. But the monks apparently made strenuous attempts to do just that.

They argued that drinking whey and water was fine, with some consumption of milk.[39] However, they had a bit of a row over the place of ale in their diet. Dublittir argued that members should be allowed to drink ale at certain times. Máelrúain vehemently opposed this idea and would not consider it in the slightest because ale equals enjoyment equals sin, to which Dublittir quipped that his monks would still get into heaven.[40]

While Máelrúain might have been morally opposed to drinking ale, and more to the point, its enjoyment, other monastic communities held it in high esteem. To that end, let's return to St Columban. In his *Monks' Rules*, he states that if a monk spills ale, he has to cough up a supply for 'an equal number of days what he had been accustomed to receive lawfully for his own use'. He must also realise that he'd lost his ale-quaffing privileges due to his own actions and had to drink water instead.[41] The horror of drinking water over ale! This tells us how highly valued ale was to the monks following the rules of St Columban, so much so that it was a sacrifice to give up this ale and drink water instead.

Medieval Europeans did not necessarily think that water was dangerous. They drank water, as we saw in the writings of Hildegarde von Bingen. The whole 'ale was safer than water' myth implies that ale was boiled, rendering it 'safer'. But medieval ales weren't necessarily boiled, though they could be. Also remember that we're still talking about a time well before the arrival of germ theory. That all-important bit of knowledge that revealed that microscopic organisms cause disease wasn't floating around in the medieval period. Instead, diseases could be caused by unbalanced humours, poison, miasma, planetary misalignment or that old perennial favourite, God's wrath, to name but a few commonly believed causes.

That said, medieval people knew that water could be unhealthy or dangerous in certain circumstances. They linked it to the Black Death, for example, but in that instance the water was believed to have been poisoned. Some medieval writers also advised against drinking water in the instance of specific illnesses, like we saw in von Bingen's writings. Suffice it to say that while medieval people drank water and it was an important part of their diet, many of them may have just preferred ale in many circumstances, not to mention that it might have had significant nutritional value.

In any event, Columban finishes his rules by saying that if a monk spills ale on the table, it's essentially okay to just say sorry.[42] Columban also tells the monks that they should 'drink such as to avoid intoxication'.[43] Much like we saw with our Tallaght vs. Finglas monks and their debate on drinking ale, the goal here was to avoid too much enjoyment. Having said all that, some Irish monks were exceedingly fussy about their ale and it all centred around enjoyment.

Sedulius Scottus was part of a contingent of Irish monks who went to the European continent, likely to escape the Vikings – or that's how the story goes. He wrote about his journey in one of his poems, '*Flamina Nos Boreae*'. Importantly for our purposes, he most likely wrote this entire poem of complaint to Bishop Hartgar, who he stayed with during his time in Liège, Belgium.[44] This work was all about the ale he was served there in the mid-9th century and he had a lot of opinions, none of them particularly positive.

Sedulius notes that the beer produced there was weak, which in turn made the drinkers so.[45] He accuses the ale of being completely unpalatable and utterly undrinkable, arguing that it made those who consumed it sad. He makes several references to Roman mythology by invoking Ceres, who was the goddess of agriculture, fertility, the harvest and, most importantly for us, grain. In fact, in his poem, Sedulius accuses the ale of pretending to be her child, which it decidedly was not. Essentially, he is lamenting the fact that the ale is not sweet and has no relation to Ceres, perhaps insinuating that it has no relationship to actual grains and is made from some unknown quantity.

The final reference that reveals something about this Belgian ale is that he says it was born of the Cedron, a river that appears in the Hebrew Bible as well as the Christian New Testament. Its name means 'dark' or possibly 'dusky', which suggests that the ale was cloudy, as Max Nelson also noted. If we trust Sedulius' description of this brew, we might get an idea that it was a bitter, weak, cloudy ale that was pretending to pass itself off as something better than it was.

And what did Sedulius suggest doing about this horrible beverage? He said that God should wipe it from the earth. In fact, he thought that the ale should be drowned (though precisely how one drowns a liquid is not yet known). Sedulius hated this beer so much that he wanted it to be tortured for eternity in the same way drinking it apparently tormented him.

So what does this reference reveal to us? Well, it certainly tells us that Sedulius was *dramatic*. That's an awful lot of words to say the beer is weak and bitter. I've had some drain-pour beers in my day, but I've never been tempted to wish the beer should be cruelly tortured. I have certainly never read a review on Untappd hoping that the beer could be hidden in the River Styx or drowned in the rivers of Hades. Perhaps someone should up their game.

One of the interesting things Sedulius does touch on is the differences between the style or even the quality of ale he was getting in Ireland versus what he found in Belgium. In that regard, he might be dead on. The ales would have been different, though not necessarily better or worse, though he clearly had a strong preference for those from home, as he emphatically proves in his (not a single bit melodramatic) poem. To dig a bit deeper on what the ale would have tasted like in early medieval Ireland, we turn to our next chapter and our study on brewing in the secular and legal sources.

MY DRINKING HORN IS BETTER THAN YOUR DRINKING HORN

IF YOU LIKE TO DRINK BEER – and I'm going to go out on a limb here and assume you at least have a passing interest in it – then you're probably familiar with drinking games. Flip cup, cards, quarters. At this point, beer pong could almost be an Olympic sport. In fact, there was actually a World Series of Beer Pong featuring players from more than 15 countries that ran from 2006 to 2019 in Las Vegas, not to mention the more local competitive circuits all over the world, like the famous Swiss Series of Beer Pong.

Many of us like to liven up our pints with a bit of friendly competition. It's all meant to be just a bit of fun, not taken too seriously, and nothing where the risks are too high. Medieval people weren't all that different. They, too, liked to play games, but with one glaring difference: for some, the stakes couldn't be higher.

To say King Bricriu was a bit devious would be an understatement. The man fancied himself something of an evil genius, manipulating those around him according to his various whims. You can almost picture him as a cartoon villain, rubbing his hands together in glee as he manoeuvred people into competition with one another. To put a fine point on it, though, he wasn't quite as crafty as he believed himself to be; more Doctor Evil than Doctor Lecter, if you see what I mean.

Nevertheless, after inviting three formidable warriors to his feast, he decided to pit them against each other by withholding the champion's portion, a particularly excellent selection of food and drink. This share was desirable not only for the delicious fare it promised, but also for the high status attached to those who consumed it. Naturally, shenanigans ensued.

The story comes from *The Feast of Bricriu* and the three warriors in question were Cú Chulainn, Conall Cernach and Lóegaire Búadach, who tried to outdo each other in a series of competitions in Munster, Connacht and Navan Fort, including vying for who had the prettiest, fanciest, most expensive cup as proof of their victories.[1]

As part of these tests, the three warriors had been sent off to Connacht to be judged by the infamous Queen Medb herself (whose name, incidentally, means 'the intoxicating one') and her husband, Ailill. They invited each warrior individually into their palace and presented each hero with a cup: to Lóegaire, one of bronze with a bird chased in white metal (silver); to Conall, one of white metal (silver) with a bird on the bottom; and to Cú Chulainn, one of gold decorated with birds and a massive precious stone.[2] It is over this drink that Medb grants each the 'feast of a champion' and tells each one that he and his wife are to precede all the Ultonian warriors and ladies, respectively. Each warrior then drinks all the wine in the cup, thus sealing the deal.[3]

But Medb and Ailill neglect to mention that they promised each warrior the champion's portion and that they gave each warrior a cup. Nor did they mention that each cup had an increasing value, one being bronze, the next silver and the final one gold. This surprise would not go over well later, when the hero who had won was to present his token of having done so and therefore be assigned the champion's portion. It reads like a kind of medieval pissing contest, with the gist being 'my cup is better than your cup, and therefore so am I'.

When the winning man is instructed to present his token, Lóegaire holds aloft his cup of bronze with a silver bird on the bottom, declaring himself the winner. Not to be outdone, Conall Cernach shows off his cup made of silver, which he proclaims to be far superior to Lóegaire's cup, and therefore it is he, not Lóegaire, who has won. At this, however, Cú Chulainn enters the fray, declaring his cup to be the finest and holding aloft his very fancy version of red gold with a bird on the bottom made of a large, precious dragon-stone.[4] After seeing this, Lóegaire and Conall accuse Cú Chulainn of, horror of horrors, *purchasing the cup*. They argue that he did not earn the cup from Medb and Ailill, but bribed them. And so they choose violence and draw their swords.[5]

At first this may seem like a ridiculous story of male posturing. You might also be wondering what a bunch of expensive cups have to do with our study of beer history, besides the obvious usage. Well, according to scholars, drinking alcohol was such an important part of early medieval European societies that it was a way to identify who was in charge. Bettina Arnold argues that the consumption of alcohol was 'central' in Celtic cultures and that it played a critical socio-political role.[6] Arnold contends that alcohol and its service could not only be a way to reinforce existing kingship, but to even establish new leaders.[7] Many scholars like Arnold, including D.A. Binchy, Charles Doherty and H. Wagner, have examined these links and reached similar conclusions.

This is evident in our story of Bricriu and the three warriors, which might have mirrored what was happening in lived reality. Historian Michael Enright analysed many early medieval Irish myths and argues that these may have reflected real life, concluding that the political hierarchy could be established by the rituals surrounding who drank what and when.[8]

Modern readers might find the story in *The Feast of Bricriu* a bit extreme, if not downright silly, but the outcome of such competitions was important to medieval audiences. The rivalry between the three warriors was something they would have understood and accepted. It was part of life as a medieval Irish king and the way they understood power and how to keep it. It isn't all that different from our modern beer games. We might not be establishing who the most powerful ruler is, but you'll certainly get bragging rights for winning a game of beer pong these days.

The cup competition determined who got the champion's portion, meaning the best food and drink but also – and this is critical – the higher-ranking social position in the hall. This story also introduces us to the concept of gift exchange and the importance of hospitality, both of which were fundamentally intertwined with ale in the Irish Middle Ages. Indeed, hospitality was an essential part of being a king, as we will see.

The entire practice of brewing and drinking ale, from what malt you used and what kind of ale it was to the cup you drank from and the order you drank it in, could all be signals of your wealth and status.[9] This continued for centuries, well into our modern era. Simply put, people used ale as a way to claim, manipulate and maintain power, and at the centre of all this were women.

ॐ

Lugh was the god of sun and light, an awe-inspiring figure in Irish mythology often depicted as a young warrior. While he can steal the spotlight in most any story, in this tale it's another figure who catches our eye.

In this instance, depicted right next to the seated Lugh is the Sovereignty of Ireland, portrayed as a young woman with a crown of gold, with a silver vat of red ale decorated in more gold, a gold dipper and a further cup of gold before her. The story is called *Baile in Scáil*, or *The Phantom's Frenzy*. Dating from the 9th century, in this tale the god Lugh presents to the King of Tara, Conn, a listing of all the rulers of his territory forevermore. However, the power of this ritual lies with this woman, the Sovereignty of Ireland. She is the host for this event. She serves all the drinks, calling out to Lugh to name the kings to reply to the question 'who shall this cup be given?'. Thus in this way did she name all the kings of Ireland until Judgement Day as she went about serving ale in Lugh's house.[10]

While this story is certainly fictional, given that we haven't reached Armageddon and we have long since left the monarchy behind, women serving ale as a way to establish the social hierarchy, as seen in this tale, likely existed in early medieval Ireland, according to many historians like Enright, Dillon and Arnold.[11] H. Wagner argues that in Celtic society, queens offered alcohol, like ale, to their chosen king as part of the inauguration ritual, much like we see here in this fictional story.[12]

The sheer breadth of examples of this ritual in Irish mythology supports this argument. Another prominent instance is in the Book of Leinster, which contains the tale of 'The Exile of the Sons of Usnech', in which the wife of Feidlimid, heavily pregnant and all, attends her husband and the men of Ulster with drinking horns of ale as well as food.[13] Enright concludes that a high-ranking woman would serve alcohol to her male counterpart (husband, father, brother) as part of an important status ritual: these high-ranking women would often serve these men while talking about their superior qualities, thus establishing his top position in the social hierarchy. Those who were served afterwards and drank were conceding their subordination to his leadership, according to Enright.[14] Basically, what it boils down to is he who drinks first has the power. You can observe this ritual across many cultures, including the three we will touch on in this book: Irish, English and Scandinavian. From the Viking sagas to the famous *Beowulf*, women serving ale and giving speeches was a ubiquitous and also prized position in this period.

If we return to our chapter's opening story, we find our crafty Bricriu up to his old tricks again, though this time he's targeting the wives of our three heroes: Fedelm, wife of Lóegaire; Lendabair, wife of Conall Cernach; and Emer, wife of Cú Chulainn. He invites all of them and their respective husbands to be the first into the banqueting hall without notifying the others, once again engaging in his favourite pastime of creating unnecessary drama.[15] Just like being the first to drink ale sent a clear signal of one's status, so did the first entrance to the hall itself, so the role was jealously guarded and fiercely competitive. In response to this slight, the 'Women's War of Words' followed, in which each woman bragged about how amazing she and her husband were. She who gave the best speech won.

Fedelm goes first, extolling her virtues and those of her husband, Lóegaire, who she declares is 'more famous than heroes, in number of victories greater'.[16] Lendabair, wife of Conall Cernach, makes sure to include the following: 'Big is his shield and triumphant, majestic his gait and commanding.'[17] However, Emer is not to be outdone and contends that she is 'the standard of women, in figure, in grace and in wisdom'.[18] She proudly recalls her husband's prowess, declaring 'blood from his spear is spurting, with life-blood his sword is dripping'[19] and that 'battles of bloody battalions, the world's proud armies he heweth'.[20]

Basically, it's just a lot of boasting, but for an important reason. While this example doesn't directly speak of ale, it does involve feasting and the mead hall, and these Irish women are using their speeches to not only establish their own prestige, but also that of their husbands within the feasting hall. This is a way for the upper echelons of women to hold and negotiate power,[21] and that power was intricately intertwined with drinking rituals.

In the *Táin Bó Cúailnge*, or *The Cattle Raid of Cooley*, Cú Chulainn, Emer's husband, had managed to enrage Queen Medb. In this story, Medb and her husband, Ailill, are trying to figure out who can defeat him. They finally decide that the only person is Cú Chulainn's own foster brother, Fer Diad. Unfortunately for Fer Diad, they basically force him to join them at their tent. He comes and they purposefully sit their daughter, Finnabair, next to him, where she plies him with drink and kisses and basically convinces him that he is her one and only, seducing him into compliance.[22] After a time, Medb and Ailill make their move to bribe him to do their bidding with all manner of material objects, including Finnabair as his consort.

Medb uses the serving and acceptance of alcohol as a way to determine who would rule and also to solidify alliances. This also demonstrates the link between women and hosting. Medb is literally a legendary woman – her exploits are revealed in the early medieval Irish mythological cycle – and she is certainly a high-status figure. Whether she was real or not, this link between status and hosting does seem to indicate that this may have been the lived reality for the author of the tale. This reiterates the idea that serving, at least the serving of certain guests, was a treasured position for women within medieval Irish society.

Many of us have owed rent to a landlord at one point or another. I'm assuming you paid with cash or some sort of bank transfer. But what if you paid your rent in beer, glassware and parties? Doesn't sound like a bad deal ... until you look into the sheer amount of things you'd need.

The *Lebor na Cert*, or *The Book of Rights*, is a 12th-century text that lists the entitlements of kings in medieval Ireland. During this period, Ireland had many kings of varying degrees of status and power. The highest-ranking kings were owed something from the lower-ranking kings as part of their rents; equally, the higher-ranking kings in turn owed things to their subordinates as part of their entitlements.

As scholar Charles Doherty explains, gift-giving was a critical part of the social fabric of early medieval Ireland.[23] Doherty says that this was a way to create ties between kings and subjects. Accepting a gift was accepting the king's superiority, while giving the gift was establishing the king's dominance.[24] Essentially, it's identical to the drinking rituals we talked about above, just on a larger scale. In return for the gifts, the subject would offer tribute to the king. Doherty argues the point of all this was to create and maintain alliances.[25] This is echoed by Arnold, who contends that the 'generosity' of a chief was part and parcel of his status – it was an expected part of his relationship to those who served him.[26]

Ale was central to these gifts in the *Lebor na Cert*. For instance, the King of Fernmag is listed as being owed six ale horns, among other things.[27] The King of Muirthemne was also entitled to six ale horns.[28] Six seems like a reasonable number, but the numbers grow and grow, with some kings owed 40, 50 or more based on their status. For the King of Cashel, 'if he be king of Ireland', the book lists the following stipends that he owed to other kings: 100 horns to the King of Cruachain, the same to the King of Ulaid, 50 to the King of Ailech and 30 to the chief of the Tulach Óc.[29] This is among other things. For example, the King of Cruachain is also owed 100 swords, 100 horses and 100 tunics. This perhaps gives us an idea of precisely how valuable these drinking horns could be if they were around the same value as a horse.[30]

This entitlement to these horns, ostensibly for drinking things like ale or mead, is demonstrated over and over in the *Lebor na Cert*. In fact, there are more than 130 mentions of drinking horns in this text. But drinking horns aren't just modes of ale consumption. Binchy and Arnold both contend that they were symbols that represented sovereignty over a place or people.[31] As Doherty argues, the drinking horns represented authority.[32] Sometimes these horns were so important, they were magickal. Or at least that's how the story goes.

Áed Oirdnide, King of Erin, had to travel to Connacht in order to get the area under control, but during his journey, his drinking horns, along with his servants, were lost in Eas Ruaid, a river.[33] Áed was apparently quite a stubborn man and refused to drink from any other vessel except for a horn because 'he never drank a draught from any other vessel, since he was weaned from his mother', and he certainly wasn't going to start now. This was a problem because he was visiting Angal, the King of Corca Tri, and couldn't easily get any replacements. So Áed opted not to drink at all.[34]

This could not be borne. King Angal became greatly distressed because if he couldn't provide for his guests – if he couldn't be trusted to hold a great feast and be a respectable host – then he might not be able to be a good king. This whole ordeal called his honour into question. So Angal's wife urged him to set out on an adventure to Guaire mac Colmain at Durlas, 'for that was the home of hospitality and generosity from the time of Dathi onward', to get a drinking horn for Áed.[35]

When the king left the fort, a stone fell away, revealing the three best drinking horns in all of Ireland, called the Twisted Horn, the Litan and the Eel. They had apparently been hidden by the Christian god until he lifted the veil for Angal because he had been deemed worthy.[36] So not only did Angal get new drinking horns for Áed, he got some magickal ones at that and Áed was finally able to drink his ale, or mead, or whatever he wanted.[37]

This story comes from 'The Three Drinking-Horns of Cormac úa Cuinn', found in the 15th-century *Liber Flavus Fergusiorum*. It's an excellent case study on hospitality. It's likely from the Ulster Myth Cycle, which comes from oral traditions dating from the 8th to the 11th centuries, and once again tells us that these horns – and by proxy, drinking ale – played an important role in medieval Irish society.

If you want to see what one of these valuable drinking apparatuses might have looked like, look no further than the National Museum of Ireland–Archaeology in Dublin, home to the Kavanagh Charter Horn, which dates to the 12th and 15th centuries. An impressive drinking horn with intricate metal decorations, this example is not to be missed on a visit to the museum. Unfortunately, not many examples have survived to our modern day. The very nature of the material the horns are made from makes this difficult because keratin disintegrates over time.[38] What survives are often decorative items attached to the horns, such as metal rims.[39] A good example of this can be found in the remaining terminal mounts (the decorative bits located on each end) from a drinking horn from Lismore, Co. Waterford.[40]

Of course, drinking horns weren't just for ale. There's that whole pesky thing about needing water to survive, and you had to drink it from something. Also mead! And milk! Milk was particularly popular in medieval Ireland. Regardless of exactly what they were imbibing, drinking horns were for the elite. But even among the drinking horns themselves, there were cheaper versions as well as pricey numbers. For example, there could be less elaborately decorated horns, such as the one found in Clonmore, Co. Carlow, or wooden ones such as the one found in Ballinderry, Co. Westmeath.[41]

Less wealthy people obviously needed to be able to drink too, so other vessels would have been needed. However, while little remains from this era, we do have some records for possibly less expensive drinking vessels. They could be simple wooden mugs or goblets, which can also be found in the National Museum in Dublin.[42] There was also a unique vessel called a mether. Methers were two- or four-handled drinking vessels that could be carved out of a single piece of wood (or made up of pieces) and were designed to be drunk from by the corners. These could have been used by both the highest echelons as well as the lower ranks. Often a king would begin a ritual where he passed the mether around the hall, with the idea being each person drinks a small amount and sends it on until it makes a complete loop around the hall.[43] This again represents an important tradition around the consumption of what was likely a form of alcohol, such as ale or mead.

Men weren't the only ones entitled to drinking horns. The *Lebor na Cert* also holds entitlements for ale-drinking horns belonging to queens. In fact, we are told that the King of Airgíalla and his queen are both entitled to the third drinking horn that went to the King of Tara.[44] At the very least, it suggests to us that queens in medieval Ireland also drank ale, participated in the feasting and were an integral part of this system of gift exchange.

To dig even further into the Queen of Airgíalla receiving drinking horns, a song later on in the text reveals that not only was this queen to get every third horn of ale, like her husband, but that she was entitled to this allowance 'from the other queen' – that is, the Queen of Tara.[45] What we have here is an exchange of drinking vessels between queens. This tells us that these queens held a high status within this framework and that this gift exchange was not only important for men, but also for women in their society's upper echelons.

More importantly, if the *Lebor na Cert* is accurate, the queens in medieval Ireland negotiated power with each other, and not just as a proxy for their male counterparts. This supports what we saw with the 'Women's War of Words', with queens vying with each other for their titles and prestige. And so, it is through drinking that women could navigate their social status with each other, related to, but also somewhat independent from, their spouses.

When you think of the perfect relaxing winter evening, many of us won't need to look much further than a hot bath, a nice warm fire and some lovely ale – something to keep away the chill from the rain and cold outside while you unwind. In fact, there are entire social media accounts devoted to the concept of beers to have in a bath or shower.

We aren't all that different from our medieval counterparts. Over 1,000 years ago, the author of *The Triads of Ireland* told readers that the three essential necessities for a man's household are 'ale, a bath, a large fire'.[46] *The Triads* are the author's thoughts on various topics, each listing three things, hence the name. Archaeologist Bettina Arnold notes that numerical symbolism was important in Celtic society, particularly multiples of three, which we have also seen in the *Lebor na Cert*.[47] Another great example in *The Triads* is of the 'three wealths' of fortunate people. These are listed as a 'ready conveyance, ale without a habitation, a safeguard upon the road'.[48] I interpret 'ale without a habitation' to mean the ability to access ale without having to make it yourself or having it be prepared at your own house, which in turn means you'd have enough money or power to acquire ale whenever you needed it, to be able to receive hospitality wherever you go.

This draws attention to something else we have seen several times in these stories: hospitality, or more to the point, the tragedy of failing to be a good host. In fact, refusing to provide hospitality was a violation for which the full honour price was owed, according to the *Corpus Iuris Hibernici*.[49] There was even a specific title for those who hosted somewhat professionally in early medieval Ireland. Called the *briugu*, this was a man, of varying social status, who provided his guests with hospitality.[50] There were different levels to this. The *briugu cedach*, that is, the 'hundred farmer', is defined in the *Uraicecht Becc* as:

> He is no 'brewy' who is not possessed of hundreds; he warns off no individual of whatever shape, he refuses not any company, he keeps no account against a person, though often he comes. Such is the 'brewy' who has equal 'dire' with the king of a territory.[51]

The term 'brewy' here is the translation of *briugu*. This text goes on to state that the *briugu leitech* has double or more than the *briugu cedach*. This man must always have 'an ever-full cauldron', from which he 'grants everyone his proper portion' and that it is 'perpetually wet', meaning full.[52] This likely refers to food, as it was commonly boiled, but we need to remember that alcohol (specifically, ale and mead) was also critically important in hosting activities. Kings travelled their domains to visit the houses of their clients, where these clients were expected to host them and provide feasts, though it's clear that kings were supposed to be mindful to only go where clients could handle hosting their numbers (although this wasn't always the case; as we will see in future chapters, it caused more than a few problems).[53] In turn, the clients provided the king with food-rents so that he could host feasts at his own place.[54]

We also have evidence for the importance of feasting in general in early medieval Ireland. And where there are feasts, there's ale. For instance, in the 9th-century 'Liadin and Curithir', Curithir, a poet, has an alefeast for Liadin, a female poet from Corkaguiney.[55] Some of these feasts were so big or famous, they were known by name. According to D.A. Binchy's reading of an account of the Battle of Moira, there were three famous feasts to be had in Ireland: Feis Temra, Feis Eamna and Feis Chruachna.[56] Binchy conducted an exhaustive study of the origins and reality of the famous Feast of Tara, which is mired in myth and legend, and concludes that this feast was a 'symbolic mating' with a goddess to cement a king's right to rule.[57]

In *Mesca Ulad*, a tale from the Ulster Cycle of myths, the feast of Samhain in Emain Macha given by Conor had 'a hundred vats of every kind of ale'.[58] In this story, we are told that Conor had become the 'arch-king' of the Ulad, so Emer, that famous wife of Cú Chulainn, told her husband that they needed to prepare his feast to acknowledge his kingship. Emer said, 'It is time to prepare his banquet of sovereignty for him now ... because he is a king for ever.'[59] Like we learned earlier, Arnold argues that the feast was a way to reinforce social rank.[60] We can see that in action here with this feast made by Cú Chulainn and Emer, who served up 'one hundred vats of every kind of ale'.[61]

The archaeological evidence also sheds light on the importance of feasting, and in particular the concept of funeral feasts. Though this tradition was likely pre-Christian in nature, it appears that Irish ecclesiastical institutions might have looked the other way or incorporated the old traditions into the new Christian rituals in Ireland. For example, in Clonmacnoise, a high-status church settlement, six bodies were found buried with beef ribs.[62] Lorcan Harney argues that this may indicate that they were interred with some of the food items from their funeral feast.[63] Animal bones are often discovered at other ecclesiastical settlements, which scholars have linked to the idea of funeral feasting.[64] Such feasts would have most likely involved ale.

On the other hand, archaeological evidence for alehouses, and indeed for large feasting houses, is lacking. Some scholars argue that we have not found any such halls to date.[65] Anne Sassin contends that this could be for a variety of reasons, including the difficulties surrounding the interpretation of wooden buildings and the overall lack of excavation of ringforts.[66]

However, this idea has been challenged by Richard Warner, who argues that there *is* evidence for these structures in Ireland, but that they have been misinterpreted.[67] Warner's exhaustive study, comparing the literary sources, annalistic entries and legal texts to archaeology, concludes that there is indeed evidence of feasting halls. For example, he believes that the ringfort at Lissue, Co. Antrim, matches the description of a royal house or feasting house as described in the early medieval sources.[68] Meanwhile, historian Edel Bhreathnach contends that there are several potential locations for royal residences that were hosting great feasts, including Knowth, Lagore and Clogher as well as our old friend Kildare, which was often the residence of the Kings of Leinster from the 7th century.[69] While we may or may not have found the remains of these feasting halls, it matters little for our purposes so long as we know that they existed, and of that we can be certain.

What were these alefeasts like? What could we expect if we attended one? In another instance found in *Mesca Ulad*, the feast hosted by Fintan was massive, with men and women feasting and enjoying huge amounts of food and drink. There was music and entertainment, and they also had a hundred vats of every kind of ale.[70] It paints a picture of an extravagant event, something perhaps not so different from a modern beer festival or even a large wedding. But this isn't the only source.

To further help us picture what attending an alefeast in an alehouse might have been like so long ago, let's turn again to *The Triads of Ireland*.

The Triads tell us of the 'three welcomes of an ale-house: plenty and kindliness and art'.[71] Aside from telling us that the alehouse should have lots of ale and food and that the hosts should be amiable, this also tells us that we have a society that was comfortable enough, and rich enough, to make and value art. It tells us that early medieval Irish society had enough money, free time and, importantly, safety to be able to focus on the creation of things for their own sake. The importance of art is echoed in a later triad that stated that one of the three taboos of a chief is 'an ale-house without story-telling'.[72] Again, this emphasises the importance of art within these confines.

So we can expect to listen to some tales while drinking our ale in medieval Ireland – that is, if we're important enough to be invited in the first place. We should also anticipate that we will be treated kindly and that there will be an abundance of food and drink.

The relationship between storytelling and art in the alehouse is echoed in the *Tecosca Cormaic*, or *The Instructions of King Cormac*. This text dates to the 9th century and is a series of questions and answers between King Cormac and his son, Carpre. Most importantly, Cormac lists the 'dues of a chief and of an ale-house' as being the following:

> Good behaviour around a good chief,
> Lights to lamps,
> Exerting oneself for the company,
> Settling seats,
> Liberality of dispensers,
> A nimble hand at distributing,
> Attentive service,
> To love one's lord,
> Music in moderation,
> Short story-telling,
> A joyous countenance,
>
> Welcome to companies,
> Silence during a recital (?),
> Harmonious choruses.[73]

While the dialogue is fictitious, it can tell us a bit about what an alefeast was like – or at least about what the author wished it was like. We can once again see the emphasis on music and storytelling. The service should be excellent and quite liberal, and when people perform, they should be given respect by way of silence. Like *The Triads*, Cormac also emphasises kindness – that the leader should be good company and ensure that everyone is having a good time.

But what is an alefeast without ale? So important is ale within feasting that Cormac states that 'banqueting without ale' is 'a crime in the gatherings of the world' and instructs Carpre that he should never give feasts without brewing ale.[74] This is echoed in the 8th-century law text *Críth Gablach*, which states that a king who could not give ale on Sundays was not fit to be king – and not just a little bit of ale, but an overabundance of the stuff.[75]

Nonetheless, given the reflections in the text of the legal records and other literary sources, we could conclude that Cormac's instructions for alehouses to be a possible, if not idealised, reflection of what alehouses and drinking in feasting halls may have been like in early medieval Ireland. This once again leads us to conclude that ale had a prominent place in this society.

While scholars like to bang on about how ale served an essential nutritional purpose, people drank to get tipsy and enjoy themselves, much like we do now. Cormac also states that 'frequent assemblies' and an 'abundance of wine and mead' are part and parcel of kingship.[76] He also argues for the 'liberality of dispensers', just like our *Triads* author, who declared 'plenty' to be one of the 'three welcomes of the alehouse'. This isn't the only time the *Triads* author emphasises the desire for lots of ale. Later we are told of the 'three fewnessess that are better than plenty', which include 'a fewness of friends around ale'.[77] For the *Triads* author, sharing might not have been caring. Or it might have been that they didn't want to get sucked into rounds and end up getting ale for all their mates and waking up with The Fear; in this, the fewer friends, the better.[78]

Not everyone was thrilled about alefeasts. *The Triads* tell us that 'three sorrowful ones of an alehouse: the man who gives the feast, the man to whom it is given, the man who drinks without being satiated'.[79] The man who throws the party is likely sad because of the expense. The man who keeps drinking and is never satisfied, well, that's self-explanatory. But why is the recipient of the party so unhappy?

Medieval people weren't so very different from us, and much like in our own celebrations, sometimes talking to so many people and being the centre of attention is exhausting. It may appear that the writer of *The Triads* could simply be an introvert expressing their own hostility to the matter, but it's more likely that because the party was thrown for them, the expectation was that they would return the favour at a later date, which, given the culture of gift exchange, is highly probable. Or the guest of honour may have had to undertake or participate in certain activities that may have seemed daunting or undesirable. Whatever the reason, it tells us that festivities could be given for specific people, similar to our modern-day birthday parties.

Much like *The Triads,* the author of *The Instructions of King Cormac* reveals who else he thought was miserable in the alehouse, and with it, his bias. Among other things, he contends that women were:

> feeble in a contest,
> viragos in strife,
> prodigal at a feast,
> sorrowful in an ale-house...[80]

Cormac concludes that it was better to whip, beat, crush, scourge and generally be horrible to women than to be kind or loving; just a *tiny* bit misogynistic, is Cormac.[81] His sexism spills over to the alehouse, where we are told that women ruin the joyous, happy atmosphere with crying and by generally wasting food and drink – grave sins against the sanctity of the space. This diatribe against women reveals the magnitude of the author's prejudice, but it also tells us that women were involved in feasting rituals and were patrons of alehouses.

Women certainly drank ale in the medieval Irish period. The author of the *Corpus Iuris Hibernici* states that the smell of malt could trigger a pregnant woman's desire for ale.[82] A woman who was expecting was supposed to be able to access food that she required, and she was entitled to access ale.[83] For example, we have the story of the mother of the famous Irish satirist Aithirne Ailgesach. She entered the house of a king and pleaded with his brewer for ale, which she was refused three times (there's that all-important number three again). At this time, the child she carried cast a spell so powerful that all the casks burst open and the ale flooded the floor, reaching upward of their ankles,[84] and she was able to drink as much as she pleased. That will teach you to come between a pregnant woman and her cravings.

And how did they drink their ale? An entry in *The Triads* is particularly interesting here: 'three cold things that seethe: a well, the sea, new ale'. It may tell us that ale was served cold, not warm, as some have speculated. It may also give us an indication about the yeast and the fermentation process (hence the seething).

I agree with scholars like Fergus Kelly that ale had a key nutritional role in early medieval Irish culture.[85] Ale would have been a valuable resource from a dietary standpoint, but it was also certainly consumed for political or ritualistic reasons as well as just for fun. For example, in the late 10th-century story 'The Lament of the Old Woman of Beare', the titular old woman mourns her age and appearance, talking about her wedding feast and times she enjoyed drinking ale in her youth. She reminisces about the past in a morose tone: 'Time was when many cloths of every hue/ Bedecked my head as we drank the good ale.'[86]

As previously stated, some of these alefeasts were literally part of what people were owed. Turning back to the *Lebor na Cert*, we see entitlements due to the King of Tara, who may also sometimes be a very high-status king of Ireland, but not always. Here we see that the King of Ulaid owed him a feast on every seventh Samhain and that he was to show up with 'twelve vats of each kind of ale' and not to stint on the food either.[87] This is echoed just a few stanzas later in that the King of Naas also owes a feast to the King of Tara, this one to be with 20 vats of each kind of ale.[88]

All these parties sound like a good time with plenty to drink, but what I really want to know is what kinds of ale were to be had. In Dillon's translation of the lists of taboos for the Kings of Ireland, which also included positive or 'lucky things', one of the five 'lucky things' for the King of Leinster was the ale of Cualu,[89] while the King of Connacht got to drink ale specifically in the area Dillon believes to be between Croagh Patrick and Clew Bay in Co. Mayo.[90]

Both of these texts mention vats of each kind of ale, but they don't tell us what these are. This might imply that the author knew or that it was well-known to the audience, so no more explanation was needed. It's also possible that the author was vague on purpose and didn't know exactly what they were talking about. Either way, it's a fascinating turn of phrase and may suggest that various kinds of ale were not only known, but that, at least for high-ranking kings, a set variety would have been expected to have been made. Again, this could be what the author wished was true versus reality; or they could just be making things up. Like in modern times, instead of knowing the ins and outs of brewing and that specific brewers made specific beers, our fair writer could just have been covering their bases and saying 'every kind of ale', meaning every kind available to this particular king that they made in his kingdom.

However, other sources support the idea that a variety of ales were available in early medieval Ireland. For more insight, let's turn to a poem that Irish scholar Eugene O'Curry came across that may offer some clues as to what they were brewing. The origins of this text are unknown, as is its date of composition, but because it was written to the Scottish prince Cano Meic Gartnáin, who was killed in 688 CE, it possibly fits into our early medieval time period. And it talks about a lot of different kinds of Irish ale: over 10 different varieties drunk all over Ireland. For example, the poet states, 'He shall not be a king over Eriu, Unless he drink the ale of Cualand', perhaps echoing that 'lucky' ale for the King of Leinster.[91]

While most types of ale are delineated by the people who brewed them or how they drank them (there are mentions of 'shining goblets' and 'deep horns'), there are also some clues as to what kind of ales they drank. For example, the line 'By the gentle Dalriad it is drank / In half measures by [the light] of bright candles' may suggest a really strong kind of beer because of the size of the measures. But it's the last stanza that really stands out for us:

> The Saxon ale of bitterness
> Is drank with pleasure about Inber in Rig,
> About the land of the Cruithni,
> about Gergin,
> Red ales like wine are freely drank.[92]

What might first jump out at you is the mention of that Saxon bitter ale. This tells us that there were possible trade relations between the two peoples and that it was imported, but also that this kind of ale was desirable. However, D.A. Binchy argues that this wasn't just a list of various ales, but instead represents the areas that Cano Mac Gartnáin had sovereignty over.[93] So this might be symbolic as well as describing different kinds of brews. Yet given the time period, different locations would have had ales that would have varied as a matter of course. It simply wouldn't have been possible for all the brewers all over the island of Ireland to brew the exact same ales, full stop. This leads us to believe that the variety of brews available was not only accidental, it was desired.

O'Curry speculates about the inclusion of hops in this Saxon bitter ale, though he notes that the poem doesn't answer this question.[94] There are no references to hops being used for flavouring in Ireland. They are not a native plant, so it's highly unlikely that they were used in the early medieval period, though they were around a bit later. That said, ale does not necessarily need hops to create the bitterness, as other additives could have fulfilled this role. This lack of hops might have impacted the brewing process, as hops are added during a boil; in fact, you *need* to boil hops. If you aren't adding hops to a particular ale, then there isn't necessarily a need to boil it, as indicated by Icelandic scholar Tofi Kerthjalfadsson in the medieval English ales he and his team recreated. Instead, we have what is called raw ale. If the early medieval Irish weren't adding hops at all, it's possible that they might not have boiled the wort (the liquid created from the malt after mashing in). Boiling would require a lot of fuel, plus it would be unnecessary without this ingredient. It seems most likely, then, that these early medieval Irish ales were potentially raw ales.[95]

We don't know for certain what was used in place of hops, if anything at all, to bitter the brews in Ireland, but there are some interesting speculations to be pondered. O'Curry suggests that perhaps buck-bean, which was found near some raths (early medieval forts), 'was probably used in Ireland at an early period to flavour beer'.[96] That said, this doesn't seem like an entirely convincing argument for its use in ale production, so I did a deeper dive on this topic. Bog myrtle, or sweet gale, is another possibility and was a popular plant used in brewing elsewhere. This sweet gale was used throughout Europe as part of the ale production process, so its inclusion in Irish ale may have been a possibility.

However, we can gain more insight by using archaeological evidence to determine which herbs may have been used in medieval brews. This proves to be quite tricky, as plant material doesn't often hold up over millennia, which makes this idea difficult to ascertain. However, Susan Lyons conducted a study of archaeobotanical evidence from urban medieval Irish environments. In her study, she found a wide variety of plants, including fennel, dill, black mustard, mint, marjoram and yarrow.[97] There were also a number of wild herbs that may have been used in this period, such as fat hen, nettle, charlock, black bindweed, redshank and knotgrass.[98] While a lot of this evidence comes from the high and later medieval period, it's possible that these ingredients were used in early brews as well. Herbal additives may have been incredibly context-specific and these herbs might have varied greatly, even within households, depending on the meal, mood and availability. Seasonality would have been important too, though of course, herbs can be dried and used later. However, the point needs to be considered that they didn't bitter their brews or use herbal additives as standard.

One source that may indicate that ale was brewed without herbs is the poem 'King and Hermit' about the 7th-century King Guare and his brother Marvan, who had decided to become a hermit instead of a warrior. In this tale, Marvan tells his brother that he has 'ale with herbs, a dish of strawberries/of good taste and colour/haws berries of the juniper/ sloes nuts'.[99] This may suggest that ale didn't include herbal additives in the brewing of it, but rather, that they were something to be added later, like we add spices to dishes. Perhaps herbal additives were somewhat uncommon, given that in this poem they are mentioned specifically as a descriptor of the ale, or they might have been reserved for higher-ranking people. Or maybe herbs were only used in certain circumstances or depending on the drinker's or cook's own personal preferences, much like we do today when we measure garlic with our hearts instead of the two measly cloves many recipes call for.

Another thing that may suggest a variety of ales was available is in the names themselves. There is some debate about which words in Old Irish actually pertain to ale, as in the malt grain beverage. For example, scholars have translated the word *lind* to mean both a generic term for alcoholic drink but also ale.[100] This is different from the term *beoir*, which may mean 'beer' or 'black beer' and might come from the Norse word *bjórr*. However, this is when things get a bit tricky, because *bjórr* may refer to a kind of hybrid ale or even mead (we'll talk more about this in Chapter 3),[101] so it might not actually mean ale as we would know it now.

The early medieval Irish had a variety of names that have been attributed to this drink by scholars like Binchy, such as *cuirim* and *laith*, a more formal, maybe even regal, term.[102] The antiquarian O'Curry argues that *ól* and *cuirm* might mean different things, with *ól* being a 'simple fermented, slightly sour decoction of malt ... and that the wort of the *cuirm* was boiled with some bitter aromatic herbs'.[103] Again, the possibility is raised of not using herbs or of herbs being used only in specific circumstances.

In the fragment of the ancient tale of *Tochmarc Emire*, or *The Wooing of Emer by Cú Chulainn*, we have the following entry:

> Now, once the men of Ulster were in Emain Macha with Conchobor drinking the iern-gual (iron-coal). A hundred fillings of beverage went into it every evening. This was the drinking of the 'coal' that would satisfy all the men of Ulster at one time.[104]

Kuno Meyer's translation declares that the *iern-gual* 'was the name of a huge copper wine-cask, so called, "because there was a coal-fire in the house at Emain when it was drunk"'. However, in contrast to Meyer, O'Curry suggests that this entry refers to a coal house, from the early medieval English word *aern*, meaning 'house', and *gual*, the Old Irish for 'coal'. Instead, this entry might say something like: 'Now the men of Ulster were drinking in the coal house, which was filled with 100 servings of ale every evening.' O'Curry argues that what they were drinking was instead a reference to ale, specifically *ol n-guala*, which means 'ale of the coal', and was likely called that because the wort was boiled over a charcoal fire.[105] He supports this argument by highlighting that Conchobar Mac Nessa and his army 'sat around a fire and quaffed their ale'.[106] He also argues that this *guala* could mean the name of the wort-boiling pot itself.[107]

In any event, when it comes to translation, things can get complicated, with words changing their meaning depending on who is doing the work. It makes figuring out precisely what each potential word for ale means quite tricky. But one thing is certain: there wasn't only one kind of ale to be had in medieval Ireland.

To return to O'Curry's poem, we also see that 'red ales like wine are freely drank'. Irish red ales are second only to the ubiquitous stout in terms of beers associated with the country. But the red ale here is something separate from the others, which again suggests a variety of ales and that this type was a specific kind made in a certain location. Red ales get their colour from the grains, so specific malts were likely used in the grain bill to make these brews. So let's take a look at possible grains used in early medieval Irish brewing.

The archaeological evidence reveals much about what kinds of malt could have been used, with clear indications of barley, oats, wheat and rye found in early medieval contexts. Historian Cherie Peters argues that rye was highly prized, so it's possible that it would have been included in high-status ales.[108]

The *Bretha Déin Chécht*, a medieval Irish medical text, may also offer some insight into the variety of grains and their accorded statuses.[109] In particular, it starts with the classification of people by virtue of their status into nine categories, which according to Binchy's translation are as follows:

- The highest classes of people – the supreme king, bishop and master poet – are associated with wheat.
- Next, the superior king, a poet a step down from the master level and a priest get rye.
- Then we have a grain of *siligo*, which according to Binchy apparently means a well-angled or soft barley, for the king of one tribe, a deacon and a poet of the third level, and every equal person among the other poets and clergy.
- Binchy's translation tells us that the fourth-level grain means soft barley of the Western Isles (there are lots of varieties of

barley here) and that this belongs to a subdeacon, a poet of the fourth grade and the *aire ard*, or 'high lord'.
- Next, a grain of red wheat belongs to the *aire túise*, which means a 'lord of leadership', a 'lector' and a poet 'of the fifth grade' and all the people of equal status to them.
- Regular barley goes to *aire déso*, or 'lord of vassals', and the people of equal status to this man.
- Now apparently we have reached the commoners, though still lords of a kind, with oats for a *bóaire,* aka a cow lord, and all equal to him.
- The *ócaire*, or young lord, and all those who are equal to him get peas.
- Finally, a *fer midboth*, 'a man of middle huts', who was a newly semi-independent boy or young man living on his father's land, gets beans.[110]

We can see that, at least in this text, there was a strong link between social class and kinds of grain. Whether this is reflected directly in brewing is another matter.

It's possible that the brewing of ale mimicked this idea of status and that ale created for higher-status men was made with higher-status grains, such as wheat and rye, but I'm not convinced that lower-status men were drinking ale made only from peas and beans. However, I should point out that in all these ranks, none of them are female and none of them are enslaved, so even though there is a clear hierarchy at work here, they all still had something of a social position in early medieval Irish society.

That said, Europeans did make pea beer, but peas were only part of the grain bill. It's actually a long-standing tradition in several places. Beer historian Martyn Cornell has an excellent overview on pea beer, and notes that the earliest mention he found was in Gervase Markham's *The English Housewife*, dating to 1615.[111] This lists the grain bill for this beverage, which includes peas along with oats, barley, malt and wheat.[112] So if a lower-status person needed to brew, they may have chosen to supplement their brews with peas or beans.

What is most important for our purposes is their inclusion in a 1758 Irish Parliamentary ban on making distilled spirits using, among other things, 'beans and pease'.[113] And we do have clear archaeobotanical evidence for peas in this era.[114] So there you have it. I think pea and bean beer was certainly possible, even if not particularly widespread.

❧

Quality control is an essential part of commercial brewing these days. Customers won't buy your beer again if you can't make a consistently good product that isn't infected or awash with off-flavours, so breweries need to make sure what they're putting on the shelves tastes excellent every time they make it. Thankfully, now we have all manner of ways to ensure this is the case, such as temperature control, strict cleanliness guidelines and even scientific testing. Our medieval companions didn't have access to any of that. They had to find other ways to make sure they were brewing the best they could, so they tried to control what they were able to control, which is why they had intricate tests for malt.

The *Senchus Mór*, one of the Brehon Law tracts, contains a detailed regulation for malt. A quick note here: the Brehon Laws were largely used orally and adapted for particular situations. They were prescriptive in nature, which means they were what the author hoped things should be, not necessarily a reflection of lived reality. That said, these laws certainly make it clear, at least for the author, that controlling the malt was an important part of the brewing process, which is why there were three tests for malt.

> Three tests concerning malt; one test for it after being dried without being ground; another test for it after being ground before it is made into a cake, that its taste and soundness may be known; and a test for the mash before it is put to ferment. If no unsoundness is perceived upon it in these three tests, no fine for failure shall lie against the tenant for it, if he sues for test; but even though the test be applied, it is right that the restitution with 'cric'-fine shall nevertheless be paid by the tenant.[115]

This means that the malt was tested throughout its lifespan, even into what we would now interpret as the first stage of brewing: the wort.

The first test happened after the malt had been made but before it was ground for brewing. The second test was done after it had been ground but before it was made into a cake that people tasted to see how it was faring, perhaps similar to the Sumerian *bappir*. If the malt passed these two tests, it was given the green light to be used in a brew. Then after the mash had been completed and the wort made, but right before it was left to ferment, it would be tested one more time. If the malt, and now the unfermented wort, had passed all the tests, then the brewer, and the tenant commissioning the brew, had done their due diligence. This meant that the tenant was exempt from certain fines, as he could not be sued for failure regardless of how the ale turned out. However, if the malt failed at the test stages, then the chief could still sue and be owed a penalty.[116] According to Binchy, these tests would have been performed by the ruler's brewer, known as the *scoaire*.[117]

There is a lot more to these laws, including details about something called lawful versus unlawful houses, where the tests were performed and if anyone had witnessed the tests (or if the person just claimed they did them). Fines would be given to those who failed to do the tests, especially those who failed them altogether, didn't care and went ahead and served their guests the bad ale resulting from the poor malt anyway.[118]

In summary, the medieval Irish tried to control what they could in the brewing process so that they didn't make bad ale, because serving your guests bad ale meant you had to pay some hefty fines, including the *cumbal*. The *cumbal* literally meant an enslaved woman, so the *cumbal* price is equivalent to the cost of a woman who was either kidnapped and sold or born into slavery, because slavery was rife in early medieval Ireland.

So why did these tests focus so much on the malt and not on the finished ale? This was largely because the malt could be controlled. Its production and creation was a well-regulated and known quantity, whereas people didn't yet know how yeast created ale. They weren't entirely sure what the process was or even what yeast itself was, so this part couldn't be precisely controlled. Therefore, you couldn't be punished if everything went bad during that part of the brewing process.

Let's not forget infections, off-flavours and other mishaps that would have been hard to control before the advent of modern technology. The Brehon Law authors seem well aware of this fact, so it's apparent throughout the legal tracts that brewers should control what they can, meaning the malt and wort. This also reinforces the idea that adding herbs wasn't part of the strict brewing process. Given the problems you'd face if you presented bad ale to your guests, it seems likely that there would have been some legal guidelines regarding the inclusion of specific herbs if it was a part of the brewing process that they could control. These detailed regulations of malt give us some valuable insights into the importance of ale. After all, if the ale wasn't of any great value, it's unlikely the legal authorities would have spent so much time discussing these issues.

And who was making this ale? Returning to our tales of Brigid, it's clear that brewing was included in the duties of nuns and those in monastic communities, but what about secular society?

According to the legal texts, professional brewers were quite high status. Large households, such as that of a king or monastic orders, had their own brewers. From early medieval Ireland, when professional brewers are mentioned, they are male. Binchy argues that brewing was a prestigious role taken on by the upper echelons of society, but that the wealthier lower classes must have engaged in it as well.[119]

This is echoed by earlier antiquarian scholars like O'Curry, who notes that 'brewing of beer appears to have been the privilege of the *Flaths*' (*flaths* are the wealthy and powerful families). But O'Curry states that because of the hosting requirements of the *briugu* that we explored earlier in this chapter – notably, that he must always have an ale for kings, poets and the like – they must have also brewed.[120] O'Curry also notes that any high-ranking monastery had their own brewer, called a *cirbseoir*, who would make beer from their clients' malt.[121] This seems to be reflected in our study of brewing monks and nuns. However, Brigid's nuns didn't seem to have a designated brewer for the alefeasts, which may have been what the whole issue was in the first place. Of course, her monastic community was also a new institution.

However, while there were certainly professional brewers, I want to expand our understanding of who brewed beyond these roles. These positions did not preclude the fact that women could – and would – brew ale for their own households. As the historian Kelly notes, both men and women may have been involved in household brewing. I would argue that brewing could have been a female task when it was done for one's own household. Since brewing was so important, the legal sources like the *Senchus Mor* offer clear insight into the desired amount of oversight into the task, but this was certainly more applicable to high-status brewers or those whose final product was going to high-status people. Lower-status individuals might have abided by a completely different set of rules and brewed for themselves in their own households on a much smaller scale with very little in the way of oversight, much like homebrewers do today. This brewing role, as it was throughout the medieval world, might have fallen to women.

Simply put, when brewing held a higher social standing or higher rate of pay, it often fell to men. When it was part of the daily household chores, it was likely performed by women. This could be why the only brewers mentioned in accordance with these high-status roles are male, but we just don't know for sure.

For some, brewing might have taken place in dedicated areas in their homes or even in separate buildings. In the early medieval period before 800 CE, there were round houses constructed within raths, that is, a settlement site, usually of a single family, surrounded by circular earthworks enclosed by a kind of wooden fencing. Some of these excavations have indicated a second round house connected to the first that may have been used as a kitchen.[122] This space could have also been used for brewing if it wasn't carried out in the main space, or indeed even outside.

From the 9th century, house shapes changed and they became rectangular. Aidan O'Sullivan and Triona Nicholls speculate that these structures could have been divided into rooms. I would say it's possible that brewing for household use happened within a division of these rooms, or equally, another building altogether.

Hearths and fireplaces are readily apparent in early medieval settlement structures. According to O'Sullivan and Nicholls, some hearths can be identified by a use of stone or a build-up of ash, while others are clearly formally delineated by stone borders.[123] Further, excavations have indicated that there were outdoor hearths and fireplaces that could also have been used for brewing purposes.[124]

Outbuildings also offer insight into brewing or malting in this early medieval period. In Ballymacash in Co. Antrim, there is a rath that has several outbuildings, one of which had a kiln for drying grain.[125]

Before we go on, I want to note that the ways in which people brewed and related to ale in early medieval Ireland, at least in Irish-held regions, likely persisted in some form for centuries. Brehon Law lasted well into the early modern period, so when we discuss brewing going forward amidst several colonisations, keep in mind that things for Irish-held Ireland might not have changed that much with regard to women and serving rituals, the role of ale and how they brewed, which is why we have two chapters on this topic.

Now that we are moving on to the series of invasions that the Irish were subjected to, we have a firm foundation for understanding what these colonising forces were met with. And so we venture forth with the first of these groups: the Vikings.

CANNIBALISM, HUMAN SACRIFICE AND OTHER THINGS TO PAIR WITH ALE

800–1100 AD

IT WAS CLEARLY A TRAP.

A message sent by Guðrún's husband, Atli, to her dear brothers, Gunnarr and Hogni, was designed to lure them to his side in exchange for unfathomable riches. Gunnarr was the King of the Burgundians and had already amassed a dragon's horde of wealth, so Guðrún had hoped that they would deny the summons outright. As a measure of insurance, she sent along a ring wrapped in wolf's hair to warn her siblings of the danger.

Alas, they did not heed her warnings, as brothers are often wont to do. Instead, curiosity overruled their common sense as they travelled to Atli's court. Guðrún rushed to intercept them and beg them to leave, but it was too late. Her husband had the brothers seized. Hogni fought bravely, killing eight men before he was inevitably subdued.

After his men had taken the brothers into custody, Atli demanded Gunnarr reveal the location of his own riches in exchange for his life. In reply, Gunnarr demanded Hogni's heart, knowing their lives were forfeit. At first they brought a heart they had cut from Hjalli, a known coward. But Hogni was as strong and brave a man as had ever existed, so it was instantly clear to Gunnarr that this was not his heart. In response, they cut the heart from Hogni, who laughed in their faces as he breathed his last. Brave to the end, he died a good death.

Gunnarr, now faced with the reality of Hogni's demise, revealed that this had been his plan all along. He'd realised that they weren't going to leave this place alive, so now he alone knew the location of the treasure and he would take it to his grave. Atli then tossed Gunnarr into a snake pit, where he faced his death playing a harp.

So Guðrún prepared a feast – and her revenge. She called her two sons to her side, children she had borne to her husband. They were central to her plan.

It was with vengeance in mind that she greeted her husband, arm extended with a golden cup of wine to welcome him to the feast, as good a wife and hostess as ever. As Atli gorged himself on wine, ale and meat pies, Guðrún waited. She watched silently throughout the evening as the teeming masses in the hall laughed and joked, each breath an offence to the death of her brothers. As the night progressed, her pain compounded until she could bear no more and broke her silence. She rose and addressed her husband, casually informing him that the meat he was so enjoying and had greedily devoured was in fact the flesh of his sons, slaughtered with more dignity then he had allowed her brothers.

With this revelation, everyone in the stunned hall took to weeping. Their all-consuming grief was only managed with the overconsumption of more and more ale and wine. No one came for Guðrún, so she moved silently through her home, freeing her husband's dogs and the people he had enslaved while giving away all his possessions. She then crept into her husband's room, where she found him passed out from grief and drink, killing him easily.

She left through the hall, passing all those who had earlier stood by as her brothers had been taken from her, now asleep from an overindulgence of drink. Rage once again engulfed Guðrún as she grabbed a burning stick and flung it into the hall. She waited to see the fire begin in earnest before she walked out the door and slipped away into the night. The fire consumed the hall; no one escaped. Her revenge was complete.

This is a dramatisation of the story of the *Atlakviða,* a poem whose date is somewhat contentious, though it possibly originates as early as the 9th century.[1] You might already be familiar with one of the main characters of the poem – Guðrún's husband, Atli – as he is none other than the famous (or rather, infamous) Attila the Hun. Of course, this tale is not factually accurate and was written, even at its earliest date, some 300 years after Attila's lifetime. Though his death in 453 is shrouded in mystery, a contemporary account by Priscus does put him dying at a feast, though it's suggested that instead of eating his children and being murdered in his bed, he possibly died of a nosebleed.[2]

While this folklore is a fascinating tale of blood-soaked vengeance, in between all the murdering and maiming we have a story that centres on drinking traditions. As this tale shows, women and the role of serving ale or beer were an integral part of Scandinavian rituals of power.

Let's return to our opening story. If Guðrún murdering her children and feeding them to her husband isn't gruesome enough for you, it gets even worse; so much worse. Another version of the story is told in the Eddic poem *Atlamál*, where Guðrún says:

> You know their skulls
> you hold as ale bowls.
> I do have your drink
> I have claimed it with their blood stains.[3]

In what amounts to possibly the most disturbing beer mugs ever, Guðrún turned her sons' skulls into the ale bowls they were drinking from, while also possibly mixing her children's blood into the ale. This isn't the only instance of skull cups in the Viking saga materials; there are a few. In the *Völundarkviða*, for example, we find skulls of children turned into silver-plated drinking vessels.[4] While there is limited archaeological evidence for skull cups all over the world in any time period, the truth is that these stories from the Viking age are most likely just that: stories.

However, they do reveal some truth behind the lore, some facet of lived reality for women in the Viking age. Throughout the saga materials, women are depicted as serving ale. Even the Valkyries were getting in on the act. The *Gylfaginning* tells readers that in addition to choosing the slain for Odin's hall, the Valkyries' duties were 'to bear drink and mind the table-service and ale-flagons'.[5] In the *Grímnismál*, they are also depicted serving ale.[6] It wasn't just legendary figures charged with serving this brew. In *Njál's Saga*, Bergthora, Njál's wife, serves the guests food and drink.[7] In *Egil's Saga*, Hildirida serves ale to the men who have come to her house: 'then Hogni gave orders to bring in cauldron/tun and strong ale; and Hildirida, the daughter of the householder, served ale to the guests'.[8]

A final example occurs in the *Heiðarvíga Saga*, where we find Thorbiorn Brunison being served ale by his wife. Unlike our previous examples, where people are being served well, Thorbiorn is so mad at what he believes to be his wife's poor hosting that he thinks she's an unspeakable evil that would bring him apples from the orchard in hell.[9]

To be clear, women in medieval Scandinavian society weren't only interacting with ale by serving the stuff. It was just one aspect, albeit a common one in literature, that we can find in these sagas. Women were also consumers, creators and ritual users of the beverage in other ways, and it was those traditions that the Vikings brought with them when they arrived on Irish shores in the early years of the 9th century.

The Vikings came, saw and conquered portions of early medieval Ireland and left an undeniable mark on its culture, including its rituals around ale. Scholars have been debating the impact of the Viking settlement on the cultural identity of Ireland for years. Some believe that the Irish had a greater influence on Viking life than the Norse did on Irish culture, whereas other scholars go so far as to suggest that the Irish and Norse remained culturally distinct.[10]

While initially the Vikings likely held onto their own traditions, many scholars, including me, argue that the invasions and settlement eventually led to the Vikings adapting and adopting Irish culture.[11] Irish and Norse Viking culture were similar in a lot of ways, which in turn naturally lent themselves to being blended. It was easy for the newly arrived colonising forces to take on aspects of Irish culture because of these overlaps in traditions, and this is clearly apparent in the ale-serving rituals.

[49]

In Chapter 2, we looked at the role of women serving their husbands as a way to acknowledge and solidify their right to rule. 'The Tale of Deirdre' or 'The Exile of the Sons of Usnech' from the Book of Leinster opens with the wife of Feidlimid serving the men of Ulster.[12] Queen Medb herself demands 'strong ale and sound and well malted, warriors' keep'.[13] And don't forget the story about the Sovereignty of Ireland, who served and named every ruler until Armageddon with ale.

Guðrún also names Atli as chief and invites him into the feast, thereby performing a similar role. Later on in that saga, Guðrún also seems to be praising Atli's virtues, similar to the speeches of the three queens at the feast of Bricriu in the 'The Women's War of Words', where they boast about themselves and their husbands. However, in a perverse twist on this ritual, Guðrún, instead of engaging in a speech designed to reiterate Atli's power, mimics this style of address to mock and debase him, using the phrasing 'giver of swords' to inform him he is eating his own children. In this aspect, Viking and Irish culture have many similarities.

We don't have to only rely on the written sources to see evidence of this serving role for women and beyond, and in fact, we shouldn't. Most of the literary sources for life during the Viking Age were written long after it – some by 300 years or more – so as you can imagine, they aren't always exactly reliable; they can be full of bias. On the other hand, they aren't completely fictional accounts either, especially as they relate to some aspects of beer history. We have to try to disentangle fact from fiction, and one of the best ways to do that is by comparing the tales to the archaeological data.

We certainly have archaeological evidence for bowls, cauldrons, ladles and other serving equipment in Ireland. A burial in Ballyholme Bay on the shores of Belfast Lough found in the autumn of 1903 contained a copper alloy bowl alongside two single-shelled oval brooches, jewellery that was often associated with high-status women.[14] When bowls are found in a Viking furnished burial (that, is, burials made by Scandinavian colonists in Ireland), it's often alongside other goods associated with these elite femininities.[15] According to Sheila Raven, their presence in these burials, along with other 'luxury' vessels associated with liquids, might be a direct representation of a woman's role in serving beverages. On the other hand, it could be a washing set.[16]

The two other items related to feasting were found at Church Bay in Rathlin, Co. Antrim, where three Viking burials were found. Discovered prior to 1851, one of these possible graves contained a copper alloy ladle and a composite copper alloy and iron artefact that was a vessel, maybe a cauldron.[17] Cauldrons weren't that uncommon in the broader context. They were used for boiling meat, which seems to have been the preferred method of cooking in the Viking era.[18] However, they could have been used for making ale and possibly also serving it. For instance, in *Egil's Saga,* we saw that Hildirida brought in the ale in something like a cauldron.

Ladles are less commonly found. In Norway, 15 imported copper alloy insular ladles have been found in burials; again, this demonstrates a method of cultural exchange.[19] The National Museum of Ireland–Archaeology has a number of ladles in its collection, including some from ecclesiastical origins, such as the Derrynaflan ladle, which is made of bronze and has a built-in strainer.[20] Others have a more secular context. The fact that a cauldron and ladle were together in the Church Bay example may suggest that this was a serving set. As we saw with Hildirida, it's possible that the cauldron was used not only to serve ale, but potentially also to brew it.

Much like today, brewing was not a one-size-fits-all activity. There wasn't only one way to brew using all the same equipment, with the same ingredients and in the same amounts. Instead, there were a variety of approaches. Merryn and Graham Dineley have conducted extensive research into the Vikings' brewing methods. Using both saga materials and archaeological finds, they have pieced together several possibilities, including purpose-built brewhouses located beside feasting halls that had previously been identified as other types of structures, such as saunas or latrines.[21] They also conclude that ale could be kept in large vats close to the hall for consumption and was transported from these vats using buckets,[22] perhaps something similar to what the National Museum of Ireland–Archaeology has on display, though whether they were used to serve ale is anyone's guess.

These bigger batches of ale weren't the only ones made. People also brewed at home for their own households, making smaller batches of ale in kettles or cauldrons, possibly over fires (more on the precise brewing techniques in a bit).[23] Some scholars, like Joan Elisabeth Rosa Brusin, contend that large and small batches were brewed in tandem, with each serving different functions: the larger brews to be served at feasts or rituals and the smaller ones to be used within households.[24 '] Hildirida's brewing cauldron was a nice manageable size, something she could have easily carted around or used for brewing for her home. According to folklore, however, not all Scandinavian brewing cauldrons were so conveniently transportable. In fact, one was so deep, it would give the massive Lake Baikal in Siberia a run for its money. The otherworldly stories surrounding it would probably do the same.

In the *Hymiskviða,* a poem in the *Poetic Edda*, the gods get together to perform a magickal ritual to figure out who among them has the best place to throw a feast, as you do. They determine that Ægir's hall is the best spot for revelry.[25] Ægir is less than enthused, to put it mildly. Hosting is a metric ton of thankless, boring work and he isn't particularly inclined to undertake it. So he issues a challenge, declaring that the other gods need to find a massive kettle to brew the ale, thinking they won't be able to find one. And at first, they can't. But then Tyr remembers that his father, Hymir, has a brewing kettle, 'a mighty vessel a mile in depth',[26] also referred to as 'whirler of water', which is fun to say 10 times fast.[27]

Now of course I don't think that Vikings were actually brewing in kettles that were a mile deep. Can you imagine mashing out? The absolute size of the shovel you would need! I don't even want to think about the cleaning. As I said, this was as deep as Lake Baikal and probably just as haunted. Clearly this was for giants (or gods, as the case may be), but it does suggest to us that kettles were used in brewing. The phrase 'whirler of water' suggests a stirring or churning brewing process as well, perhaps reminding us of our own mashing-in practices. Additionally, the kettle is referred to as 'hard hammered', which suggests it was made of metal and hints that the brewing might have taken place over a fire.[28] At least it's one possibility. I can't imagine the size of the fire needed for a mile-deep cauldron. In any event, there's more than one way to crack an egg. Enter: rocks.

In *Historical Brewing Techniques: The Lost Art of Farmhouse Brewing*, Lars Marius Garshol writes extensively about making beer on, well, farms. He argues that for much of history, many people would have made beer on their own properties for their own households. He found that many of the old farmhouse techniques – those from the 20th century that might have roots extending much farther back into history – are still in use throughout parts of Europe.[29] One of Garshol's key arguments is that, unlike today, in history there was an incredible number of different brewing techniques. Traditions varied from farm to farm, even producing a variety of ales. And one of the most important and widespread techniques in use in Europe was using hot stones to heat the mash. These potential shattered brewing stones have been found in deposits dating from the 7th to the 17th centuries, though Garshol argues that this is only part of the story.[30]

Some of the medieval Scandinavians were probably brewing by using hot stones, as evidenced by Geir Grønnesby's analysis of cultural layers in Trøndelag, Norway. Here, Grønnesby concludes that the remains of these cracked stones found in these layers could have been used for brewing purposes and that this practice was likely widespread.[31] Merryn and Graham Dineley also argue, like Grønnesby, that hot rocks could have been used in wooden brewing vessels, as evidenced by the multitude of these cracked stones found at many sites, including that at Jarlshof, Shetland, where hundreds were found located close to the drinking hall.[32] Might they have brought this technique with them on their way to Ireland?

The answer to that is somewhat complicated. You see, the Irish themselves already used hot rocks, or at least they had centuries prior to the Viking invasions. *Fulachtaí fia* exist throughout Ireland, with most dating to pre-historical times. *Fulachtaí fia* are water-boiling cooking sites where hot stones were used to cook food.[33] Basically, these stones were heated up, then put into an adjacent water trough to raise the temperature of the water.[34] Some archaeologists have argued that this could have also been a way to make ale, similar to the hot rock brewing of the Vikings. In fact, the Moore Group conducted a successful experimental brew using the *fulacht fiadh* method and concluded it was likely used in Bronze Age brewing.[35] But that's more than 1,000 years before the period we're discussing in this chapter.

Is it possible that this practice carried on into the medieval period? The evidence for that is scant, at least at these dedicated sites. Alan Hawkes did a survey of 1,022 *fulacht fiadh* sites in Ireland and found that there were none with an absolute medieval date.[36] He argues that there is 'no support' for the 'claim of a continuation of use from historical times'.[37] Some historians argue that the early medieval written sources that reference the term *fulacht* might simply equate to various forms of cooking, such as spit roasting or using a cauldron, and not this specific method of boiling and hot stones at all.[38] In fact, it was Geoffery Keating, writing in the late 16th and 17th centuries, who associated this term with this cooking method, and Keating is quite biased, to say the least; he was much more interested in lore and myth than historical accuracy.[39]

It's possible that a variation of hot rock brewing was revived with the arrival of the Vikings, but perhaps not in the context of *fulachtaí fia*. Since using hot stones in brewing is clearly apparent in Europe in the medieval period, it's definitely something to consider, but the archaeological evidence is sorely lacking. At least for now.

The 19th-century Irish poet John Locke was a massive history geek. Writing about 'rummaging old books' to discover various hidden bits of historical trivia, his fascination with the Vikings is contagious.

In 1859, Locke recalled a story that had been told to him about *Beoir-Lochlonnach*, a kind of heather ale, a beverage the Danes 'drank to intensify their valour'.[40] We have to be careful with Locke, as he is rather biased and woefully misinformed, though well in line with the expected standards of his age. He says the legend was regaled to him by a local from Rughelmore in Co. Kerry, where he had personally seen Danish brewing vats in 1847.[41]

Apparently, the medieval Danish were quite cagey about how they brewed, and kept it a secret from the Irish. According to the legend, after the Battle of Clontarf in 1014 CE, only three men alive – a father and his two sons – knew the secrets of Viking brewing. After his capture, the father was tortured to try to get him to spill the beans, which he refused to do, saying his sons would kill him just the same. So the Irish killed his sons. Now, being the last remaining person with the secret, he said:

'Now my purpose is accomplished; youth might have yielded to the fear of death, and played the traitor, but age has no such terror,' and so heroically suffered death; the secret of making the heath-beer perishing with him.[42]

This seems remarkably similar to what happened to Guðrun's brothers. In any event, Locke wasn't completely convinced of the veracity of the tale, arguing that the word *Lochlonnach* was actually *Luigenach*, from *luighe*, meaning 'cauldron', such as one a person brews in. But his source was insistent: 'he assured me that he was nearly one hundred years old, and had heard from his grandfather, who had also lived a great age, the same explanation of the term which he communicated to me.'[43]

And what was the brewing process? Locke was told that they used the *fulacht fiadh* as part of their creation.[44] Heather was placed in the cauldron to steep, after which another bitter herb, called herb bennet, was added. But there is no mention of cereal grains or of this being an ale. That said, this could simply be an omission by Locke of what he (or his informer) believed was obvious. Or, more likely, it's simply folklore.

The famous Irish historian D.A. Binchy believes there to be some truth behind all the myth, arguing that, 'Apparently the invaders brought with them some special type of beer, which eventually gave rise to the widespread folk-tale about "Viking" or "heather" ale.'[45] O'Curry argues that 'the heather beer' that the 'Danes' are supposed to have made from the common heath is a myth, believing that it could possibly be a substitute for hops, but that there isn't evidence for its use in that capacity.[46] However, the Moore Group decided to use this as the basis of a recipe to make their own version of a heather ale. They used the hot stone method to brew and added ling heather and bog myrtle, which also turned out quite successfully.[47]

Let's return to Binchy's comments about a specific kind of beer that the Vikings might have brought with them to Ireland. It's likely that there were a few different types of beverages known and drunk by the Vikings that might be called ale, or within what we modern people might deem to be this family of beverages. This distinction appears in texts like *Alvíssmál*, the Eddic poem written around the 12th century. This is the story of Thor and Alvíss (which means 'all-wise'), a dwarf who was seeking Thor's daughter's hand in marriage. As part of his inquiry, Thor asks Alvíss what the names of ale are in all the worlds.[48] In reply, Alvíss names six distinct kinds: *öl, bjórr, veig, hreinalög, mjöð* and *sumbl*. Essentially, this stanza says that men call it *öl*; gods call it *bjórr*; the Vanir call it *veig*, meaning 'drink' or, more directly, 'The Foaming'; the giants call it *hreinalög*, which means 'bright' or 'pure draught'; in hell it is known as mead, or *mjöð*; and finally, the sons of Suttungs call it *sumbl*, which literally means 'feast', maybe referencing feast draught.[49]

Much like we saw with the early medieval Irish, this not only implies that a variety of alcoholic drinks were known in the Viking period, but also a variety of ales. Most of these mentioned are otherworldly and don't necessarily correspond to something humans would have been consuming. It's likely that those consumed by giants or the Vanir weren't beverages that everyday people would expect to encounter; instead, these are mythical brews, perhaps made in those mythical giant cauldrons we just learned about. Nevertheless, this answer might still hint that during this period, a variety of ales were available in the Viking world because several of them, notably mead, *öl* and *bjórr*, would have had real-world examples.

Öl itself was a type of ale. Much like the Irish, the Vikings would have had different forms and kinds of this ale, likely brewed with slightly different grain bills, additives or using hot rocks or other brewing methods. Mead is an alcoholic drink made by fermenting honey mixed with water. This leaves us to consider the meaning behind *bjórr*, a drink whose exact ingredients are somewhat contentious among scholars, though most agree that later usage in relation to the Hanseatic League (a medieval organisation of merchants that acted not only as a kind of alliance, but also as a defensive network) does refer to hopped ale.[50]

The term *bjórr* was not common prior to the 13th century, but was in use from about the 10th century.[51] For example, in our opening story about Guðrun, she was drinking *bjórr*. However, Christie L. Ward argues that in earlier instances, it meant a kind of cider.[52] In contrast, Jesus Fernando Guerrero Rodriguez argues that *bjórr* was a sweet drink and that if it is indeed related to the early medieval English *beor*, then it was likely a 'brew or wine fortified with honey'.[53] That said, as Guerrero Rodriguez argues, this doesn't mean it didn't have malt; it was possibly a braggot. Braggot is not ale mixed with mead, as is commonly believed, or at least in the medieval Irish and English contexts; in all the recipes I've looked at so far, this has not been the case. Instead, braggot is ale that is mixed with honey and spices and left to ferment again. But Guerrero Rodriguez argues *bjórr* could have equally been a fermented fruit-based beverage.[54]

Another contentious beer is *mungat*. Guerrero Rodriguez defines it to mean a strong ale.[55] However, some scholars, like Gianna Chiesa Isnardi, argue that it means a homebrewed ale, possibly a small ale with a low alcohol by volume (ABV).[56] A lot of this is based on the folklore, so we should once again turn to the archaeological record, and specifically, what we can find in Ireland to see if there is any corresponding data that may hint at the types of ales made.

There is certainly evidence of barley and other possible cereal grains used for brewing in Viking Dublin.[57] A study of macroscopic plant remains from 10th- and early-11th-century deposits from Viking Dublin, in particular from Fishamble Street, found that barley was the most abundant, followed by oats and wheat.[58] The evidence doesn't stop there. Mary Valente found that the Book of Uí Maine, a 14th-century Irish work, contains a poem about what was owed in tolls by those merchants who wanted to trade in Dublin with the Viking kings, including 'a pack horse load of malt'.[59] This rent or tribute payment demonstrates that they were using Irish malt, and this likely came into use in the brewing of ale. Valente argues that this demonstrates that the Vikings were integrating Irish conceptions of kingship into their ruling practices, as these items, like malt, were commonly demanded as part of Irish tributes.[60] This same source states that the Norse kings of Dublin collected tax from the inhabitants, including 'a horn of mead from every vat'.[61] Overall, Valente contends that the Vikings got their required malt and grain through a combination of trade, tax and raiding.[62]

We can possibly see here that the creation of alcoholic beverages was alive and well in Viking Dublin. Indeed, scholar Siobhan Geraghty found that the Vikings in Dublin needed 10,000 acres of grain to keep up with bread-making needs, to say nothing of the requirements for their ale consumption.[63] We also know from another Irish source, *The Circuit of Ireland by Muircheartach Mac Neill, Prince of Aileach*, that grain and cereals were being stored in Viking Dublin in large quantities.[64]

As for additives in Viking brews, Locke's legend and his investigation postulated a few, including tormentil, herb bennet, ling heather, myrcia or wild hops.[65] It's reasonable to suggest that they used local herbal additives like juniper or bog myrtle.[66] Merryn Dineley argues that yarrow, angelica and meadowsweet could also have been used.[67]

The Viking historian Else Roesdahl argues that hops were in some use during this early medieval period in Scandinavia as well as in Viking York, but like much of Europe, other herbal agents, such as juniper, were commonly used for flavour and bittering.[68] Hops were also known to be in Britain, at least during the 10th century, as evidenced in the Saxon remains of the boat found in Graveney, Kent, which was found to be carrying a cargo of hops. These might have been destined for brewing, but they could have also been intended for medicinal use. However, hops weren't prevalent in English brews until the later Middle Ages, after the introduction of Flemish ale by immigrants from that area. More interestingly for our purposes, the kings of Viking York and Dublin were at one time one and the same, so it's possible that there was some limited use of hopped beers by people who lived on both islands, given the close links to both cities by the leaders. It's more likely that people brewed with what could be acquired more locally, so perhaps they used many of the herbs that we explored in Chapter 2.

So now we have an idea of what they brewed, how they brewed and where they brewed. But who did all the brewing? The answer is complicated.

Calling back to our story in the *Hymiskviða* about the giant mash tun, this bit of lore also references women serving ale; indeed, the 'bright-browed one brought beer [sic: ale] to her son' is Tyr's grandmother.[69] But women weren't just serving ale. They could also be brewing it.

According to many scholars, including Jenny Jochens, the majority of brewers during the Viking period were most likely women, at least in some contexts. This conclusion is largely based on the fact that brewing was often dominated by women throughout Europe in the medieval period because it was a task associated with domestic skills. There are notable exceptions and high-status brewers were often male. Essentially, as is often the case in the medieval period, if brewing was done within the household or as a kind of side hustle, it was usually done by women. When it was an important task, with an accompanying higher status and higher financial benefit, it was often done by men. This is not to say that brewing wasn't an important part of the life and social rituals in either Irish or Viking culture – it certainly was. Rather, there is perhaps a marked difference between those who did it as a full-time job and those who did it more informally or only occasionally.

We find support that women were brewing in *Hálfs saga ok Hálfskrekka*, or *The Saga of Half and His Heroes*, the story of a king named Alrek and his two wives. Alrek was already married to Signy but was struck by the beauty of another woman, Geirhild, who he came upon 'brewing ale', so he decided to marry her too. As you can imagine, this went over rather poorly with his current wife. The king, in his infinite wisdom, realised he couldn't remain married to the pair of them 'on account of their squabbles', so he decided to 'keep the one who made him the best ale when he came home from summer's raiding'. There we have it: marital status decided via a homebrew competition. As a beer judge myself, I can safely say I have never been at a competition with such high stakes.

To try to win, Geirhild entreated with Odin, who decided to spit on her ale. As a result, she won the contest and remained as Alrek's only wife (though I'm not convinced she was the real winner in the end, as he seems to be a rather poor prize).[70] If the saga sources are to be believed, this shows us that women were certainly brewing ale. Indeed, the author presents it as completely unremarkable that Geirhild was brewing, nor is it depicted as shocking that Alrek's other wife, Signy, would be able to brew as well.[71]

Women weren't the only brewers. Men were still depicted as making ale in this period. It just might have been that, like elsewhere, the majority of people who brewed were female. We also see other possible references to men brewing in the saga sources, but I don't necessarily agree that all of these are meant to mean that the man is physically doing the brewing. For example, in *Egil's Saga* we see the following: '*Fór Yngvarr þá heim ok bjó til veizlunnar ok lét þá öl heita*', which translates to 'Yngvar then went home, prepared for the banquet and called for ale'.[72] Some translations have '*ok lét þá öl heita*' as meaning 'brewing ale', but in my opinion it seems more likely to mean 'called for ale (to be served or brewed)'. Later on in *Egil's Saga* we see references to Thord, a male character, who had ale brewed at his household in anticipation of hosting a banquet. Again, there is no specific reference here to who exactly is doing the brewing, but it isn't Thord.[73]

There are other, clearer examples of men brewing, which we'll get to in a bit. We have only begun to scratch the surface of Viking brewing, because besides simple consumption, ale also often served an otherworldly function, a magickal role. Especially in death.

The ghosts totally killed the vibe, coming to their funeral alefeast dripping wet, freezing cold and hogging the fire. They didn't even talk to anyone, and worst of all, they began to kill people.

The *Eyrbyggja Saga* tells the story of a man called Thorod Scat-Catcher and his men, who had gone out fishing when a storm came upon them. All were lost to the crashing waves, their bodies consigned to Davy Jones's locker. At least for a little while.

Just like the Irish, the medieval Scandinavians also celebrated funeral feasts, and these celebrations required a special ale, called *erfiøl*, or funeral ale. Scandinavian drinking traditions started at birth with a *barnøl*, or christening ale,[74] and ended with your death and an ale made especially for your funeral. You came in with a beer and went out with one. During the Christian period this *erfjøl* became known as *sáluøl*, or soul ale (or beer), and included the role of a priest in the course of the ceremonies.

So after Thorod and his men died, their surviving relatives gathered to make this brew for the funerary rituals. Luckily for them, it was close to Yuletide. Yule, or *Jól* in Old Norse, occurred roughly from mid-November to early January. It was a crucial holiday in the Viking belief system and was associated with complex rituals, including the *Jólablót*, literally 'Yule sacrifice'. For the festivities, special ales were brewed, drunk and sacrificed to Odin as well as other gods of the Norse pantheon including Frey.

The *Heimskringla*, or *The Sagas of the Old Norse Kings*, was composed by Snorri Sturluson circa 1230 CE. Within this text is the saga of King Haakon of Norway, who lived from approximately 920–961 CE. This is where we learn of the harsh penalties if one fails to cough up the goods for Yule. According to Haakon's law in the saga, '*Ok skyldi þá hverr maðr eiga mælis öl*', which I've translated to 'and every man is obliged to have a measure of ale', or else '*gjalda fé ella*' – or else they have to pay *fé*, which is the Old Norse word for 'assets', 'livestock' or 'money'. *Mælis öl* is the important phrase here, which means 'measure of ale'. According to Richard Cleasby and Gudbrand Vigfusson, this means about six and a half gallons. Essentially, Haakon is stating that every freeman of a certain status is required to have this amount of ale brewed for the Yule festivities.

Haakon's ruling isn't only found in sagas, but also in law codes such as the *Gulaþingslova*, a medieval Scandinavian legal text. The law required freemen of a particular rank to come together in groups of at least three to brew for alefeasts, one of which was to be held on the Holy Night. If three winters passed without this occurring, the man will have 'forfeited his goods to the last penny', and if he further refuses, he is then banished from Norway entirely. In short, you had better make that ale.

This has parallels in Irish culture, where we saw the Easter ale festivities of St Brigid and the early Christian Church. Of course, this wasn't limited to Easter – other holidays also involved alefeasts. Let's not forget that when the Scandinavians converted to Christianity, they brought their traditions with them. In Ireland, this could mean that they took up the Easter alefeasts and also transferred the brewing of Yule ales to the making of Christmas ones, as they did elsewhere. These celebrations, and their calls for specialty ale, might be yet another parallel cultural trait that allowed for the further mixing of ale traditions in Viking Ireland.

Returning to our story about Thorod and his men, because Yule was close at hand and the Yule ale had already been made, the surviving relatives repurposed it for the funeral, as it was the more pressing matter. But when the feast commenced, the attendees got a bit of a surprise, for none other than the dead men arrived in the hall. At first, everyone was happy with this development. After all, they concluded it was good luck to attend your own funeral feast, and Ran, the goddess of the sea, would be particularly pleased.[75] File that one away for future haunting purposes.

But then the dead wouldn't leave! They returned night after night after night to the funeral alefeast, hogging the fire and ignoring everyone; just hanging out, bringing down the vibe and draining their descendants' coffers. It's one of my favourite tales, a sort of early version of the Ghosts of Christmas Past, haunting their living descendants and feuding with the local zombies, causing death and illness, until a lawsuit is brought against them.

Funeral ales aren't limited to ghostly apparitions. Or the Vikings. They even continue into our modern era. A wake in Ireland often calls for beer, and many people mourn the death of a loved one with a trip to a pub. Funeral beers are, and were, incredibly important, and not just for the dead. In fact, they could be part of a kind of physical performance of the dead's last will and testament. Most importantly for our purposes, these rituals around funeral ales and inheritance ales don't come just from fictional tales. They are also found in more reliable sources written in perhaps the unlikeliest of places, like on giant stones.

Sometime between 200 and 450 AD, a man called WodundaR died.[76] He left behind three daughters, who not only had to pick up the pieces in the wake of their father's death, but also had to make sure he had a proper send-off. So they erected a monument of stone, a testament to his life and legacy. Immortalised upon it in runes are only two sentences. The first sentence on one rock face names their father and the runic stone's purpose as a memorial. The other sentence declares that his three daughters are his heirs, and as such they had done what heirs were meant to do in the centuries after WodundaR had died: they made him a funeral ale.[77]

The *Gulaþingslova* records that 'when men are dead and the heir will make ale (or beer) after (them)'.[78] This concept comes up over and over again throughout the tales of the Vikings. Our zombies weren't just interrupting their own funeral, you see – they were also interrupting their survivors' inheritance ceremonies. In *Fagrskinna* we are told that the heir, or heirs, of the deceased are to commission a funeral ale and that they can't officially claim their inheritance until after they have consumed this ale and made their oaths. Here we also see the use of the *bragafull*, which is typically translated as 'best cup' or 'chieftain's/king's cup', which both represents the actual cup and the process of toasting the deceased. A *bragafull* toasting was linked with the concept of *minni*, that is, remembering; it literally means 'memory'. These toasts and consuming the ale were critical components of funerary rituals and inheritance rites.

These funeral ales are found throughout the Viking sagas. From the *erfiøl* on the death of the powerful woman Unnr, who was once married to a Viking king of Dublin, which was served at her grandson's wedding in the *Laxdæla Saga,* to Mord in *Njál's Saga,* who states, 'I mean to drink in my heirship after my father', they are ubiquitous.[79]

In Chapter 2, we saw how the Irish engaged in funeral feasts from animal bones found alongside human remains in the archaeological excavations at Clonmacnoise. Funeral feasts were one of the many ways that these two groups of people could have shared their cultures. And not just in death. Everyone has to eat ... and drink. And many people like to do so with their friends or family. You need look no further for a way in which the Vikings and Irish blended than the ritual of the feast. Like we saw in Chapter 2, drinking rituals could establish the political hierarchy and allegiances both within and without cultures. This means the Irish could have invited the Vikings into their rituals as a way to accept them and also as a way to fit them into the pre-existing mould. Simply put, it was a way that they could integrate.

Feasting was central to the fabric of political and social traditions in medieval Ireland, and the same can be said for the Vikings. Feasting was part of the duties of householders and was linked to the formation and maintenance of friendships as well as alliances. That this was a way for these cultures to meld is not a unique argument; many scholars make similar contentions. For example, Sarah Semple, Alexandra Sanmark, Frode Iversen and Natascha Mehler contend that feasting and eating together was a way to solidify and create alliances in late pre-history.[80]

This isn't so different from our own lives. We feast at weddings, christenings, communions, birthday parties and even funerals. We use beer as a way to celebrate but also to commiserate. Everything going wrong? Meet your friends for some adult beverages. We go for a beer after long meetings or for after-work drinks. We meet potential new employers at conference drinks receptions and we network over pints of beer. We, too, form alliances with ale at their centres, like our ancestors did hundreds of years ago. While the stakes might be a bit different – perhaps a job offer instead of a war – we still use the bonding ritual of drinking to build networks of a kind.

I cannot stress enough how important the ritual of feasting was in both Viking and Irish medieval culture. The rituals of drinking were deeply entwined with politics. Some of these feasts weren't small-scale events, but rather huge assemblies of people with specific political functions, and they lasted for weeks. In Scandinavian culture there were things called, well, *Things*. These were assemblies of Viking freemen and leaders that also heard legal cases, like the *Althing* in Iceland. The *Althing* was likely started around 930 CE and *still exists today* as the Icelandic Parliament. This makes it one of the oldest-running parliaments in the world, which is frankly just an incredible *thing*. (See what I did there?) But the most important thing about the *Thing* is that they drank and brewed ale.

The sagas tell us that eating, drinking and feasting were important parts of these assemblies, which has also been confirmed by archaeological evidence.[81] Drawing in many attendees of all genders, the *Althing* at Thingvellir in Iceland was critically important in both political and social realms and was held for about two weeks in the summer.[82] Ale brewed at the *Althing* was commonly made on the spot. In her study of Thingvellir, which was the site of the *Althing*, Natascha Mehler found that among the craftspeople present were ale brewers.[83] There's even a reference to there being a brewery at the *Althing* in the saga *Orms þáttr Stórólfssonar*.[84]

With regard to the *Althing*, the sagas even tell us of a specific brewer present called þórhallr.[85] He was also known by his nickname Ölkofra, which literally means 'Ale-hood', based on his occupation as a brewer and his penchant for wearing a hood to cover his face. He made his money selling very bad ale at the *Althing*.[86] Apparently competition was not fierce, which may also suggest that there weren't that many brewers at such events if he could still make money selling horrendous ale. What is perhaps the most interesting part of this story is Ölkofra's alleged involvement in arson. You see, the local leaders attempted to wage a judgement against him for apparently creating a blazing inferno that annihilated an entire forest. William Sayer argues that this was an 'inversion' of the idea of the leaders being generous dispensers of ale that instead they 'prosecute its brewer'.[87]

In Ireland, Dublin had a specific hill that was artificially made where these assemblies were held, called, unsurprisingly, the Thingmote.

Later, it was known as the Hoggin Green and various other anglicised interpretations. It was purportedly located around what is now College Green, Church Lane and Suffolk Street and existed well into the 17th century.[88] In the medieval period, this would have been outside both the Viking earthwork defences and the later city walls. However, it was still quite close to the city itself. To give you an idea of the geography if you aren't familiar with Dublin city, Dublin Castle, where Viking-age fortifications have been found underground, is about a 10-minute walk away. It's probable that they brewed within the settlement and brought the ale out with them to the location of the meeting.

This assembly, and the importance of feasting at it, is another link that has parallels between Irish and Viking cultures. The medieval Irish practised their own version of the *Thing* called the *óenach*, which also functioned as a social and political assembly.[89] Feasting and the rituals of drinking were an important part of Irish culture and the political hierarchy, and they were important in Viking society too.

We turn now from celebrations and parties to something else that was common in early medieval Ireland: slavery.

Both Viking and Irish societies in the early medieval period engaged in the practice of enslaving people. However, as historian Clare Downham argues, there is no evidence of large-scale slave-raiding before the Vikings arrived. Instead, people were enslaved because they were prisoners of war, to pay debts or because their parents had sold them so they wouldn't starve to death.[90] Of course, none of these reasons makes the practice justifiable or negates the fact that it wasn't terrible for the enslaved people. We are already somewhat familiar with the idea of parents attempting to sell their children, as we saw in Chapter 1 in the case of St Brigid, whose father tried to enslave her because he couldn't control her, while in Chapter 2 we talked about a penalty for serving bad ale called the *cumbal*, which is an enslaved woman or her worth.

The Vikings engaged in raids specifically to enslave people, and after their arrival, the Irish also took up this form of slavery.[91] We have plenty of evidence for this practice in Ireland in the archaeological record. For example, archaeologists have found a 10-metre-long iron chain with an attached collar near a crannog in Ardakillen Lake in Co. Roscommon, which is now in the collection at the National Museum of Ireland–Archaeology.

It was within this appalling practice that we also find the ritual use of ale. While it was likely that enslaved people were forced to brew as part of their duties to their enslavers, they also did so to free themselves. The Norse used ale in the practice of manumission. Specifically, the legal text the *Gulathingslov* details the practice of 'Freedom Ale':

> If a thrall takes up land or sets up a home, he shall give his freedom ale, [serving the brew of] nine measures [of malt] ... Now if the owner seems willing to let him give his freedom ale, he shall ask him before two witnesses whether he may give his ale and he shall invite him with five others to the feast that he plans to give his freedom ale...[92]

To summarise, in order to be freed, a thrall (i.e. an enslaved person) must serve their enslaver this freedom ale feast. Not only was the brewing of the ale itself important, but the alefeast and serving of ale were also critical parts of the emancipation. This plays a crucial role throughout the legal texts and is mentioned numerous times in connection with strict legal codes and rituals. This mirrors our funeral feast. A key part of all these ale traditions is the ritual aspect, the practice by which beliefs were mixed with physical practices to create a kind of performance. One of the central components of many of these feasts was magick, or more specifically in the Viking world, *seiðr*.

The year 2014 marked 1,000 years since the Battle of Clontarf was waged, and with it came all manner of commemorations: re-enactments, concerts, talks, guided tours, even a memorial coin. The battle in 1014 has been invoked over the years, notably in 1914 as a nationalist anthem of how Irish people defeated foreign invaders. We know that this narrative of Irish versus Viking isn't true – there were both Irish and Viking warriors on both sides of the battle – but nevertheless, this myth persists.

The man at the heart of the story, Brian Boru, can probably lay claim to the title of Ireland's most famous king. The battle, fought on Good Friday, has been famously immortalised in *Cogadh Gaedhel re Gallaibh* = *The war of the Gaedhil with the Gaill, or, The invasions of Ireland by the Danes and other Norsemen*, a propaganda text written at the behest of Brian's great-grandson, Muirchertach, some 100 years after the events took place. While Brian is certainly the star of the work, as he is meant to be, it's the women of the text who really stand out. These women include Gormlaith, wife of Brian, who rightfully incited her brother (unsuccessfully) to go to war against him for slighting his family honour; or the Badb, also known as the Morrígan or Nemain, who was responsible for stirring up violence and bloodshed in battle, striking fear in or granting courage to warriors in the wars to come or even predicting a death.[93] But it's one of the background characters, one who only features in a mere three sentences, who offers hints into Viking and Irish beer history. You see, the Vikings on all sides of Clontarf not only brought with them their warriors and their violence, they also brought their magick.

The *Cogadh* tells us the story of the wife of a Viking leader: 'Cluainmicnois was taken by his wife. It was on the altar of the great church she used to give her answers. Otta was the name of the wife of Turges.'[94] Though this book was written much later than the initial Viking incursions or the events it talks about, and although it's full of bias, as it's a propaganda text, this entry does suggest that Otta, a Scandinavian woman married to a Viking leader, was engaging in these *seiðr* rituals.

To paraphrase the Viking scholar Neil Price, if you asked a Viking if they believed in the gods, it would be like asking them if they 'believed in the sea'.[95] However, as Price argues, there was not one central religion or set of beliefs for these people. These could vary greatly, though there were some commonalities. These beliefs were intricately juxtaposed with a practice called *seiðr*, a kind of shamanism.[96] From the feasts to the more mundane practicalities of the day to day, these rituals informed all aspects of their lives.[97] *Seiðr* was practised at every level and in some way by everybody, from leaders like Otta to common people. However, it's clear that there were also professional practitioners who gained status from such a task. These people are defined as those who travelled around society and devoted their lives to the practice.

The *Cogadh* isn't our only evidence for the practice of Viking ritual magick in Ireland. Archaeology also lends credence, particularly for female wielders. Scholars have established that for these practitioners, *seiðr* held real social and political power. Of particular interest to the study of women's power is the *vǫlva*, or 'wand carrier', who would have been a female professional practitioner who wielded something we now call a *seiðr* staff.

At the Kilmainham Viking burials in Dublin, what I have argued to be a *seiðr* staff was found alongside a whalebone plaque in the mid-1800s.[98] *Seiðr* staffs were used for rituals and symbolised high-status *seiðr* practitioners.[99] Functioning like a wand, they possibly worked to concentrate the wielder's power. References to these staffs are found throughout the saga materials and can also be located in the Norwegian Law Codes of the 12th century, the *Eiðsivaþingslov*, which declare that,

'No person shall have in their house staff or altar, charms or sacrificial offering, or nothing that is concerning heathen religion.'[100]

The whalebone plaque is another artefact linked to magickal practice, specifically the rituals involved with textile creation.[101] These two objects together support the idea that ritual magick practice was happening in Ireland by Scandinavians. Additionally, all those bowls, cauldrons and ladles are also linked to magickal practice because it was embedded in just about every part of Viking life. This is just the tip of the iceberg.[102]

So we know that women (and men too, for that matter) were practising forms of Viking magick in Ireland, which informs our study of ale history in many ways. First, as we have already seen it was part of the rituals like inheritance beers and Yule ales; these would have all been tied up with *seiðr*. Even brewing itself might have been a magickal tradition. Archaeologist Bettina Arnold argues that in Iron Ages cultures, especially among the Celts, there was a belief in smithing as a form of 'transformative' magick – that is, the process of turning something into something else was intrinsically magickal. She contends that this might be viewed as the masculine equivalent of female beer brewing, which 'transformed' water and grain into such a socially important beverage.[103]

It wasn't just making ale or symbolically consuming it that made it part and parcel of ritual traditions. It was also what happened to you once you drank it. As Price argues, Viking practices were shamanic in nature, and part of this meant reaching altered states of consciousness for performing rituals.[104, 105] This could be achieved in various ways, but one that was easily attainable was through the consumption of ale.

This last story is a dark one. Its content, Viking human sacrifice, is not for the faint of heart. The alleged evidence in an Irish context comes from a burial in Donnybrook, Dublin, which was discovered by construction workers in 1879 and was subsequently studied by William Frazer on October 3rd of that same year.[106] According to Frazer, the grave contained a man with an 'unusually powerful frame' with two other burials a 'short distance away' containing much smaller individuals.[107] This led him to conclude that the smaller bodies were women and that the larger body was a great chief of some description.[108] The archaeologist R.A. Hall re-examined the Donnybrook burial in 1978 and goes so far as to argue that the smaller burials were women who were the 'penalty exacted for his loss'.[109]

Some historians argue that human sacrificial rituals may have involved ale. To support these claims, they cite the case written by Ibn Fadlan, a Muslim diplomat who travelled to northern Europe and encountered the people known as the Rūs in the early half of the 10th century.[110] Ibn Fadlan recorded the death of a great man of the Rūs and what he argues was an example of 'voluntary' human sacrifice. After this leader died, an enslaved girl purportedly chose to accompany him in death, though how much agency the girl had in this decision (likely, none) is highly debatable. She drinks and feasts for several days while his body and burial boat are prepared.[111] On the day of the ceremony, the girl, along with a dog, two horses, two cows, a cock and a hen, is killed by the so-called 'Angel of Death', who Ibn Fadlan refers to as a 'witch'.[112] This is after what amounts to several days of rituals, including sexual assault, culminating in this brutal end for the girl, who was consequently stabbed and strangled to death.[113]

After putting her body on the boat along with the other sacrifices, the closest male relative to the deceased man walks backwards with a torch covering his anus to light the boat on fire and complete the funerary ritual.[114] This might sound familiar to you, as this tale is the basis for the idea that the only way to have a Viking funeral is to put a body on a boat and light it on fire, which, by the way, is categorically untrue. Many people were simply buried or cremated elsewhere. But I digress.

In this story, Ibn Fadlan refers to what the Rūs were drinking as *nabidh*, which is a fermented drink from his own culture of varying alcoholic content, though here Ibn Fadlan states, 'For they drink *nabidh* unrestrainedly, night and day, so that sometimes one of them dies with his wine cup in his hand.'[115] This tells us that this beverage was clearly quite intoxicating. Further, he states that the family used one-third of the dead man's wealth to make the ale to be drunk on the day that the girl was murdered.[116] It's clear that what Ibn Fadlan was seeing was likely the brewing, serving and consumption of *erfiøl* (funeral ale).

In his accounting of this burial, the enslaved girl spends the days before her execution singing songs and drinking copious amounts of ale.[117] This tells us that the consumption of this ale was an important part of the funerary traditions. The drink also plays a key role in the more detailed rituals of the burial. It's said it was enclosed with the dead man and was removed later as part of the ceremony. Indeed, new ale was placed in his grave as part of the festivities as well as bread, meat and onions. In fact, the enslaved girl drinks ale as part of her death ritual.[118]

Saying spells over ale as part of the ritual or the consumption of ale was a way to reach an altered state of consciousness necessary to complete the practice. Here she is likely drinking as a way to calm herself, but also because it allowed her mind to reach a state that would be more amenable to her transition from this life to the next, much like condemned criminals would sometimes be given drinks before their executions. The fact that the woman who was sacrificing her, who inevitably was a magick practitioner, used ale as a way to guide the girl into the next part of her existence speaks volumes about its importance in this ritual. We can see here that ale was used as a way to gain the altered state of consciousness necessary for the rituals inherent in Viking society, so it's a reiteration of the importance of ale within Viking culture. That is, of course, if this story is to be believed. This tale also brings to us the idea that the Vikings engaged in rituals of human sacrifice that made use of ale.

But what does this have to do with Ireland? Well, the truth is very little. Setting aside the facts that Ibn Fadlan was talking about the Rūs, Swedish-descended Scandinavians who may have jettisoned their own culture to adopt the local one, and that the archaeological evidence for human sacrifice is scant and unconvincing throughout the Viking age, the Donnybrook burial itself is likely not human sacrifice, contrary to what some have argued in the past. The only reason the two potential sacrificial burials have been called 'female' is due to their location and the size of the skeletons compared to the central 'warrior' burial. Frazer himself was unable to examine the bones, as they had quickly become entangled with the rest of the bodies in the burial mound and many were broken, with the notable exception of the skull. There is no hard evidence that these burials were smaller or female, no statements to prove this except the word of workmen who were not skilled in archaeological excavation, nor perhaps experienced in the nature of Viking burial itself. There has been no analysis of the bones, so there is no way to determine if these bodies were even biologically female, much less gendered that way.

In short, there is little evidence that these were women, much less sacrifices. Their small stature could mean they were children or simply smaller people buried close by because they died in battle at the same time, or of disease, or so they could absorb some of the status of the central burial. There are any number of reasons, so this is not a case of a human sacrifice ritual involving ale. Even if there was no human sacrifice, it's likely that funeral ale was brewed as part of this ceremonial burial.

Given the importance of the brewing and consumption of ale to the Vikings, it's logical that they were probably brewing their own ale, in their own traditional styles, in the early days of settlement. However, as time wore on it's likely that the Vikings merged their brewing traditions with those of the Irish during their process of cultural assimilation. In doing so, they also combined their rituals as they converted to Christianity and jettisoned some of the old ways. Since the traditional ale practices in both cultures were often similar, this wouldn't have been a particularly difficult endeavour once the huge obstacle of religion in particular was changed.

And now, just like our zombie fishermen who came in and wouldn't leave, we turn to another group of guests who overstayed their welcome: the medieval English.

WHEREIN WE DISCOVER THE FIRST TIME THE BRITS WERE AT IT[1]

1169–1400

JULIANA HONICODE WAS FINALLY GOING TO GET HER DAY IN COURT, and she had a plan – or more precisely, a loophole.

In 1308, Juliana, along with four other women, Blissina Lotrix, Mabilla Arnalde, Elena de Donne and Joan Tyrell (as well as some 20 men), found themselves facing off against the powerful Abbot of St Thomas the Martyr in Dublin. And why did they find themselves in legal hot water? Because of ale, of course.

To understand this case, we have to backtrack a little more than 100 years to John of England; yes, the infamous King John of Magna Carta and Robin Hood fame. The English had originally come over to Ireland in 1169. They had been invited at first, welcomed by an Irish king who wanted to get his position back in return for land and his daughter Aoife's hand in marriage. But the English weren't exactly great guests. Instead, they used their invitation to wreak havoc, aiming to capture much more than they had initially been asked to help retake. At first they were mildly successful in their endeavours, colonising parts of the island before eventually being pushed back into the area around Dublin and a few other select locations during the period we're covering in this chapter. Of course, this would drastically change in later years.

Before he was even king, John of England created something called the tolboll in Dublin in 1185, less than 20 years after the initial English invasion. This was so important that he reinforced it over the ensuing years. The tolboll, as his 21 April 1201 decree states, instructs the ale brewers of Dublin to pay to the Abbey of St Thomas the Martyr a toll of ale and mead – specifically, a gallon and a half of the 'best ale and mead and as much of the second' from all the taverns in Dublin.[2] To be clear, the Abbey of St Thomas was massive. It had vast swathes of land, called Liberties, outside the city walls of Dublin in addition to farms elsewhere. The Abbey was an incredibly powerful entity, so keeping them happy would have been important to the king, not to mention the religious implications of being in good standing with the local men of God.[3]

The tolboll wasn't a unique concept to Dublin. In 1384, King Richard II granted to Joan, Abbess of Othir, 'custody of a gallon from any ale-tavern in the town of Skreen, to have for as long as it is in the K's hand' (the 'K' in this instance is referring to the king).[4] This is reiterated in 1386 to have a gallon of any ale for sale from the alehouses of Skreen.[5] We even saw something similar in one of the stories about St Patrick in Chapter 1, no matter how fictional it might have been, which tells us that the author might have been familiar with these or similar grants.

Local secular rulers also made similar provisions. In medieval Newtown Jerpoint, the following law was made: 'that if the burgesses wish to brew ale, the lord or his bailiff is to have twelve gallons from each brewing ... and a quarter of each gallon when they are sold'.[6] This is comparable to what we found in the tolboll, except perhaps a much higher amount of ale to be taken, though this makes sense given that a burgess would have been a high-ranking person in the town. They would likely have had the funds to be making larger brews in each instance, so they could afford this toll per brew. In theory.

Demanding that portions of brews be given in charity to holy houses, or as a kind of tax to local leaders, was not uncommon in medieval Ireland. Therefore, the relationship between St Thomas and the brewers of Dublin wasn't particularly unusual, except for the fact that it all appears to have descended into a bit of legal chaos.

The 1308 suit was brought by the abbot against the ale brewers of Dublin for failing to provide him with his ale and mead. Several of the defendants argued that they were exempt from this tithe because their tenements, defined in the medieval period as a piece of property with a building on it where the person normally lived, simply didn't exist at the time of John's creation. They had been wasteland, and therefore could not be subject to it. This was quickly chucked out of the court.

But our Juliana had another plan. She told the court that she held her tenement of an inn, and inns, as she argued, were exempt from the tolboll. She probably congratulated herself on the pretty glaring loophole she had found.[7]

She wasn't the only one to search for ways to get out of having to pay this fee. The tolboll proved to be wildly unpopular among the brewers of Dublin over the years, including moves in 1524 and 1527 to get the whole thing revised. In these later instances, the brewers argued that in previous centuries, like Juliana's time, fewer brewers brewed more than, say, 30 to 40 bushels in each brew, so the cost of the tolboll was reasonable to bear. Now, however, the brewers argued that 'now none within this cittie of Dublin brew nott past two bussellis, four other eight att the furdest att a brew, which ys spent for more in parte in ther housis and soo nott in the case that owght to pay tolboll'.[8] In other words, there were significantly more brewers now in Dublin, and those that did brew, brewed less, and generally made ale only for their own households.

This is particularly interesting because it sets out a premise that in the early days of the English colony in Ireland, a few brewers made a lot of ale for the people of Dublin. Then, as time went on and the city grew, more and more people brewed, and they brewed less, so the tolboll was becoming too much of a burden for them to bear. Indeed, they argued that most of what they were brewing was meant for their own households. So in contrast with what you might find in, say, urban London in the 1500s, where brewing was becoming an increasingly commercial enterprise, the opposite appears to have been happening in Dublin. More people were brewing less ale for use in their own homes.

The commissioners agreed and changed the law, stating that now only those who brewed 16 gallons or more – that was also meant to be sold – were to pay the custom of the tolboll.[9] The tolboll would continue to be an annoyance, although a less powerful one, all the way up to the 1530s, when Henry VIII dissolved the monasteries altogether and the Abbey of St Thomas ceased to be.

Unfortunately for Juliana, this legal change happened long after she needed it. The early 14th-century court found that because her tenement wasn't directly connected to the inn itself, it was not exempt, so she had to pay up. Unlike the other female defendants, she and Blissina Lotrix didn't incur additional fines. The other women had to pay for their insolence: Mabilla Arnalde owing two marks; Elena de Donne, 12 pence; and Joan Tyrell, 20 shillings. In the end, all the defendants had to cough up the beery goods. The notable exceptions were that John Sampson, William Botiller, William Callane and John de Castleknock did not owe for the tolboll of mead, but only because they never made it, which is fair enough.[10]

۞

If you wander around Dublin, you might find it hard to see remnants of the medieval past at first glance. Georgian architecture and its uniformity, beautiful as it may be, seems to dominate much of the city's streets. But if you look a little closer, you can still find traces of the old city, although you might have to look deeper – much deeper. Perhaps even well below street level.

The city is host to monuments to the medieval English crown, however much in ruins many of them may be. Dublin Castle, built by none other than King John of tolboll fame, still looms in the skyline, reigning over the city centre. Of course, what remains visible of it, with the notable exception of the Record Tower, is much newer than its medieval foundations. Still further, we find Christ Church Cathedral and St Patrick's Cathedral, visual memories of the once-overwhelming power of the Christian Church. Even the remains of the medieval city walls, like those found on Cook Street, give us glimpses into the past and the wars fought to control the city. But finding glimpses of regular people can be a bit more difficult, at least on the surface.

We can find hints of regular life in street names that mark the passing roads. Most notable for us is Winetavern Street, stretching up from the River Liffey towards Christ Church Cathedral. To be honest, it doesn't look like much now, but this road has been in existence since the 13th century, and as the name suggests it was once lined with taverns.[11] In the medieval period, it was sandwiched between the city walls, punctuated on the bottom by Prickett's Tower and the Quay Gate, which allowed ships to dock and unload their goods for the city, and on the top by the old city walls with the Winetavern Street Gate, which people would go through to get to the newer, enclosed parts of Dublin and vice versa. Though back then, it went by a slightly different name. The incredibly wordy title 'Ordinances by the Common Council of Dublin on the Friday Next After [Sept 21] The Festival of St Matthew the Apostle, 1305', found in the *Dublin Chain Book*, tells us that one of the city watchmen's territory covered the 'Church of St John to Bouestrete, as far as the gate in the Tavern-street' (the emphasis on wine wasn't always present).[12]

One of the houses of the women in that 1308 tolboll court case might very well have been here on this street, or even someone who paid their tolboll in full. It's difficult to track down these average brewing men and women, as they usually only appear in written records when they ran afoul of the law. In addition, no houses remain standing from that time. Instead, their remains lie buried under layers of roadworks and construction, built on top of each other, one after another, for centuries, creating the cityscape that we see today. To learn more about the lives of brewers in medieval Dublin, we have to dig a little deeper – literally.

Winetavern Street is a mere shadow of its colourful past. The last pub to stand on the street that was named for them closed many years ago and what's left doesn't reflect the importance of the street's place in beer history. At least on the outside. Archaeological excavations of the street from the 20th century revealed much of its history. From the 13th century, archaeologists discovered pottery from England and France – bowls, platters and pitchers to hold wine, mead and ale[13] as well as barrel staves, coins, glass vessels and pottery sherds.[14, 15] All of these tell the story of the taverns that operated there, which, in addition to specialising in the sale of wine, could have possibly also served ale at some point.

Before we get too far ahead of ourselves, we need to briefly discuss one of the biggest problems with identifying medieval drinking spaces by archaeology. Finding one medieval pitcher, for example, only reveals to us that at a period in time, this specific item was lost, forgotten or purposefully discarded. It alone does not tell us what the space was where it was left. For that, we need to look at structures, the remains of timber buildings or stone foundations, or whether one particular piece of pottery was combined with many others of the same type. A large cache of pottery sherds, pitchers, bowls and barrels might hint that this was indeed a place where people drank. Or it might mean it was a rubbish bin.

Matching this with historical data is also key. We must understand the place within its context. For example, in medieval Dublin, in many cases there wouldn't be any archaeological differences between the structure of an actual alehouse where a woman sold ale to her neighbours when she had some available versus someone's home who didn't brew. We must be incredibly careful about assigning a value or even a date to an extant building based on archaeological data; otherwise you could go to Winetavern Street, open a pub tomorrow and say it had medieval origins just because medieval drinking artefacts are buried beneath the ground.

So how do we define these spaces? This can be a bit of a philosophical question. I saw someone online talking about it being like the Ship of Theseus – you know, the one where a ship gets replaced one plank at a time until none of the original material remains, leading us to question if it's actually still the same ship. Archaeologist James Wright has written extensively about the myths around medieval buildings in his book *Historic Building Mythbusting: Uncovering Folklore, History, and Archaeology*.[16] Besides the stories of castles and churches, he did a deep dive into some of the purported oldest pubs in the UK to find the truth behind the folk stories. We can learn a lot from his book and apply it to our own public houses in Ireland. This is not to say that the lore surrounding pubs isn't also important, because it is – these stories tell us a lot about the culture that told them – but we must be careful to disentangle what the archaeology is *actually* saying from what the tales perhaps wish it did. We know there were taverns on Winetavern Street because of the archaeological evidence but also because of the historical information and, of course, the very name of the place.

A few blocks away, up on Bridge Street, is the Brazen Head pub, which is one of the most famous pubs in Ireland. It lays claim to a long and storied history. The earliest written reference to a place called the Brazen Head relates to a fine that was given to Richard Fagan and his wife in 1613 on 'one massuage and garden; called the Brazen Head, in Bridge Street, in the City of Dublin'. Timothy Dawson argues that this building likely existed before this, putting its date somewhere in the 16th century.[17] However, the evidence for the Fagans' fine comes from a much later source, dating to 1700.[18] Precisely what this Brazen Head functioned as is another story. For the Fagans, it was likely their home. Is it possible that they brewed on location for their own household or even for sale? Certainly. In fact, it's quite likely (more on why this might be the case in Chapter 6). According to Henry Berry, the earliest mention that has been found referring specifically to a Brazen Head Inn was in 1668.[19] But buried underneath the paths and pavement, we can still find hints of beer history.

In the 13th century, Bridge Street was outside of the medieval city walls. It got its name from, you guessed it, the bridge that linked the south and north sides of the River Liffey. Once known as Ostman Bridge, it now (ironically for our purposes) bears the name of Father Mathew, the chief proponent of temperance in 19th-century Ireland. Because of its location outside the city walls, it probably wouldn't have been home to any buildings because they would have been vulnerable to attacks.[20]

In 1989, excavations took place on an 8 metre by 3 metre site near the Brazen Head.[21] According to Howard Clarke, in the medieval period this site would have been just south of the Carles Inn, but in his 2002 revised edition of the medieval Dublin map, he removed this inn from Bridge Street because he wasn't sure of its precise location.[22] Regardless, the 1989 excavations on Bridge Street Lower revealed 1,198 sherds of medieval pottery from Dublin and even imports from France and

England.[23] For example, archaeologists have concluded that among the Dublin hand-built glazed ware, this represents a minimum of 25 jugs.[24] And that's just of one kind. The report from these excavations concludes that a decent number of pitchers, tankards, jugs or bowls were originally formed from these remains. They even found a barrel lid![25] All these finds, combined with other evidence like shoes and even skeletal materials, led researchers to conclude that in the 13th century, people lived on Bridge Street.[26]

Of course, people who lived in medieval Dublin would be drinking ale. The evidence from the Bridge Street excavations turned up many possible vessels – tankards, jugs, pitchers – that could have been used to drink and serve ale. The harder part of the equation comes into play when we begin to expand on this question to wonder if they were also brewing here. It's certainly possible. After all, many people would have done so in their own houses with their kitchen equipment, so there wouldn't necessarily be any glaring evidence of brewing. It's possible that someone at some point in the 13th century was brewing on Bridge Street, but we can't say for certain one way or the other. Regardless, they were certainly drinking ale – ale that would have had to be purchased from their neighbours somewhere, likely from something like an alehouse, but maybe not by that name.

This is where things can get a bit tricky in Ireland, particularly in Dublin. As I've said, temporary alehouses can be almost impossible to identify because they were simply part of someone's home, a space a woman might open up because she had extra ale to sell to those around her. Plus prior to the 15th century, at least in English contexts, an alehouse was generally not somewhere people drank on the premises.[27] Peter Clark argues that with the advent of the 1500s, alehouses sprung up that served people on site, with the clientele mostly focused on common people. These places were also often part of someone's home, with spare rooms or even cellars serving as drinking spaces, so the lines between public space and private could be quite blurred.[28] You could also stay at an alehouse, though as Clark notes, the accommodation was often poor, with the options being the floor, the table or in bed with the landlords.[29]

As we saw in Chapter 3, alehouses in Irish-held areas could be establishments of high rank, places kings or lords drank in, and houses of professional hosts. These alehouses could be more permanent spaces, buildings dedicated to drinking, though perhaps sometimes still part of someone's home. Alehouses in Ireland predate the arrival of the English, and the Vikings too for that matter. These places mentioned in the Irish sources would have looked a bit different than a woman opening up her home when she'd brewed a bit more than her own household needed, as we saw in the English colonies. They might have been more permanent spaces or halls where people often hosted events, rather than a place where a person went to purchase ale.

In England in particular, a tavern was often meant to mean a place that primarily sold wine. We can see hints of that on Winetavern Street in Dublin. However, as noted in the tolboll, the people who had to pay this tithe were those who brewed and those who kept taverns. This would repeat well into the early modern period, when people who sold ale in Dublin were often referred to as keeping taverns, not alehouses. So in Dublin at least, taverns were also places where you could buy ale that had been brewed on site.

As we will see in Chapter 6, the brewing women of Dublin who sold ale referred to their establishments as taverns. This was a major bone of contention for one English immigrant to the city, who believed they were giving their drinking places a higher rank than they deserved. Taverns were meant to be posher types of places, unlike the more rough-and-tumble alehouses.[30]

On the other hand, inns were places where people stayed. They were also often bigger houses. John Hare argues that inns served as a space for travellers with stables and room for their goods, and catered to a more wealthy clientele, such as merchants or government officials, than the alehouses.[31] Hare contends that inns weren't only places to sleep, but also a kind of informal market, and sometimes even a bank.[32] And as the tolboll says, they were also sites of ale brewing.

But you could also stay at a tavern, or even an alehouse, and both could have food as an option. The clientele could differ greatly, as could the quality of the food and drink offered. The lines between these kinds of spaces change over the years and vary depending on context, though many scholars have tried to establish the clear differences between the three, like Peter Clark's book *The English Alehouse: A Social History, 1200–1830*.

Confused? Here's a summary: alehouses, taverns and inns in Ireland were potentially all places where you could stay the night. Taverns in England catered to a wealthier kind of clientele. In Ireland, many places that would be called alehouses in England were called taverns here for one reason or another. Alehouses in England were often spaces in someone's house that were opened up when the woman had spare ale to sell. These spaces could even be in a cellar and were for common people. In Ireland, these spaces in Irish-held areas could be more permanent and were host to feasts and festivals as well as kings and other high-ranking officials. Inns were different kinds of establishments, while also offering food, a place to stay and beer, though as the tolboll declares, their brewing was exempt, making for a clear legal delineation between the two.

Regardless of your social rank or what kind of establishment you visited, many people went out and had a drink or two with the express purpose of enjoying themselves. Drinking spaces were much more than just for drinking. They were also undoubtedly for fun.

Who doesn't love a good story? Many of us have probably spent a night or two out at the pub regaling each other with tales of our recent exploits while enjoying a few pints. We go to pubs to share our triumphs, to commiserate our losses and to entertain each other with funny anecdotes. In short, we go to have a good time, to escape everyday life, if only for a little while. And so did medieval people.

> Make glad my friends, you sit to long still
> Speak now and glad and drink all your fill
> You have ihird of men lif that live in lond
> Drink deep and make glad, you have no other need
> This song is y-seid of me
> Ever blessed may ye be[33]

Drink deep, be merry. There is nothing else you need to be doing right now, so enjoy yourself, Friar Michael of Kildare told his listeners. These lines come from 'Satire', one of a collection of verses, now known as *The Kildare Poems,* likely written by our friar in the 1330s. 'Satire' was presumably designed to be read out loud, perhaps while people were drinking, as this final stanza indicates. Contrary to what some might tell you, medieval people certainly drank ale to get ~~drunk~~ 'glad'. 'Satire' encourages the drinker to have a good time and maybe get a little tipsy. But just as there are writers like Friar Michael encouraging listeners to let loose, there are also many ecclesiastical authors railing against drunkenness.

As long as people have been drinking ale, there have been monks lecturing them about sinning. There were warnings against such behaviour in the *Regimen Sanitatis Salernitanum*, which was originally composed sometime in the 12th or 13th century before making its way to Ireland in the late Middle Ages. In any event, this text deals with drunkenness – specifically, the concept of getting drunk once a month, which apparently some voices of the day argued was a good idea, to which the writer says this was a terrible notion because moderation is key; otherwise it's harmful.[34]

The text then goes on to talk in some depth about who should be able to drink, noting that old men should be able to drink as much as they want because they are old and know precisely how much they can handle.[35] In contrast, the 'youths' should only be drinking in moderation because they can't cope with it: 'it is like putting fire upon the head of fire on weakly wood'.[36] However, like so many texts, this is wishful thinking (or should we say, wishful drinking?). We can be certain people liked to drink for fun and to get a little (or a lotta) inebriated. This was apparent when Friar Michael invited people to drink deep and be merry; many certainly did.

While the final stanza in 'Satire' is a lovely message for listeners to drink up and enjoy themselves, the rest of it is a satirical rant at various modes of employ. To be frank, Friar Michael mocks, denigrates and generally takes the piss out of a plethora of medieval occupations. In between having a go at nuns, potters, bakers and tailors, he takes aim at our brewing women:

> Hail be you brewsters with your gallons
> Potels and quarts over all the towns!
> Your thumbs take much away, shame has possessed the gyle
> Be careful of the cucking stool, the lake is deep and dirty.[37]

When the English invaded and colonised parts of Ireland, they brought with them many things, including their biases. One of these was the very real fear of cheating alewives. In my book *The Devil's in the Draught Lines*, I explore the relationship of this anxiety of brewing women ripping off their customers in English art and literature. Paintings were made of alewives doomed to hell, plays were written with brewing women consigned to devilish marriages and sculptures were created of cheating brewsters cavorting with demons. To be clear, there was a general fear throughout England of people in the food and drink trades ripping off their customers; this wasn't limited to alewives. It's just that alewives also got a healthy dose of misogyny on top of that.[38]

Friar Michael is echoing these biases here with his line 'your thumbs take much away'. He is referring to the way in which ale was sold while also alluding to some dishonest behaviour.[39] Friar Michael then goes on to make a witty double entendre. The Middle English word *gyle* means both 'a trick' and also 'fermenting wort', so our fair author is again referring to the supposed cheating nature of these brewsters as well as to the wort that they make for brewing.

Of course, Friar Michael isn't just mimicking something from across the Irish Sea. The fears that women who brewed were cheating their customers or selling in false measures aren't just found in funny poems designed to make the listeners laugh. They can also be seen in the laws. The *Chain Book of the Dublin Corporation* contains a 1305 code that states the following in Anglo-Norman French, translated as, 'Every woman brewer must pay two shillings yearly, unless exempted by the Bailiffs. Fine for making ale inferior to the quality required by the assize, fifteen pence.'[40]

The assize of ale was the set of laws that regulated the price, quality and size of portions for sale. Similar to the Brehon Laws and their tests for malt, the assize was set to ensure there were some kind of standards of ale-making and that customers weren't being ripped off. The assize was a foundational part of brewing in medieval English-controlled Ireland and was often repeated throughout the years, with noted punishments for violators – violators who often just so happened to be female. We know this because the laws were written about women, and women only, but that's not because women were the only ones breaking them; it's because women were overwhelmingly the only ones brewing. An even earlier 14th-century legal code states: 'The fine on any woman-brewer for inferior ale is fifteen pence for the first offence, two and six pence for the second, and for the third, suspension from her occupation for a year and a day.'[41]

These two codes, made around the time of the legal action by the Abbey of St Thomas against our brewers regarding the tolboll, seem to suggest that women dominated the brewing trade at the time, at least in Dublin. To be clear, they weren't just afraid of women selling in false measures or not brewing in accordance with the assize. They were also deeply concerned that they were adding weird stuff to their brews, things that should not be in there, in an attempt to cut corners. *Ordinances by the Common Council of the City of Dublin*, also written in the early 14th century, states that 'no woman-brewer shall brew with straw under penalty of 20 shillings'.[42] Was brewing with straw widespread? A reaction perhaps to a famine or otherwise poor harvests? Maybe. It might also have been a more general fear or a more isolated instance that caused the law to be put on the books.

These laws and regulations weren't limited to Dublin, not by a long shot. Towns and urban centres throughout English-held Ireland passed similar measures to control brewers. In 1306, the people in the town of Kilmehallok, Co. Limerick (which is likely Kilmallock), tried to skirt regulations of the assize of bread and ale by hiking up the prices. We are told that before the Justiciar arrived, ale was to be sold for one penny, whereas after he came, it was sold at one penny and a halfpenny 'to the damage of the Justiciar and the people coming there before him the King's mandate'.[43] So the brewers of the town were collectively fined 40 shillings.

This is echoed in 1316–18, where we see this statement in the *Dublin White Book* under the 'Grievances of the Common Folk of Dublin': 'The assize of bread and ale to be more strictly kept, the assay to be made more frequently than heretofore, and transgressors to be speedily punished as in former times.'[44]

Here we see references to punishments, and perhaps not just a fine. If we return to our poem 'Satire' written in Kildare, Friar Michael warns his audience that alewives should 'Be careful of the cucking stool, the lake is deep and dirty'. This suggests that brewing women who cheat their customers, at least in Kildare, might find themselves on the wrong side of this cucking stool, which was a kind of chair used to punish women. They would be strapped in and left to the jeers and humiliation of the crowds. The cucking stool could also involve dunking the person in water, though the specific term for this method, 'ducking stool', comes into use later. However, the line from our Friar Michael referencing the lake does suggest that these alewives would find themselves brought to the lake, strapped to this chair and dunked in and out of the water.

So it wasn't just fines brewers had to fear, but corporal punishment too. I haven't found any evidence of a Kildare alewife being strapped to a ducking stool, but as we know, absence of evidence is not evidence of absence. Elsewhere in Ireland, there might be some truth to Friar Michael's warning, as the *Corporation By-laws of Kilkenny* decreed in 1333 that if an alewife sells a false measure a third time, she will be subjected to the *swynglingstol* for corporal punishment (this also seems to be referencing a cucking stool, but again, water might not have been involved).[45] Friar Michael might have been referencing a very real punishment for cheating brewsters who ripped off their customers, at least after a certain number of offences.

One last point before we move on: all these legal decrees and ordinances reference women, and women only, in this period of the 14th century – the same period of the tolboll case where we saw 20 men listed as defendants alongside only five women. To reconcile this, we need to consider the legal practice of coverture.

Under the English law of coverture, women's legal identities were often subsumed by their husbands, meaning they could stand in for them in legal cases, such as the tolboll. Gillian Kenny argues that under common law in English-held Ireland, married Anglo-Irish women had very little power (perhaps in contrast to their Irish counterparts, who could own property). They were subject to their husbands, who most of the time controlled all their property and money but could not sell or give them away, etc., without their wife's permission.[46] In other words, a wife had to consent to her husband's distribution of her properties, but how much agency they really had in these interactions is debatable, as Kenny points out.[47] If they weren't under their husband's legal guardianship, they could have been under their father's or brother's. Therefore, of the 20 male defendants charged with not paying the tolboll, they might not have been the ones who had actually done the brewing. Instead, it's more likely that their wives were the ones making the ale or that they were brewing together as a couple.

Confused yet? This legal practice makes teasing out economic history in this period incredibly complicated, but we shall try.

As I wrote about in my book on UK brewing history, *The Devil's in the Draught Lines*, during the medieval period it was primarily women who did the brewing. Though their husbands might have physically owned the brewhouse, it was generally the women who did the actual activity, either entirely by themselves or with some aid from their spouses. In England, Scotland and Wales, brewing was viewed as a natural extension of the household duties in the medieval periods, and even later, so it fell to women to engage in the trade. They might make some extra to sell to their neighbours as a kind of side hustle, but it was a way to supplement their family income, not generally a way to make loads of money on their own.[48] There were always exceptions, though, especially in medieval Wales.[49] As time wore on in the medieval, and later early modern periods, brewing became more lucrative as it became increasingly commercialised and professionalised.[50]

In Ireland, while it was certainly the case that brewing was seen as an extension of household duties, and thus it often fell to women to brew, based on the size of the brews, it might have been more lucrative than it was for some of their counterparts across the Irish Sea. Given that we know from the 16th-century case that people were brewing less than they had in the medieval period, it may suggest that brewing was at least better paid in the High Middle Ages than it was later. It's an interesting point to consider.

In the tolboll legal case, we can see coverture in action because William Donne might have been the husband or father of Elena de Donne, and it was he who the court ordered the abbot should recover against for Elena's deceit, so it was he who owed that 12 pence fine.[51] While only five of our plaintiffs in the case were female, this may have little to do with who was actually brewing. Which is not to say that men didn't brew; they certainly did. However, it's clear that women dominated the brewing trade if the legal sources are to be believed (and I suggest they should be).

From these, we also know what the expectations were for these women who brewed in the 14th century. You needed to keep to the assize. You needed to sell by specific measurements dictated by the King of England himself. And under no circumstances were you to brew with straw. But what, then, were you supposed to brew with?

Sarra lived in the 14th century. And that's just about all we know of her. We don't know when she came into the world or when she left it. We don't know if she ever married or had children. We don't know her hopes or dreams or wishes. We don't even know her last name. We know just one more thing: that between 1 August 1344 and the same date the following year, the Priory of the Holy Trinity delivered seven crannocs and six pecks of grain for her to make malt, as it appears she was the one responsible for this operation at Grangegorman.[52]

When I introduced you to Winetavern Street earlier on, I mentioned how Christ Church Cathedral is at the top of the hill. And Christ Church, perhaps more than any other ecclesiastical body, offers direct insight into brewing in medieval Ireland.

You see, what is now Christ Church Cathedral was once home to the Priory of the Holy Trinity. A priory is a small monastic group consisting of a prior and a close group of associated monks. Small though it might have been, the Priory of the Holy Trinity was quite wealthy, holding thousands of acres in Co. Dublin, including farms at Grangegorman, Glasnevin and Clonkeen – farms where malting and brewing would take place.

Even within the city walls, the priory left an indelible mark on brewing history because the grounds themselves were the possible location of at least two brewhouses over the centuries: one on St Michael's Hill East, dating to around 1591, and another on Christ Church Place, dating to around 1327.[53] If that's not enough, the basement of the cathedral likely functioned as a tavern at some point. Historian Gillian Kenny found that in 1423, Juliana Loveryn, a widow, and a merchant called John Warying leased, among other things, two cellars under Christ Church in Dublin. She argues that because church cellars were often used as taverns, this might have been the case here, given the timeframe and who leased it.[54]

Christ Church was home to one more important thing to the history of beer in Ireland: the *Account Roll of the Priory of the Holy Trinity, Dublin,* dating to the years 1337–46.[55] The *Account Roll* details all manner of things, including food supplies, purchases and payments. We even learn that the prior liked to order takeaway pies from the shops just down the road on Cook Street, delivered to his rooms.[56] Much like we do now. And in the midst of all these fascinating insights into daily life is brewing. More precisely, we learn exactly what malts they were using in their brews and a little bit about the women who made them.

References to malt litter the pages of this text, with shipments of grains made to people, often women, who made the final product. Grain was sent to women like Leticia Marcold for drying malt or to Sarra, who we've already mentioned.[57] The amounts given to these women varied but were often between four and seven crannocs, though this isn't particularly helpful because what made up a crannoc varied in the Middle Ages, ranging from eight bushels to eight pecks over the years.[58] Suffice it to say it was not a small amount.

The *Account Roll* also tells us what women who malted might expect to be paid. A woman who worked as a maltster on one of their manors received 3 shillings for this as well as other work from August 1st to the Sunday before May 19th.[59] This might seem very low, but to give you some perspective, at the same place, a cowherd earned 2 shillings, a plough driver 4 shillings and a sergeant 5 shillings.[60] The priory even sometimes borrowed malt, receiving some from Alice Raggeley 'as a loan' because of an upcoming visit from the archbishop.[61]

From these records, we can also see the types of malt that they used, with wheat, oats and barley making frequent appearances, but also something called hastivel, a kind of early-ripening grain that was grown around Ireland. Hastivel doesn't just appear in the *Account Roll*. It also pops up in the *Justiciary Rolls* in 1308, where it was described as 'sown' with wheat on five acres belonging to Eustace de Glenmethan and worth half a mark an acre (compared to beans and peas, which were worth 4 shillings an acre).[62] Later on in this same source, we have the case of Walter Reyth in Cork, who was the purveyor of victuals for the king's use in Scotland. He contracted marriage with one Juliana Colle and as such received from her, among other things, 1 crannoc of wheat malt, 2 crannocs of oat malt, 4 crannocs of hastivel, 1 crannoc of best malt (*de bras capitali*) and 2 crannocs *de bras cursal*.[63] So a woman brought five different kinds of malt with her dowry.

The grain bills for these brews might have been complex and were certainly not limited to only one type of malt. These *Rolls* detail that while a generic 'malt' is often mentioned, likely a reference to barley malt, there are also more specific kinds of malts used in the same brew: 'Also in ale brewed on same day, 1 peck of wheat malt, and 10 pecks of oat malt'.[64] This sort of grain bill – one peck of wheat malt and one crannoc of oat malt – is echoed in later accounts.[65] But these grain bills could be more complicated, although this can get a bit tricky, because it can become hard to discern whether this was in one single kind of ale or if they were brewing multiple kinds at the same time. But for argument's sake, let's assume that these malts were for one kind of ale at least some of the time. I think this makes the most sense because the records refer to a specific ale made because a certain visitor is coming. They also brewed multiple times a week, so perhaps they made different ales on different days. Regardless, on Wednesday, 16 September 1344, '...in ale brewed against the coming of the Prior, 2 pecks of wheat malt, 1 crannoc of hastivell malt, and 10 pecks of oat malt'.[66]

These ales were also made to be drunk young. This is not unique to the priory, but is reflected throughout the medieval Irish world. Ales without anything to act in a preservative manner, like hops, would spoil somewhat quickly, certainly after a few weeks. We can tell from this example at the priory that the brew day for this complex ale was September 16th. The prior arrived on September 20th and remained there until October 8th, when the 'prior went away to Dublin'. This means that the ale that was brewed on September 16th was drunk sometime within that three-week window. It's possible that this was brewed because the prior was coming and was going to be a drain on their stores, so it was necessary to brew extra, not necessarily to be drunk while he was there, but to replace what he drank after he arrived. But I don't think this is the case, given that we know that brews in both England and Ireland at this time were made to be drunk young because they spoiled so quickly.

We know what the malt bill might have looked like and we have an idea that these ales all had a relatively short shelf life. We also know that at least in Christ Church, they brewed with great frequency. But how precisely did they brew?

This is a more complex question. Experimental archaeologists and historians the world over have been trying to recreate medieval European ales for quite a while. This is surprisingly difficult because instructions on precisely how to brew are relatively non-existent. This is because brewing was something that was taught, particularly when it was the domain of women, by sharing the knowledge from mother to daughter, parent to child, or even housekeeper to servant. Much like cooking and baking, there wouldn't be a manual on the process. Rather, oral tradition and technique were taught and passed down in families or among workers. It wasn't a process that was usually written down.

In his book *Amber, Gold and Black*, Martyn Cornell writes about historical English brewing techniques and ingredients, and it's likely that the English brought similar traditions with them when they invaded and colonised Ireland. But how exactly did they make their medieval brews? Well, like the ingredients themselves, this likely varied greatly. For example, they might have used a basic infusion mashing process. They might not have boiled the ale because without the inclusion of hops, there wouldn't have been a need to, as Cornell argues.

Perhaps one of the best examples, and one of the very few available, comes to us from the *Treatise of Walter de Bibbesworth*, a text composed by the titular knight for Dionisie de Muchensi to instruct her stepchildren. One of the key things he writes about is how to make ale, from the malting process to the creation of the wort. Here we are told that ground malt is added to hot water until the woman brewing the ale is happy with the wort. After this point, Bibbesworth indicates that he cannot go into more detail.[67] From this text, Cornell was able to extrapolate how a medieval ale might have been made: the ale remained unboiled, it included a deliberate addition of yeast and no herbal additives were used in the actual brewing process.[68]

I have a bit of experience with medieval brewing because a few years ago I experimented with recreating an English small ale from the Middle Ages. I used a recipe created by Tofi Kerthjalfadsson in 1998, available on the Carnegie Mellon University website.[69] Kerthjalfadsson based his recipes on two substantial bits of information from Judith Bennett's work *Ale, Beer, and Brewsters in England: Women's Work in a Changing World 1300–1600*, specifically, the household of Elizabeth de Burgh, Lady of Clare, and the case of Robert Sibille the younger, who went to court at Kibworth Harcourt for ripping off his customers.[70] The recipe was fairly easy to follow, just lots of adding water at various stages in the brew.

But this was just one way that brewing could be done. As we have seen in previous chapters, there were a number of different ways ales could be made, depending on the size of the brew and the ingredients, so this could certainly change, not to mention various brewers would have had their own tricks of the trade. Therefore, the brewing in English-held Ireland likely mimics what Cornell has found in England. Elsewhere, in areas where Ireland was still controlled by the Irish, it was likely done as it had been done in the previous centuries, carrying on the old traditions well into the centuries after the invasion and colonisation, though it's also possible that they picked up some of the English techniques as well. And vice versa – the English were certainly using native ingredients like malts.

As they say on TV, don't try this at home, kids.

To combat dysentery, the *Materia Medica* says to add marrow to ale. Add orache to hot ale to help your cough. Combine hyssop and absinth, and boil with ale to cure mercury poisoning.[71] Add pennyroyal, elecampane or calamint for abortions.[72, 73] If you want to 'expel the melancholic humour' and clear up your period, add the root of sowthistle with cornflower, tansy roots, mouse-ear hawkweed, roots of houndstongue, germander, a pinch of fumiter and some roots of bugloss all mixed together with a mortar and pestle, and combine with strong ale and honey.[74] If your heart needs comforting, it instructs readers to add houndstongue to ale.[75] Hot ale mixed with spurge will 'accentuate every medicine that purges the phlegmatic humour'.[76] The juice of ribwort added to ale helps with bladder lesions.[77] Of course, do not under any circumstances follow any of this advice because it comes from a 15th-century text with very little knowledge of disease and is therefore liable to kill you. I repeat, do not try any of these at home. Ever.

With that warning, the *Materia Medica* is an Irish medical text written in 1415. It's slightly outside of this chapter's timeframe, but nonetheless it provides a critical component to launch our investigation into which herbs, if any, people might have been using in their ales. This text includes 292 different herbs and their uses. Ale features prominently in the medicinal recipes in this text. The book also offers a variety of ways to consume ale: strong, fresh and hot. Critically, *fermentum,* i.e. leaven, a brewer's yeast, is mentioned, including how it's made of wheat flour, salt and water.[78]

The question of herbal brewing additives is a wily one. It's possible that Irish people were using herbs as part of the standard practice for brewing. The translator of the *Materia Medica*, Micheál Ó Conchubhair, speculates that sea wormwood was possibly used for bittering ale.[79] It's possible that herbal additives varied as greatly as those used in the medicinal ales.

In England, author Martyn Cornell concludes that 40 or 50 types of plants, including wormwood, broom, yarrow, sweet gale (bog myrtle), marsh or wild rosemary, long pepper, fennel, laurel berries, peony seeds, ground ivy, sage, mace, thyme and clove, might have found their way into medieval brews.[80] There is also some evidence that herbs were added not as part of the brewing process as such, but after. In fact, herbs could be added much later, long after the fermentation process was completed, to be steeped in brews like teabags, perhaps using whatever herbs they liked or had easy access to, as we saw with medicinal beers.

But not only these, perhaps. In William Langland's *Piers Plowman,* for instance, Beton the Brewster beckons Sir Glutton into her establishment, derailing him from his route to church and calling out to him that she has both good ale and good gossip. He responds to her entreaties by asking if she has any spices, to which she replies that she indeed does, including pepper, garlic and fennel seed for fasting days. Could he be talking about spices to put in his ale? Possibly – Cornell believes this meant that these spices were added to ale after it was brewed and served.[81] Of course, the inclusion of garlic in this list hints that this might not be referring to what you might want to put in your ale. Or maybe you do.

Because we now include hops in nearly every beer on the market today, we often think that the absence of them in a brew means that something else must be added as a matter of course. But this is simply not the case. It's possible that adding herbs wasn't part of the actual brewing process and that they were only added later, or not at all.

Cornell contends that in England it's possible that often no herbs were used in brewing.[82] The *Materia Medica* seems to support this because all these herbs were added to a base ale, which in turn might suggest that herbs weren't added to the ales prior to their transformation into medicine because they might interfere with this new medicinal cure. In addition, the Brehon Laws, which specify nearly everything, don't make any mention of herbal additives in Irish-made ales, so it's quite likely that there was not a standardised method, as we saw in Chapter 3.

It's not only the Brehon Laws that make no mention of specific herbal additives. The Christ Church *Account Roll* also makes no mention of herbs to be added to their ales. These records are meticulous in detailing precisely what malts from their stores went into their ales and when, so if great quantities of one single herb were regularly used as part of the brewing process, it would seem that this would have also been mentioned. Again, these herbal additions might have come later, or perhaps for some, not at all.

Regardless, the *Materia Medica* does provide us with a fascinating insight into how herbs were added to brews in order to create these medieval medicines and cures. They believed that these medicinal ales could cure any number of diseases, from dysentery and lesions to a wicked cough. The one thing it doesn't seem to offer is a cure for the Plague.

Friar John Clyn likely settled into his new home in Kilkenny sometime in the decade before the Black Death hit in 1348. Born in Leinster, he had moved around Ireland and had served at one point as the guardian of the friary in Carrick, according to Bernadette Williams.[84] Clyn probably wouldn't be all that remarkable in our history of Ireland except that he happened to be writing an annalistic account of the area during the time when the Plague hit Ireland. Clyn has ended up being essentially *the* source for the bubonic plague and its happenings in the country.

> But I, Brother John Clyn of the Order of Minors and convent of Kilkenny, wrote these notable facts that happened in my time in this book ... and so that notable deeds do not vanish with time and disappear from the memory of the future, observing these many evils and the whole world resembling a wicked place, waiting among the dead until death comes, thus I have rendered into writing just as truthfully as I have heard and examined, so the writing does not perish with the writer, and the labour die together with the workman, I leave parchment for the work to continue, if by chance in the future surviving men remain, and anyone of the race of Adam could avoid this pestilence, and continue the work I began.[83]

Clyn stopped writing at some point, stating, as the quote above says, that he was leaving pages blank for those who might have survived the 'pestilence' to continue working on his annalistic account. This quotation is particularly poignant; it reveals a man who thinks the world might very well end with lines like 'in case anyone should still be alive in the future'. He was indeed 'waiting among the dead for death to come'. Whether Clyn died from the Black Death after writing this is something of scholarly debate, but shortly after completing these entries in 1349, we see this morose speculation written by someone else later: 'It seems the author died here.'[85]

Regardless of why Clyn stopped writing, before he did he offers an incredible insight into life, and death, during the Plague. This account can help us to understand how something so horrific might have impacted all parts of daily life, from what people ate to where they lived and even how they brewed.

Clyn tells readers that in Dublin from the beginning of August, thousands of people died. In fact, he even begins to talk about himself, to say that he is a first-hand witness to the death and destruction wrought by the Plague and that he is essentially waiting for it to come for him. He is seeing this all happen in real time. In this text, Clyn makes a particularly haunting claim of those dying of the Plague being carried away with those with whom they had just issued their deathbed confessions.[86]

This depiction is reminiscent of Continental authors. According to Marchionne Di Coppo Stefani, a Florentine statesman writing in the late 1370s and early 1380s, 'Child abandoned the father, the husband the wife, wife the husband, one brother the other, one sister the other.' As in Ireland, towns and cities were annihilated, leaving only the remnants of still-burning fires and corpses rotting in their beds. Di Coppo Stefani states that there was nothing else to do in Florence but to bury the dead: 'And then more bodies were put on top of them, with a little more dirt over those; they put layer on layer just like one puts layers of cheese in a lasagne.' And this, my friends, is why I can no longer eat lasagne without imagining piles upon piles of rotting, mouldering bodies in plague pits. This image now haunts me.

As for brewers, many of them would have died alongside their neighbours during this medieval pandemic. But it didn't affect everyone the same way. Maria Kelly wrote a critical work on the Black Death in Ireland and argues that it didn't affect the Gaelic Irish to the extent that it decimated the English colonists. Gaelic Ireland – that is, Ireland controlled by the Irish – was largely pastoral. There were exceptions to this, likely in areas close to important religious sites, but by and large, Irish-controlled Ireland was made up of pastoral and rural communities, which means they were spread out and didn't have as much contact between people, so the Plague simply couldn't spread as easily.

In contrast, the English colonies largely consisted of towns and villages. For example, by 1300, 330 chartered boroughs existed and there was high population density around Kilkenny, New Ross and

Waterford as well as Cork, Dublin, Co. Kildare, Co. Tipperary, Co. Limerick and Co. Louth. In medieval Kildare alone, there were 15 villages.[87] This focus on populations in urban centres all contributed to the devastation of the Plague, simply because there were more people around to spread it to, full stop.

Geoffrey Le Baker, an English chronicler who wrote about the Black Death, noted that the plague 'fell the English inhabitants living there in great numbers, but barely touched the pure Irish who lived in the mountains and upper parts'.[88] Kelly estimates the mortality to the English was around 50% and that whole villages were completely wiped out.[89] She also found that, as elsewhere, friaries and monastic communities, like cities and towns, were hit particularly hard, largely because of population density, which made it easier for the Plague to spread.[90] Because the Irish didn't live in towns and instead had a pastoral lifestyle, they were not as badly affected.[91]

So English brewers, or those Irish who lived in English-held territories, were more likely to have been killed as a result of the Black Death. Not to mention that fear would have prevented people from buying or selling ale to their neighbours to some degree. According to Kelly, public events were cancelled.[92] Inevitably, when the disease was rampaging around Ireland, brewers, like everyone else, would see their businesses affected. People simply did not want to interact with each other for fear of catching the disease.

More rural people who brewed might have escaped the onslaught that saw people die in large numbers in the cities. They might have been able to continue their work brewing as a household chore for their families or as a servant in a more isolated castle or home. Of course, the Plague made no such discriminations and still managed to kill those in such places, though, as Kelly notes, not in the great numbers of the urban dwellers.

Thus, the Black Death had a massive impact on brewing during its reign of terror simply because it killed off many brewers, while those who managed to survive found their business impacted owing to fear and lack of contact with other people.

But it's the long-term after-effects that had a huge impact on brewing in many places in England. In the aftermath of the Black Death, the surviving workers in Europe had better conditions simply because there were fewer of them alive, so they could demand better pay. In England, scholars like Judith Bennett, Michelle Sauer and Kristen Burton argue that in the wake of the Black Death, brewing became more lucrative because those who were left had more wages and drank more than previous generations.[93]

Bennett contends that this demand for more ale meant that breweries needed better equipment, more capital and better networks, while the brewers themselves required more managerial authority – all things that single women in particular would struggle to get.[94] And as brewing became more lucrative, men got more interested. Over the centuries, brewing became a more commercial trade, with the majority of brewers being married couples or eventually men, according to scholars. This was somewhat limited to urban centres in England, while Wales and Scotland had a different experience.[95] Suffice it to say that in urban centres in England, men and couples began to dominate the brewing trade in the centuries after the Black Death.

The same cannot be said for Ireland. Kelly found that while tenants in rural Ireland, for example, did have better conditions and wages than in previous generations because of the labour shortage, it didn't reach the same level as in England.[96] Some lands became entirely vacant for years. These labour shortages in rural areas impacted the food supplies because there simply wasn't anyone to grow the food, so provisions often fell short.[97] If food supplies were impacted, brewing and malting would have been too.

Many tradespeople could no longer support themselves and left Ireland, moving elsewhere for better economic circumstances.[98] There is also the fact that the people who survived the Black Death in urban centres had lost perhaps 50% of the population and were losing more through emigration from the country.

While brewing in England became increasingly commercialised and industrialised as the centuries went on, perhaps in some way kicked off by the aftermath of the Black Death and the increased demand for ale in its wake, Ireland experienced something else entirely. Instead of seeing women pushed out of the trade, they remained an integral part of the brewing world, making ales for their own families and selling surplus to the neighbours. And as we shall see in the next chapter, for evidence of this, we don't need to look much further than death.

MALT AND
MAYHEM

1400–1600

YOU PROBABLY DON'T WANT TO THINK ABOUT YOUR DEATH TOO CLOSELY. It's an abstract concept, something that happens to other people, something distant and, we all hope, far away. It's certainly not something you thought you'd have to face in a book on the history of beer, but here we are.

On the other hand, our death can loom large. Its spectre can haunt us in the deepest recesses of our minds, maybe even scare us. It's that age-old topic of rumination in those quiet hours of the morning when the rest of the world is asleep and we lie in bed considering the whole point of it all. But generally, for many modern people, death is a foreign country, somewhere we only visit when we must before quickly returning to our comfortable homes. For medieval people, on the other hand, death wasn't quite so far removed. It walked among them, always present, ever watching.

But that doesn't mean it didn't utterly terrify them. It did. With the advent of the Black Death, medieval people developed coping mechanisms in the form of obsessing about dying a good death. They made art and carved sculptures to warn others to live a good life because otherwise they might find themselves in eternal damnation. English church paintings of the Last Judgement even depict cheating alewives in hell, not to mention the sculptures and carvings that portrayed misbehaving alewives cavorting with demons as a warning to those who brewed to be honest and trustworthy.

These cautionary tales weren't just limited to alewives. Inscriptions of 'I was as you are, you will be the same as me' – a *memento mori* (literally meaning 'remember that you will die') – were often carved on graves or placed in death paintings. *Transi* tombs – effigies depicting the entombed person as decaying, skeletal remains – were made as another stark reminder of what was to come. Death informed life, and frequent reminders pushed people to behave in a manner that might help them ensure a spot in the good place when they finally gave up the ghost.

Medieval people tried to embrace what scared them, regardless if it did little to assuage their very real fears. Even without the bubonic plague, thousands upon thousands died from illnesses we can now easily prevent. Women died in childbirth, often alongside their babies; people of all genders died in work accidents; and millions more were lost to any number of wars, famines or other atrocities. So people planned, if they could. They did that thing that many of us try to avoid like, well, the plague: they made their wills.

Agnes Laweles wasn't planning on dying just yet, but the only things in life that are guaranteed are death and taxes. So on 19 January 1476, she sat down and wrote her will. She made an accounting of all the things she owned, all her debts and all her liabilities, ensuring everything was in proper order before her inevitable demise. Then she wrote out what she was leaving to her daughters, making sure that they were well cared for in her absence. Of the many items she bequeathed to her children, she left her daughter Rose a 'mesh kewe' – a mash tun.[1]

We don't know much about Agnes and her daughter Rose. Like many of the women we have considered so far, we are offered only glimpses of their lives. But from her will, we can surmise a few things about the mother and daughter and the city they lived in. Agnes and Rose lived and brewed in Dublin. Around 20 years before Agnes wrote her will, a decree was passed in the city regarding the selling of ale, and like those issued in earlier centuries, it was directed only at women. It instructed that 'all manner of women that sell ale within the franchise of Dublin sell after the King's ale measure' – that is, the pint, quart, potell and gallon.[2] Specifically, these women were told that they must sell in these measures to 'their neighbours'. Failure to do so would result in increasing fines on the first, second and third offence, and so on.[3]

At this time, the women who were selling ale were also most likely the same people who were brewing it in the first place. A mere six years before Agnes sat down and created her will, there is more evidence that women were the majority of the ones brewing. In 1470, a similar act referring only to 'brewesteres' declared that these women should sell their best ale for 2 shillings and that they should, among other things, 'sell their ale outside their houses, and this must be sealed'.[4]

We can guess that Agnes and Rose were just two of the many women who brewed in Dublin. If they sold their ale when they had extra measures, they would have sold it to their neighbours in sealed containers, as the above laws dictate, and in the measurements set out by the decrees. Otherwise, they, like their fellow women, would have faced the fines.

Unlike previous centuries, though, there is no mention of any kind of corporal punishments here, only monetary. As in England, this might reflect the idea that cheating your customers or selling in false measures was in some ways simply the cost of doing business.[5] If brewing was a side hustle – a way of supplementing your spouse's income or a way to make some income if you were a widow or a single woman – it might have been difficult to always have the right measurements at hand, so cheating or selling in false measures might have been inevitable to some degree, as scholars like Bennett argue.[6] On the other hand, it's likely that some people cheated just because they could. Greed, as ever, was a motivator.

Importantly, as in years past, all these entries are addressed to women. And no, that isn't because it was only women who had to sell in these measures or brew according to the assize. Women were simply the majority of those who brewed.

We learned in the previous chapter that in England, the Black Death acted as a catalyst to speed up the professionalisation of the brewing trade. It was one part of the puzzle that also involved the introduction of hops and the increased importance of guilds. However, this was not a linear or all-encompassing process. It was incredibly complex and it varied greatly based on contexts. As I write in my book *The Devil's in the Draught Lines*, some areas in England didn't see this professionalisation until centuries later, particularly in more rural areas. Similarly, in Wales and Scotland, women made up the majority of brewers both commercially and at home for hundreds of years after the Plague struck, and throughout all of this, many women continued to brew at home for their own households.

The same can be said for English-colonised Ireland, where women wholly dominated the trade for many years, as we can see above. In fact, it wasn't until five years after Agnes wrote her will, in the summer of 1481, that laws and ordinances in Dublin even mention men in the brewing trade. The *Dublin Assembly Rolls* address the brewing people of the city as 'brewers' and 'brewsters', marking a clear gender delineation.[7] These brewers were instructed not to sell their ale to resellers, to 'tapsters or tappesteres' – again, gendered language – outside of their home. Instead, brewers were only allowed to have these resellers sell the brewer's ale inside their own house and, importantly, only if they were 'of good conversation and English born'.[8] This instruction is fairly obvious in its intention to prevent Irish people from working in the trade in order to limit it to the English only. This will be a recurring theme. Further, they were only to allow such 'tappesteres' to sell ale if they could pay for it. They were not under any circumstances to allow them to fall into arrears because the mayor and bailiff would not prosecute them since they shouldn't have been doing it in the first place.[9]

Of course, men certainly brewed. Some of them brewed as part of a couple with their wives and others brewed by themselves. *The Calendar of Ormond Deeds* gives us some interesting insight into the areas that were not directly controlled by the English crown, but instead were ruled somewhat independently by the local earls. In one such instance, circa either 1383 or 1405, we are told that the council received ale from five people: two men (Robert Talbot and John Lumbard) and three women (Johanna Gower, Isabella and Matilda Lybbe). There was no huge difference between what most of the women brewed and the men, with most brewing between 44 and 54 gallons.[10] Once again, we have substantial evidence that women were brewing in this later medieval period, and not just in Dublin.

Agnes Laweles wasn't the only one who had brewing equipment that she passed on to her family members. In that same group of wills where we find her entry, John Kyng and his wife, Jacoba Payn, list in their inventory a brew pan, three pint pots of pewter and 4 shillings in wooden brewing vats.[11] Those pint pots of pewter were in line with the necessary selling measure of ale, though to be clear, brewers wouldn't have been giving away valuable cups to buyers with each purchase; it could have been something to drink from in their house or for their own use. Jacoba left her daughter one of their large brass pans, possibly used for brewing.[12]

And it wasn't just brewing equipment – women also left their daughters malt. For example, Cecily Langan left her daughter Katherine one heifer, one brass pot, two measures of wheat and two of malt.[13]

Brewing could have also been a communal activity, one done in a dedicated town brewhouse or something similar. For example, in Leixlip,

Joan White left 'One three-legged pan and one trough with 2 trundles for the use of my neighbours of the said town of Leixlip, for the health of my soul and the souls of my ancestors'.[14] This trough is quite possibly a brewing vessel, or keeving trough.[15]

Some brewing pans from this period could be enormous, unwieldy circular pieces. The largest extant one in Ireland measures around 112cm wide but only 35cm deep, perhaps designed especially for brewing ales. It's not quite as massive as the one-mile-deep, fit-for-the-Viking-gods example we saw in Chapter 3, but it's still a large bit of kit. These brewing pans are quite different from our modern conceptions of mash tuns in large breweries or even a stovetop homebrew pot.

Like everything, the use of brewing pans was not limited to the English. The Irish also used such equipment in their brews. Hanging on the wall among other potential brewing pans, cauldrons and bits of kitchen equipment, this aforementioned large one is known as the Geashill Cauldron, a potentially legendary vessel and the largest extant version in Ireland discovered to date. Though unconfirmed, it's believed that this particular brewing cauldron might be one that's mentioned in the *Annals of the Four Masters*.

The story goes that in 1406, after defeating the English at Meath, Murrogh O'Conor, the Lord of Offaly, and his son, Calvach, marched to Geashill alongside some others. Here, they came upon Owen Mac Anabaidh O'Conor and his men attacking the town of Giolla Buidhe, plundering the place and making off with the town's goods. The proprietor of this town had at one point decided to borrow a rather enormous brewing pan from Calvach with which to make ale. Not one to choose his timings particularly well, he decided to return the pan to Calvach in the midst of all this violence, right while it was being stolen. Calvach accepted its return 'where it is' – in other words, he accepted he would have to get it back from the man who was so determined to steal it. Seeing the young man making off with his brewing pan on his back, Calvach launched the stone he happened to have in his hand at the fellow. It struck the pan with a noise so loud and awful, it terrified all those who were robbing the town and they fled. The fleeing bandits were quickly pursued and slaughtered.[16]

Built on the site of a chapel dating to 1095, St Michan's Church in Dublin still stands today, famous for the mummies in its crypt. These underground vaults are made of limestone, which keeps the air dry and thus preserves the bodies it contains within its walls. They have become things of legend.

The alleged Crusader is believed to be 800 years old, while there is also a 400-year-old nun, various heads of state and famous Irish revolutionaries. Bits of folklore surround these once-living people, as stories have sprung up about the bodies embedding themselves into many a haunted Dublin walking tour. It's this relationship between death and myth that St Michan's is known for today. Tourists from all over the world flocked to see these mummies and marvel that they still remained as they had for centuries, buried deep within the vaults – that is, until vandals desecrated them in 2019 and then a fire in 2024 mostly destroyed them. These mummies, at least the older ones like the supposed Crusader, showed us a real-life connection between ourselves and our past. We could quite literally see it in the faces of the people in the vaults.

However, it's not just its famous deceased denizens that make St Michan's a fascinating example of a medieval ecclesiastical building. It was once a thriving parish where medieval people came to worship, get married, baptise their children and also be buried. And in the midst of all these events, there's ale to be found.

We don't actually need to look all that far, for in 1477, Ellen Kymore wrote her will. She, like Agnes Laweles, took an accounting of her life and laid out what she wanted to happen upon her demise. But she took one extra step: she also planned her own funeral, leaving 15 shillings for bread and ale for the burial ritual at St Michan's.[17]

We know that funeral feasts were ingrained in medieval Irish culture. Some of them were such big affairs that they quite literally turned into festivals. We've seen graves with markers of feasting and we know that ale was an intricate part of these ceremonies. The Irish would continue on with their own funerary feasting rituals as they had for hundreds of years, but the unfortunate fact is that we have a dearth of written sources from the Irish themselves during this later medieval time period. But we do get hints.

In the late 16th century, an agreement made by Brian Mac Rorey and Conmeadha Mac Teige oge Mac Teige Mac Mahon, between Loghlan Roe O'Slattery and Honor, daughter of John of the Glen, stated that Loghlan Roe is entitled to 'all the wheat and liquor' provided for the funeral of John Mac Murogh O'Slattery.[18] This suggests that, as in previous centuries, ale, and probably also whiskey and mead, was central to these feasts. But like a lot of the funerals we explored in previous chapters, this agreement doesn't tell us what John Mac Murogh

O'Slattery had to say about all this. We don't know what arrangements he might have wanted for his funeral from this little bit of information, or even where he wanted to be buried, who he wanted to attend his funeral or what kinds of beverages he wanted to be served. In most of our studies of these feasts so far, we've seen very little of the agency of the deceased. Where was their voice? How did they plan their funerals? Were the funerals following the wishes of the person who had died or were they more for the living?

But in Ellen Kymore's will, we can see something else entirely: we can see her own wishes for what she wanted for her death rituals. And what she wanted was ale.

Kymore wasn't an isolated case. The English also held funeral feasts, and when they came and colonised parts of Ireland, they carried these traditions with them, making them part of the local landscape. The wills from medieval Dublin show many people leaving behind provisions for ale, or even malt to be made into ale, for their own funerals.[19] For example, Jonet Cristor left malt for her funeral at the Church of the Holy Trinity in Dublin – they were to have 10 measures of malt on the day of her burial, implying that this was to be used for making ale (this again suggests that the fermentation process was likely quick).[20] The 1467 will of Margaret Brouneusyn declares that she is 'sound in mind though weak in body' and that she leaves 8 shillings for ale for the funeral and wants her body to buried at the Church of St James of Killadoon.[21] And on and on it goes.

Both men and women left ale or malt to be made into ale for their funerals. This is a continuation of the traditions we found in the past, with the added benefit of knowing that this was something that people planned. But much like in previous centuries, someone didn't need to die to have an ale party.

Outside, three men and one woman sit perched at a long rectangular table upon which three large platters of food are placed. To the left of these dishes, a large tankard sits alone, perhaps filled with ale. Around these four central figures, a variety of other scenes are taking place: two men cook over a fire, another plays the harp and two others butcher a cow, all while a dog happily gnaws on a bone. And bent over near another roaring fire are two men displaying their unclothed backsides for all and sundry. It may appear that they are merely mooning the feasters, but these men are key parts of the entertainment. Allow me to introduce you to the *braigetór*, or the professional farter.[22] For what alefeast would be complete without a bit of ... *music*?

In 1581, John Derricke, an Englishman, published *The Image of Irelande, with a Discoverie of Woodkarne*, praising English victories and lambasting the Irish people. Contained within this work are 12 woodcuts, one of which in particular draws our eye. Called 'Mac Sweyne's Feast', this image features the chief of the Mac Sweynes with his retinue at dinner, which was probably referring to the Mac Suibhne chief from what is now Donegal.[23] While Derricke's derision is apparent in his words accompanying the images, the feast remained a central part of Irish society in this period. We learned about Irish alefeasts in previous chapters, from what kind of activities were the most fun in an ale hall and which people sapped the joy out of a party to the right kind of behaviour to engage in and how to tell a good story. In fact, we are given such a long list of dos and don'ts that we may well be able to picture the whole event as if we were there ourselves.

At this point in history, from the late medieval period into the 16th century, many of the English invaders who had stayed and colonised various parts of Ireland had become what historians call the Old English. They had intermarried with local families. They took on Irish traditions and customs. They spoke the Irish language and dressed like the Irish. Some even sided against the English with the Irish in battle. This was such a threat to the crown that in 1367, King Edward III issued the *Statutes of Kilkenny*, banning the English from all manner of things, including marrying Irish people, fostering with them, forming any kind of alliance and selling them victuals. As many scholars argue, this was largely ineffective. That ship had long since sailed.

However, as historian Sparky Booker argues, the ways in which these cultural exchanges happened weren't always consistent and wholesale. It was, as she says, 'piecemeal', with people picking up some customs but perhaps not others.[24] She found that one way this sort of cultural assimilation took place was in the custom of 'coyne and livery'.[25]

These alefeasts, which were still integral parts of Irish culture, were now also part of Old English rituals, and they still manifested as rituals of power. Cuddies were one such version, where lords, as well as their servants, soldiers and other attendants, were to be entertained at the houses of their subordinates in a feast.[26] According to scholar K.W. Nicholls, sometimes the lords didn't show up for these events, in which case these cuddies had to be shipped to their house, and could include things like whiskey and ale.[27] These cuddies were often linked with a system called 'coyne and livery' by English writers. Coyne comes from the Irish *coinnmheadh*, which translates roughly to 'billeting'; we learn about it from English writers who claim it was an Irish custom that had at times been adopted by the Old English.[28]

Historian Katharine Simms argues that in Gaelic Ireland (that is, Irish-held Ireland), money wasn't necessary for many kinds of transactions like paying rent. Instead, 'guesting and feasting' were ways these debts could be fulfilled,[29] and they were two distinct things.

Guesting, as defined by Simms, was a demand. You were being told to host and it was part of what you owed your lord, like coyne. In contrast, feasting was by invitation.[30] Nicholls argues that this system of free entertainment – coyne – was the most prevalent way to collect tax in Ireland during this period.[31] However, Nicholls also says that the line between what was voluntary hosting and what was part of this form of entertainment taxation can be hard to identify.[32]

Initially, there was actually an entire party season. This was great fun for those who were guests but maybe not so fun for those who had to throw the party. New Year's Day kicked off a period called coshering season, which lasted for around three months, when the aristocratic rank would demand their feasts.[33] According to Simms, after the English invasion, and particularly for those lords who were Old English, this coshering became a bigger burden that was no longer confined to the specific time period or a part of clientship.[34] These mandatory feasts became known as cuddies or cosher.[35]

This is echoed by Nicholls, who contends that it's possible that as time went on, this system of demanded entertainments replaced rents and tributes.[36] Booker notes that complaints about coyne being an unfair burden were common and that it was banned several times throughout the Middle Ages. However, she found that by the 15th century, the English powers that be accepted its use to some degree but imposed limits to its power – a lord could only take coyne from their own tenants, for example.[37]

In Chapter 2 we learned that alefeasts and drinking horns were given to kings by lesser kings, and vice versa, as part of their clientship. These gifts were a way to maintain their relationships and alliances. What Simms is arguing here is that these feasts were no longer just part of this gift exchange; instead, they became an extra expense, something that could be very costly for those forced to host such events.

So ale remained not just something you drank to enjoy yourself, nor just an important part of your nutrition. It was still integral to rituals around feasting and power. You were expected to have it on hand to host visitors if you were of a certain status. Indeed, it would be demanded. However, the *briugu,* or in later cases, those people responsible for public hospitality, could still be found on the island.[38]

As the Brehon Laws, those early medieval law tracts we encountered in Chapter 2, were still very much in effect, we can gather that brewing and making malt were still somewhat regulated and followed something of a prescribed method. That said, we also know that those laws were about what the author wished life was like rather than what it was actually like in reality, but we can suggest that there were probably some kinds of regulations and consequences, particularly if you made the mistake of serving your guests bad ale.

These rituals of drinking and eating together were also ways in which enemies could be ... persuaded, shall we say, to leave people alone. In Laurent Vital's *Archduke Ferdinand's visit to Kinsale in Ireland, an extract from Le Premier Voyage de Charles-Quint en Espagne, de 1517 à 1518,* he talks at some length about the violence inherent in Ireland. Kinsale had apparently been suffering years of attacks by the Irish people, who would 'pillage everything and kill all who opposed them'. But the townspeople had come up with a loophole. Now they went out and greeted them 'happily' and had a feast together, with 'good food and drink' and some souvenirs for their trouble.[39] Good food and drink would most certainly involve ale, and at a feast designed to stop violence, there was probably a lot of it.

In Sir Henry Crystede's account to Jean Froissart, a French historiographer,, he declares that Ireland is 'one of the most difficult countries in the world to fight against and subdue, for it is a strange, wild place consisting of tall forests, great stretches of water, bogs and uninhabitable regions'.[40] He states that it is nigh on impossible to fight them because there are no towns to attack and they fight in ways that we could call guerrilla warfare,[41] where they attack and pull men off horses, slit their throats and carve out their hearts, which they promptly eat.[42]

Of course, this account is full of blatant untruths as well as some serious bias, but violence was endemic in late medieval Ireland, as it had been for centuries. As the re-Gaelicisation of Ireland took place, more and more pressure was put on the English colonies as their areas of control shrank. After 1350, and indeed since the advent of the 14th century, English power had waned significantly in Ireland. After the initial incursion of the Plague in 1348, the English colonies were decimated and their power decreased greatly. The years 1350 to around 1543 (when the English sought to reconquer Ireland) saw what historians call the Gaelic Revival, that is, a return to power of the Irish.

It's in the midst of all this violence that we can find hints of the medieval brewing past.

The Viking invaders had built fortifications around Dublin to protect the city from incursions from the Irish. As the years wore on, these were turned into city walls built of stone, thick and imposing. Kings of both Irish and Norse descent added to this enclosure, and when the English came in the 12th century, the city had strong defences.

During their occupation, the medieval English expanded the walls and enclosed more of the land. Over the centuries, the walls of the city have fallen into disrepair, but if you venture down to Cook Street, for example, right behind St Audoen's Church, you can still find a huge section of the wall, complete with a gate that was built when the English expanded to include what had previously been marshland.

While the walls in Dublin predated the English invasion, other town walls were newly constructed during this period of violence. The English wanted to ensure the safety of their colonies, so they needed to enclose the towns behind these walls to help stave off attacks. But these walls were expensive and required funding that couldn't be drummed up at the drop of a hat, so just like our governments do now, they implemented a tax.

'Irish enemies' and their continued attacks on Dublin led to a 1358 patent roll granting permission to the mayor, bailiffs and community of Dublin to 'continue to levy tolls for the repair of the Tholsel, bridges and other works necessary for the city', including ¼ pence on wheat and malt, ½ pence on every leaden or iron vessel for brewing and ½ pence on every brewing cauldron.[43]

The Tholsel was an important building in Dublin, one that stood for centuries across from Christ Church on Skinners Row. It was a multitasking structure, functioning as a kind of guild hall, civic hall, jail and court. It was quite literally a powerhouse. Therefore, this tax, which included malt, wheat, brewing vessels and cauldrons, tells us that brewing played some part in maintaining the city. Unfortunately, the Tholsel itself was demolished in 1809, leaving behind only a mere trace that it had been one of the most important buildings to have stood in the city for centuries.

But Dublin wasn't alone in its use of an ale tax as a way to prevent violence to its citizens.

On 5 October 1303, Edward I issued a patent roll to the bailiffs and men of Emly 'in aid of said town' that 'they may take the following customs in that town, viz.: from each crannock of all kinds of corn, flour, malt and salt, ¼d', and importantly, 'from each tun of ale, 1d (pence)'.[44] A further example dates to 4 March 1311, when the king granted the town of Leighlin the murage (a kind of tax) to be able to build walls and towers for its protection.[45] The murage was to be taken from goods sold, including malt, at the rate of ½ pence. This entry also mentions ale: 'from each tun of ale for sale in the said town, 1d; from each barrel of ale containing 40 or 50 gallons, 1d'.[46]

Throughout the English colonies, tolls on ale and malt were used as a way to build city walls and fight against incursions. A toll in 1375 that lasted for 20 years, in some part from malt or grain (1 pence from every crannock), also helped pay for the city walls of Thomastown in Co. Kilkenny. This wall was made specifically against 'the king's Irish enemies and rebels' to protect the 'king's faithful people' whose land was 'for the greater part destroyed and plundered'.[47]

Over and over again, we see that a toll on malt was used in some part to build and maintain stone walls. The walls of Fethard, Kilmallock and Trim, to name just a few, were all paid for in some way by a toll on malt.[48, 49, 50] Most of what made up these walls has been lost to time since the city walls surrounding these places were destroyed long ago. But parts and pieces remain, if you know where to find them. In Kilkenny, Black Freren Gate and Talbot's Tower still stand. Galway still has a 60-metre section left in the Eyre Square Shopping Centre and Penrice's and Shoemaker's Towers remain. Various sections of the walls still stand in Dublin. Perhaps in some way we can still see the legacy of medieval brewing history in the stone ruins of the city enclosures.

The continued violence between the English who were loyal to the crown and the Irish and their Old English allies meant that a tax on ale, brewing equipment and malt was just the tip of the proverbial iceberg when it comes to the role of brewing and war. Earlier on in this chapter we learned about the law from the 15th century that stated that all who sold ale had to be English-born. These types of restrictions could also extend to those who bought ale.

You see, armies on all sides ran on ale. And not just that – it was an essential part of the diet for many people. So the English passed laws that forbade people from selling malt or ale to the Irish, specifically, those Irish living in areas outside of their control. A 1394 proclamation to the sheriff of Louth stated that no 'liege of the king' should under any circumstances sell, give, lend or anything of that matter ale or malt (among other things) to any Irishman that didn't live within the English-held areas, and that doing so would result in a penalty.[51]

Louth was not an exception. It was just one of many places where such ordinances came into effect. In 1382, Richard II appointed Thomas Hethe, rector of the Church of Athboy, and Nigel Naungle to look into those who were violating these sorts of laws by selling malt, grain, horses or armour to the Irish.[52] Dozens of such regulations exist in these records banning the sale of malt and ale, among other things, to the Irish enemies.

On 7 March 1408, we see a patent roll by Henry IV appointing justices to inquire as to various nefarious and criminal activities, including the selling of arms, horses, oats, wheat and malt to Irish enemies in direct violation of the statutes in place.[53] People caught doing so could find themselves becoming outlaws in a very literal sense. These people would be outside of the law, meaning that there was no legal protection for them, no judge and jury; they could be summarily killed on sight.

In the *Ormond Deeds* we learn of Thomas FitzMaurice, who became an outlaw for, among other things, giving and selling bread and ale worth some 20 shillings to the O'Brynnes, who were at that time openly at war with the king.[54] FitzMaurice was summoned five times to appear before the court to face judgement for this alleged crime, and five times he never showed up. Thus, he was declared an outlaw.

This ban on selling goods to the Irish didn't always work out so well for the towns in question, though. Kilkenny was a constant target for attacks by Irish enemies, so they appealed to their king for relief, not only for physical protection but also because they were unable to sustain themselves economically. On 26 January 1410, a patent roll from King Henry IV states that the citizens of Kilkenny pleaded with him about their 'poverty and desolation' caused by the Irish enemies and English rebels. In this regard, the people of the town said they could not afford to live because of the constraints on their merchandise. Among such restrictions, they noted that those on barley, oats, wheat and the ale that was brewed from these grains were particularly problematic for them.[55] This confirms what we already knew: that ale was a critical component to the economy. Luckily for our Kilkenny citizens, the king granted them rights to sell malt and grain, along with ale, to any people who came and went from the town, whether they remained there or not.[56] Similarly, in 1391, a patent roll gave permission to the people of Limerick to sell ale to anyone, be they English, Irish, enemy or friend.[57]

This sort of grant appears with some frequency over the century, with at least 13 instances of the king granting merchants the ability to sell to both Irish and English customers. We can see here that while attempts were made to curtail contact between the English colonisers and the Irish people, this often didn't work out quite how they'd envisioned it. Irish people were necessary at some points for their buying power. Many of the English towns needed them to purchase their goods, which included ale. Dispensations became necessary to sustain these towns, particularly during the return of Irish power. But this was not to last.

The advent of the 16th century brought with it another shift in power. Henry VIII, in between marrying, murdering and divorcing his wives, sought to reconquer Ireland. He launched his concerted campaign around 1536 and wanted to bring the entire island under English rule, with no outposts of Irish control to remain. This would be the policy of the leaders who followed him and would lead to the 1641 Rebellion and the Eleven Years' War, which ended with Ireland controlled by the English colonising forces.

In the intervening years, the rulers of England took up a variety of horrific practices designed to get the Irish to submit. We'll dive deeper into this in the next chapter, but suffice it to say that over the course of the 16th and 17th centuries, the English were quickly working to exert dominance. In that vein, let's now consider what was perhaps the most important bastion of English power in Ireland: Dublin Castle.

The castle was built by the infamous King John. It functioned as a defensive fortification and was the epicentre of English control. Over the centuries, the castle itself would fall into disrepair. At one point it was referred to by the Earl of Arran in the 17th century as 'the worst castle in the worst situation in Christendom'.[58] The castle was the official residence of the Lord Deputy of Ireland, and later the Viceroy, and was both a home and a military complex. It is here that we can find the acute intersections of beer and military power.

According to the accounts of William FitzWilliam, Lord Deputy of Ireland, in 1572, the Dublin Castle household of more than 50 people consumed 540 pints of beer a day.[59] Susan Flavin, alongside a team of researchers including Marc Meltonville, Charlie Taverner, Joshua Reid, Stephen Lawrence, Carlos Belloch-Mollina and John Morrissey, used these accounts to recreate a 16th-century beer. In a documentary project with FoodCult called *Drunk?*, which is now available on YouTube, you can watch their experiment unfold as they locate the malt, yeast and hops perfect for brewing their historical beer.

Arriving in the 16th century, hops were certainly in use in Ireland at this time. This mirrors what I found from the customs logs of Chester from Michaelmas 1565 to Easter 1566, where, for example, Simon Hand of Dublin had 200 pounds of hops imported to him on the *John of Hilbre* ship on 7 October, while on 27 March he had more brought in as well as 300 white wooden cups, which leads me to believe that Simon Hand ran a tavern or inn. I will say that not a single woman is mentioned as importing hops, which could be for a variety of reasons, including coverture.

The *Drunk?* documentary and research project is a fascinating work in experimental archaeology. The documentary itself is an incredibly insightful take on history in action. The research team also wrote up their findings in an open access journal article, 'Understanding Early Modern Beer: An Interdisciplinary Case-Study', which details the broader social context of beer in this period. They note that it functioned not only as a drink for fun, but that it was also a key part of nutrition, hence its important role in the war campaigns, as we have seen. Beer was a key component of the military might. It was a necessary and basic part of the soldiers' diet, and the armies, both Irish and English, quite frankly ran on the stuff. This is why they were forever trying to steal it off each other and control the malt trade.

The research team also found that people could drink quite a bit, with the average person consuming somewhere around six to eight pints a day. Some drank even more: the masons at Christ Church consumed upwards of 10½ to 12 pints every day, even up to 15½![60] We aren't necessarily talking about low-ABV beer either.

In any event, I encourage you to watch the documentary for its detailed breakdown of brewing techniques in early modern Ireland, something that the English likely brought with them when they colonised the island. But there's something else the English carried with them when they arrived on Irish shores: witch accusations.

The seven main charges in Ireland's first witch trial included fornicating with an incubus, stealing keys to the church and holding secret meetings there, where, in the skull of a decapitated thief, the accused would brew potions of intestines and internal organs of cocks that they had sacrificed to the demons. To this they would add things like worms, nails from dead people and clothes from baby boys who had died before they were christened. From these mixtures, they made potions to cause people to fall in love or hate, to kill or torment.

This was the 1324 trial of Alice Kyteler and her associates, brought up on charges by the Bishop of Ossory, Richard Ledrede, who accused Kyteler and her alleged conspirators of heresy and witchcraft. Ledrede had been brewing this case against Kyteler for quite some time alongside his collaborators, her former stepchildren. But Kyteler was an incredibly wealthy and powerful woman, so she wasn't going to go down easy.

You see, Kyteler had been married four times at this point. Three of her husbands had died under what many had considered to be suspicious circumstances. She was gaining a reputation as a black widow, especially because through these marriages, and deaths, Kyteler was able to consolidate her wealth even further. As for the fourth husband, he was certain he was being poisoned, a fear he voiced to his children before he, too, was consigned to the grave.

Ledrede wrote down all the proceedings so we know exactly what he accused Kyteler and the others of doing. All the ins and outs of the trial itself are beyond the scope of this book, but suffice it to say the trial was incredibly complicated and somewhat unpopular with other high-ranking men, at least at first. Eventually the bishop did get his way and was able to charge and prosecute Kyteler, or at least he tried to. Instead, she fled likely to Flanders or England, never to be heard from again. She left behind in her stead her maid, Petronella de Meath, who did not have the financial resources that Kyteler had to flee. Although some scholars argue that Petronella stayed and met her fate because Kyteler took Petronella's daughter with her, in any event, she met a tragic end: she was whipped through the streets before being burned at the stake.

Ledrede didn't have such a great life himself, as he had managed to make quite a few powerful enemies in his life, including at one time the King of England, Edward III.

What does the story of Kyteler and Petronella have to do with the history of women in beer? Very little. Of course, Kyteler, like all women in that period, probably drank ale, though given her wealth she would have certainly had access to wine. Her household staff, like Petronella, probably drank ale with some regularity and it's quite possible that Kyteler purchased or had someone brew her ale to supply her household. Historically, Kyteler and Petronella were about as connected with ale as most other women were at the time; that is to say, it was a mundane and ubiquitous part of life.

However, the folklore around Alice Kyteler still permeates the history not only of Kilkenny, but the history of beer. A trip to the city will direct you to Kyteler's Inn, with stories tying the building to the infamous woman herself. An old place with medieval foundations, the structure wasn't an inn until about the late 1630s, long after Kyteler had lived and died.[61] The pub is a wonderfully cosy affair offering traditional music and food as well as tours of the inn and history talks on Alice Kyteler herself. The inn pays homage to her with decorations invoking visions of witchcraft and black cats adorning their signage. They even have their own beer, an Irish red ale, nicknamed 'The Witches Brew' by their staff.[62]

Modern writers often link medieval brewing women with witchcraft. Pages and pages of websites feature articles alleging that medieval women brewed until they were pushed out of the trade by accusations of witchcraft. They also argue that the garb of the modern stereotypical witch is based on the clothing of these said alewives.

I have debunked both of these myths in England, Scotland and Wales in my book *The Devil's in the Draught Lines*. To briefly recap, the modern witch stereotype doesn't appear until children's books in the late 17th and early 18th centuries, well after the medieval period was over (the medieval period is roughly between the years 500 and 1500). Cats were associated with heretics long before witches, so there's no link to alewives specifically there. The pointy hat comes from a variety of possibilities, with anti-Semitism or the use of an old-fashioned capotain hat being the most plausible to me. Ale stakes weren't used in accusations of flight, and flight itself wasn't something all witches were accused of doing. Further, women weren't pushed out of brewing in the UK because they were accused en masse of witchcraft.

But what about Ireland? The Irish witch trials were quite limited, with most happening well after Kyteler's trial. Similar to the handful of trials in Wales, Andrew Sneddon argues that they didn't even reach double digits in Ireland.[63] Scholars have concluded that this is probably because there already existed a scapegoat in the form of the Irish, or Old English, and that the more recently arrived English and Scottish Protestant accusers needn't have looked any further, because in this early modern period, the formula was usually a Protestant accusing a Catholic, likely a poorer Catholic.[64] In fact, all accusations in the early modern period were made by Protestants.[65]

We can clearly see that there was no widespread campaign here. Alewives weren't put out of business by these trials, and the scope and threat of them were limited. But were there any links in the few trials between brewing women and witchcraft?

Over two centuries after Kyteler and Petronella's trial, two people were accused of witchcraft in Kilkenny in 1578 and were later executed. We don't know much about them – not their names or backgrounds or frankly anything at all. Scholars argue that they were likely either Irish or Old English based on the tensions present during this period, which may give you a hint about motivation and bias, whether intentional or not.

There was a later trial under James I of Reverend John Aston of Mellifont, who apparently was conjuring demons to locate a silver cup as well as spy on the king's enemies, but these charges were dropped.[66] A case in 1660 in Cork was brought against Florence Newton, who begged for some food and then was said to have cursed the maid when she refused, but again, there are no links here between brewing women and witchcraft accusations.

But are there any ties between witchcraft, the damned and beer? In *Satan's Invisible World Discovered*, George Sinclair tells us this story, which apparently occurred on 9 May 1698 in Antrim.

An old woman was begging from door to door, asking for food and drink to prevent her from starving. She came across a young girl, apparently the age of 19, who we are told was the best of women in birth, education and beauty. The woman begged at the door of the girl, asking for mercy and food. The girl kindly gave it to her, handing the woman bread and beer. In exchange, the woman gave her a sorrel leaf. But before the girl could even properly swallow the leaf, 'she began to be tortured in her bowels, to tremble all over, and even was convulsive; and, in fine to swoon away, as dead'.[67]

The old woman, of course, was no ordinary woman, but a witch who had laid a curse upon the girl, who was now being 'turned by the demon, in the most dreadful shapes' and vomiting needles, pins, horse dung, feathers, eggs, nails and an iron knife, among other things.[68] The witch was eventually captured and 'strangled and burnt' but refused to lift the curse because 'by reason others had done against her likewise'.[69]

According to author John Seymour, this story was likely based on a pamphlet printed in 1699 entitled *The Bewitching of a Child in Ireland*. Seymour believes that Sinclair is to some extent describing a real witchcraft trial.

The alleged witch here was seeking beer to drink, something which would have been a typical part of most people's daily diet in the 17th century. It was a basic component of their nutrition. She wasn't a witch because she was associated with beer, and asking for it wasn't strange. In fact, she knew it was a drink that would be readily available, as it was a typical and mundane part of life. It was the whole thing about cursing the person who gave it to her that brought out the accusations.

Like everything else, we must take this with a grain of salt because the people accused of witchcraft were, of course, ordinary people, likely with no magickal intentions one way or the other, and they certainly weren't killing people by cursing them. Ale itself and its creation were not viewed as something dangerous or evil, regardless of who was doing the brewing.

In fact, drinking ale could be associated with quite saintly intentions. Agnes Laweles, who we met in the opening story of this chapter, left her brewing pan to her daughter Rose, but she also left her something else: a mazer cup, which is a kind of shallow drinking vessel resembling a bowl. These cups could be simple in design or detailed and quite expensive. The small mazer that was left for Rose was valued at 6 shillings 8 pence. To put that into perspective, the nine hogs that Agnes had were worth 9 shillings, so 1 shilling per hog, so this cup was worth six and half hogs. It was certainly valuable.

Mazer cups appear a few times in Dublin wills from this period. For example, Hugh Galyane left one to his wife Agnes that was worth 4 shillings.[70] Joan Dwyer also had a small mazer cup worth 6 shillings 8 pence and Philip Taillor had one worth the same.[71] Drinking ale or other alcoholic beverages from mazers or bowls is common in the medieval period. One mazer cup from Canterbury actually had the following inscription on it:

> God and Seynt Martin
> Blysse owre ale and blysse owre wyn.
> God blesse both the[72] and me,
> and the Holy Trinity,
> Amen! So mothe yt be.[73]

So we know ale drinking or brewing wasn't associated with witchcraft in the medieval period, nor was it associated with witches in the 16th or 17th centuries in Ireland. There were no credible links to be found between women brewing and witch accusations, none whatsoever. In fact, I didn't find a tale of a witch brewing ale until many centuries later. This story comes to us via a child in the 1930s, though being folklore, the tale itself might be much older.

In the early 20th century, Ireland had an initiative where children were asked to speak with older members of their communities to hear their stories and lore. Katty Dalton, aged 13, interviewed a man called

Willie Crowe, aged 73, both of St Mullins, Co. Carlow. Willie told Katty the story of the beer witch. In this story, we learn of two men, Tom and Jack, who worked together. After such a day working, they went to the house of this alleged witch, who also sold beer. However, the beer needed sugar in order to be somewhat drinkable, but having none, our ale witch had to venture out to get some, leaving her husband behind with Tom and Jack to mind the meat boiling in the pot. She was apparently taking ages, so Tom and Jack sent her husband after her while they went ahead and stole the meat in the pot, replacing it with a poor cat they had happened to come by. Needless to say, the only two bad characters in this instance are Tom and Jack, who not only stole the meat, but killed a cat as well. Our brewing witch is not the monster of the story but is in fact the victim whose cat was murdered by two horrendous characters who also ran off with her meat.[74]

Folklore is a wonderful resource for beer history. Oral traditions passed down over the generations can hint at the role beer played in a town. As part of the local lore, we can learn a lot about how people viewed ale. Here we are told that people went to houses to buy beer, perhaps even adding sugar to the brew to make up for the awful taste, though how widespread that practice would be is unknown; it might have been merely a bit to add to the story.

However, Irish folklore doesn't stop with a single ale witch. Someone with a much more sinister reputation was also getting in on the act. The devil, it seems, always finds a way.

THE DEVIL IN
THE ALEHOUSE

1600–1700

HE HAD BEEN STALKING THE CONSTABLE FOR MONTHS, haunting his nightmares and plaguing his every move.

The man had already been forced to flee Scotland to Bangor, Co. Down, in a desperate attempt to circumvent the evil one's grasp, but to no avail. It was here, in the early years of the 17th century, that Reverend Robert Blair (who, ironically, was famous for describing Oliver Cromwell as a weeping devil) found the insensible constable in front of him, begging for help.[1] But it wasn't Cromwell who was hunting our constable, though I wouldn't put it past him. It was Satan himself.

Blair was placed quickly on his guard, as he noticed the man's eyes were like a 'cat in the night', which deeply unsettled him. He vowed to watch him closely while keeping him a safe distance away. Upon entering the church with the reverend, the constable fell to his knees in seizures. These seizures were so strong that it fully impeded his ability to speak. Blair waited and watched as the man eventually regained his speech faculties and was able to weave his tale of woe.[2]

The constable regaled our reverend with his story, of how a man by the name of Nickel Downus appeared to him in Glasgow and bought a horse from him for six pence. It was after this transaction that things became dangerous, for Downus was none other than the Devil himself and had left a bag full of silver and gold on the table for our constable before vanishing into the night.[3] After this encounter and several others involving 'many other apparitions of the Devil', the constable fled Scotland and came to Ireland, thinking to outrun him. Unfortunately for our poor constable, he couldn't trick the Dark Lord. He was swiftly found and the menacing recommenced.

And what, pray tell, did his infernal majesty want from our miserable constable? Murder. The constable revealed that the Devil had commanded him to 'kill and slay'.[4] But who, exactly, was the constable meant to kill? Anyone who came across him, with a few caveats:

> The better they be
> The better service to me,
> Or else I shall kill thee.[5]

After revealing all to Reverend Blair, the constable again fell into spasms, sobbing and screaming his pain to all who would listen. In order to remedy the situation, Blair declared that he must cease his drinking: 'I showed him the horribleness of his ignorance and drunkenness; he made many promises of reformation.'[6]

Alas, our poor constable was unable to keep his word, and it is now that we find our link between the alehouse and the Devil himself.

> For within a fortnight he went to an alehouse to crave the
> price of his malt, and sitting there long at drink, as he was
> going homeward, the Devil appeared to him, and challenged
> him for opening to me what had passed betwixt them
> secretly, and followed him to the house, pulling his cap off
> his head and his band from about his neck, saying to him,
> 'On Hallow-night I shall have thee, soul and body, in despite
> of the minister and of all that he will do for thee.'[7]

The good reverend agreed to spend Hallow-night with our constable, deep in prayer, so Satan was unable to carry him off. Our story appears to have a happy ending, as from here on out the constable apparently became a good person, giving to the poor and ceasing to drink.

John Seymour argues that this story was probably true, albeit due to hallucinations from alcoholism and spasms from delirium tremens.[8] He quipped that 'homicidal mania resulting from intemperate habits would be nearer the truth'.[9] But Reverend Blair did believe this was the work of the Devil, albeit aided in some part by the man's overconsumption of alcohol.

Regardless, this tale sets up our chapter nicely, as the 17th century in Ireland was rife with violence and death. While the Prince of Darkness himself might not have been stalking Ireland, during these 100 years another evil enmeshed itself on the island: bigotry.

He was never one to let the facts get in the way of a good story.

Despite his glaring lack of qualifications in the matter, he was determined to pen his meandering diatribes for all the world to read and marvel at. At least, that's what he may have wanted to happen. We aren't quite sure why Barnabe Rich was compelled to write three books on the Irish people, but he felt his thoughts on the matter needed to be heard, regardless of whether or not anyone actually wanted to listen.

Rich was an English army captain who had served in the colonisation of Ulster. As a result, he was incredibly biased against the Irish in nearly every aspect a person can be. In his twilight years he moved to Dublin, where he wrote his bigoted books. His first, the 1610 *New Description of Ireland*, is a horrific accounting of what he perceived to be the many flaws of the Irish. Mixed in with accusations of cannibalism and heretical beliefs is a long-winded rant on the alewives of Dublin:

> I will speake onelie of the riffe-raffe, the most filthy queanes, that are knowne to bee in the Countrey, (I meane those Huswives that doe vse selling of drinke in Dubline, or elsewhere) commonly called Tavrner-keepers, but indeed filthy and beastly alehousekeepers: I will not meddle with their honesties ... they are in the manner of their life and living to bee detested and abhorred.

Tell us how you really feel, Barnabe. And he doesn't stop there, but buried under all his insults is some truth. It's up to us to suss it out, and so we shall.

Rich tells readers that selling ale 'is the very marrow of the common wealth in Dubline', sold in 'every house in the Towne, in every day of the weeke, at every houre in the day, and in every minute in the houre'. It is so 'vendible' (sellable) that the 'whole profit of the Towne stands upon Ale-houses and the selling of Ale'.[10] Entire streets are apparently devoted purely to the selling of it, perhaps like Winetavern Street had been in earlier years.

Further, we get an idea of the sheer number of women who brew because, as Rich says, 'every Householders Wife is a brewer'.[11] This, combined with his earlier assertion that housewives are the ones selling ale, tells us that it is women who are making and selling ale in Dublin, and that the economy of the city is based entirely on this women's work. A far cry, perhaps, from other major urban centres in England, like London, where men dominated commercial brewing around this same time.[12]

Do we trust Rich, though? Were women overwhelmingly the brewers in the city of Dublin in the 17th century? And were there so many of them that every householder's wife was a brewer? Yes and no.

When we examined the tolboll in Chapter 4, we learned that in the 16th century the brewers of Dublin challenged the measure because there were more of them brewing less ale than in previous generations, so the requirements of the tolboll were too much to bear. If that trend continued (and I would argue that it did), then it would stand to reason that Dublin would have had many people brewing smaller batches. We know that the surplus of brewers was a concern for the city – in fact, in 1605, Dublin moved to ban unfree people from brewing for sale. This is a change from just over 20 years earlier, when, in 1582, we are told that for all unfree men and women brewing within Dublin and its suburbs, out of every brew of ale or beer that was marked for sale, one gallon of the best ale or beer was to go to the mayor and sheriffs for the use of the city.[13]

Unfree is a complicated legal category of people, particularly as it related to cities. As the name suggests, they weren't 'free', meaning they had fewer rights and protections than those who were free. Notably, in the medieval period they couldn't own 'free' land or win legal cases, for example.[14] Nonetheless, it clearly shows an attempt to shut out certain groups of people from the brewing trade, namely, those of lower status. The code states 'forasmuch as many inconveniences daily doth arise in this city by the multitude of brewers', unfree people were banned from brewing ale and beer to be sold and could not sell any of it either 'within the liberties of the city'.[15] Doing so would result in the constables arresting the person and sending them to prison until they could pay whatever fine the mayor laid out.[16] They could still brew for their own households, but selling it for profit was out of the question.

The language in this law is gender neutral, but I think Rich is correct in saying that it was overwhelmingly women who brewed and sold ale in Dublin at this time. First, let's look at his remark about how every housewife fancies herself a brewer. Brewing was absolutely the domain of the housewife in this period, at least in English, Scottish and Welsh households. This naturally also came to be the case in homes in colonies in Ireland, at least to some degree. In books and pamphlets from the 16th century onwards, women were encouraged not only to know how to brew, but to also know the ins and outs of maintaining a proper brewing cellar, how to malt and how to sell the final product to bring in extra income for their households. Books like Hannah Woolley's *The Queen-like Closet* and *The Compleat Servant-maid* have recipes for various brews or medicinal cures that involve ale or beer.[17]

Brewing in an industrial sense in England had become dominated by men in many urban areas, though women were brewing there to a lesser extent; for instance, women could still be brewing in more rural areas as well as on their estates and in their own households.[18] As a household task, this was most often a kind of side hustle. It wasn't necessarily a big money maker, but it was a way that women could contribute to their family's finances. It was something to be celebrated and encouraged for these housewives.

The English brought this idea with them to their colonies, so housewives in English-held Ireland were encouraged to brew ale. Rich even remarks on this being the case, stating in his second book on Ireland that brewing 'bellonges to good huswifery, that every wise womanne is to under take'.[19] Suffice it to say that brewing was the domain of the housewife in 16th- and 17th-century English colonies in Ireland. It was an expected part of her work in maintaining the household and it would have been something that women were taught to do alongside things like cooking or baking. Even women of higher rank, who wouldn't necessarily be brewing themselves, would likely have been educated on the practice because they would have been expected to supervise their households and all the tasks within it.

While brewing was the domain of the housewife and a task that all good ones should know how to do, the women in Dublin weren't doing it right, apparently. At least, that's what Rich reports. He tells readers that these women are cheating their customers. He also says that these tavern-keepers could buy malt in Dublin at half the cost it was in London and sell the drink in Dublin at two times the cost it was in London.[20] We know that Rich isn't wrong about malt and barley being plentiful, and cheaper, in Ireland. From earlier sources, we can clearly see that the crown forces were exporting malt of all kinds from Ireland in high numbers. In this era, *A Briefe Description of Ireland: made in this year 1589, By Robert Payne* remarks on the cheaper nature of supplies and indeed of life in Ireland in general; specifically, the author notes the lower cost of malt, barley and oats.[21]

More to the point, Rich tells readers that alewives had a sweet set-up that was overlooked by the mayor and his cronies. In fact, they 'wink at' the fact that it's sold at twice the cost of drink in London, even though the malt costs half as much. Rich says it's not just the 'bad sort' who are benefiting from this set-up, but 'this commoditie the Aldermen's wives and the rest of the Women-brewers do find so sweet'.[22] Everybody is engaging in what he deems to be shady practices. That said, it's the English in particular who have to be wary of getting ripped off by these alewives. This is another thing that the magistrates of Dublin apparently 'wink at'.[23] According to Rich, when the English purchase beer – and, well, everything else – they get bamboozled.[24]

Rich gets increasingly angry because, according to him, brewing and selling ale is open to any woman, 'be she better or be she worse'.[25] This was one of his biggest fears. He writes that 'it is as rare a thing, to finde a house in Dubline without a Taverne, as to find a Taverne without a Strumpet'. He refers to these alehouses as 'Nursuries of Drunkenesse, of all manner of Idlenesse, of whordome and many other vile abominations' that were, in his words, 'unfit for any man's drinking, but for common Drunkardes'.[26] With these words, he paints an interesting tableau of the alehouse as a place for vice and villainy. He once again takes aim at women, especially those 'young idle housewives' who, in his opinion, were 'verie loathsome, filthie and abhominable, both in life and manners, and these they call *Tavern-keepers*, the most of them knowne harlots; these doe take in both Ale and Beere by the Barrell from those that do brue, and they sell it forth againe by the potte...'.[27]

Rich's fears of sex work in alehouses and sex workers selling ale were not manufactured to support his diatribe. He probably brought these fears with him from England. As scholars like Susan Flavin argue, Rich's scathing commentary mirrors writings of his contemporaries in England.[28] English authors like John Skelton harshly criticised the female brewers of their day, going so far as to associate them with demons, while artists placed them firmly in hell for selling in false measures. However, they also represented a pattern made by English observers in Ireland who often decried the alleged drunkenness and promiscuity of Irish women and blamed them for being the reason why Ireland was hard to govern.[29] Therefore, Rich's vitriolic commentary must be understood in this context.

Of course, the fears of sex work in alehouses wasn't just a literary trope. The laws do tell us that some such anxiety was present; it wasn't entirely manufactured by Rich. The powers that be in Ireland could be extremely bigoted when it came to the treatment of sex workers, or alleged sex workers. For example, in 1540, the city of Chester in England banned women aged 14 to 40 from selling ale, which, according to Judith Bennett, was 'firmly' enforced.[30] Echoing this law from Chester, the most glaring Irish example of this fear can be seen in Waterford, where in 1603 a law was issued that completely banned women and girls from selling wine, 'aquavite', beer and ale:

> This lawe was made for the insuing consideracions; ffirst for avoyding whordome, Secondlie to avoyde the consealment of goods stollen, Thyrdlie for dryving away of unprofitable dwellers, and lastlie for strengthning of the Citie ffor then that all the retaylers within the Citie must be hereafter men servants and no women servants.[31]

Other places in Ireland didn't take such drastic measures, though attempts were made, especially ones targeting single women, those who were perhaps believed more likely to engage in sex work or were more vulnerable to being caught up in the trade. Dublin didn't take things quite as far as Waterford, but the city did move to punish those who engaged in sex work, particularly as it related to the ale trade. On the fourth Friday after Easter, the assembly in Dublin set out several orders, including fines that were to be due to the mayor and sheriffs of Bullring. The first thing they mention are taverns and those who set them up, especially those who give ale to unmarried women who then sell it, and 'all of them that kepethe any hores in their houses, contrarie to the lawes'. They also set out 'to punishe those unmarried women that shalbe found with child' by banishment and expulsion from the city.[32]

This is incredibly harsh. The bias and discrimination against sex workers was brutal in this period, but it wasn't unique to Dublin or even to Ireland – it was very much in keeping with the English laws at the time. In 1584, a similar measure targeted single women who sold ale – specifically, that citizens of Dublin were selling ale from their houses to these women, which resulted in a 'great inconvenience, by procuring idle and evyll disposed women to increase in this cittie' and which was also, importantly, against the law.[33]

Another entry in 1584 speaks about how some apprentices were running amok in taverns and victualling houses, 'wher they are procured by evyll disposed women to consume their masters goods'.[34] Again, let's blame the women (though in fairness, this law does also say that anyone who supports the apprentices in this carry-on and gets caught will go to prison as well). A little over 30 years later, in 1616, Dublin again moved against what it believed to be 'wicked harlottes under culor of tapping ale and beer', with fines for those householders who encouraged this behaviour.[35] Furthermore, in the same year the city issued orders to its aldermen to report on the single women in their areas selling ale because, again, there was a suspected link between single women selling ale and sex work.[36] As for Rich, he tells readers that even if a man doesn't have a wife, he will rent out his space in his house to a woman to use as a tavern. Rich doesn't look on this very favourably, stating that in order to make a profit, 'she will never be able to keepe her selfe honest'.[37]

So there was a fear, both in life and in literature, that women who sold ale were also sex workers. Because sex work was oftentimes viewed, very hypocritically, by the leaders of the time in such a hateful way, so, too, were the women who engaged in the work. They were subjected to all manner of discrimination from the laws, not to mention the very real dangers they faced in the trade. These fears combined to create laws in places like Dublin where single women were targeted for removal from selling ale, regardless of whether or not they engaged in sex work.

Even these laws had their limits. In contrast to Waterford and Chester, in Dublin the laws weren't aimed at married women, who carried on their trade as they had in previous years. While writers like Skelton got away with their hateful visions of wicked alewives, Ireland was a whole different country, with different beliefs and cultural norms, even in the colonies. Even though there may have been a fear that alewives in Dublin weren't always behaving the best, as evidenced by some of the laws we have seen, Rich took his arguments too far and found himself in the crosshairs of the wealthy and powerful men of the city. You see, those aldermen's wives had husbands – powerful husbands who weren't best pleased with Rich's thoughts on their brewing. In fact, his book caused such outrage among the elite men of Dublin that he was compelled to write an apology to the brewing women of Dublin several years later.

I'm not sure what Rich's day-to-day life looked like after *A New Description of Ireland* was published, but it seems like it must have been quite frosty or perhaps even threatening enough that he felt forced to write an 'excuse', as he termed it, for his first book. He called this second work *A True and Kinde Excuse written in defence of that booke, intituled A new Description of Ireland* and addressed this apology to knights, barons and the whole Lord Deputy of Ireland, which might suggest that he'd managed to aggravate quite a few people.

His apology is pretty pathetic by our modern standards, as he takes little accountability. He tries to dig himself out of a hole by claiming it was all a massive misunderstanding caused by one woman who 'hath forgotten to blush', making allusions to her either being wildly promiscuous or being a sex worker. This woman, he says, came out of nowhere and attacked him, 'belying and slaundering both it and me, with such false and untrue virtures'.[38] It's all her fault! He claims she spread total falsehoods that did not at all represent what he'd said in the book.

In his apology, Rich keeps telling people to just read the first book and that they'll see that the woman is spinning lies about it. I don't know what book he's talking about, because I read it and he did say all that. But no, Rich says it's all ridiculous and that he thinks the women of Dublin are the best of women:

> I speake it from my heart, I never heard women les infamed or missereported, in any citty or towne wheresoever I have travayled: so that if Thucidides rule be true, that those women are to be accounted most honest, that are least spoken of, I say the citizens wyves of Dublyne, may march in equall ranke with those women that are least steyned or misreputed.[39]

A far cry from our filthy, beastly alehouse queen, eh?

In the end, he kept doubling down on the fact that his original work was fine, it wasn't mean. The only issue he has with women who brew is when they are not the honest sort. There's no mention of the fact that he included all housewives and even aldermen's spouses in his previous rants.

In his last book on the Irish, he makes one final dig at the women of Dublin. He once again rails against the commonplace nature of sex work in alehouses. But apparently this has driven down the cost of ale, because now he says that a man can get some tobacco for his pipe, 'a pocky whore' and some ale, all for the low, low price of three pence.[40]

The Annals of Ireland from 1592 tell the story of the escape of Red Hugh, who fled captivity in Dublin with two other lads, Art and Henry, the sons of the O'Neill, by way of a rope down the privy.

They lost Henry in the mad rush to hie off before the English realised what was happening and the pair quickly became exhausted, whereby Hugh and Art sent word to Fiacha Mac Hugh (O'Byrne), who, like so many Irish, was at war with the English. The two boys desperately requested provisions and Fiacha delivered, sending them food as well as ale and mead.[41] Fiacha's friends found the boys completely encased in snow and freezing. They tried to coax them to eat and drink, with little success. This story does not have a happy ending for poor Art, because while he tried to drink the ale and eat the food, every time he did, he threw up until eventually he died. The same went for Hugh, but he tried again to drink the mead and afterwards 'his faculties were restored after drinking it, except the use of his feet alone for they became dead members'.[42]

As we've already seen, ale and beer were an essential part of nutrition for most people. From Rich's accounts, we learn much about English-controlled Ireland and those who lived within these confines, but we can also find this to be the case in the Irish source materials, scant as they may be, like the story above. From the *Inchiquin Manuscripts* we even find reference to an Irish brewhouse. Teig Clanchy, writing to Sir Donat (Donough) O'Brien on 13 August 1697, speaks of a brewhouse being constructed along with a stable by some masons.[43] The text also mentions 'drying malt against the next season'.[44] Other entries, like one from 10 March 1692 written by Laurence Chroe, also writing to O'Brien, also refer to barrels of malt and barley.[45] There are any number of entries in these texts referencing barley being grown and sold on, including people being sued on the matter.[46]

In 1598, *The Annals of Ireland* record that:

> On the morrow O'Muldoon, Magrath, and the chiefs of
> the country in general, came to them, bringing with them
> a variety of all kinds of food and liquors that were then
> generally used in that country; all those chiefs individually
> welcomed Giollaisa Maguire and served himself and those
> chiefs of Tirconnell with mead and ale...[47]

In this case, again in another feasting context, Giollaisa is ensuring that the chiefs of Tirconnell are able to be served well. He is assured that 'all sorts of liquors are in abundance, together with every other kind of ales that were requisite for the recent purpose'.[48] This was an important part of the hosting and feasting ritual, and this story tells us that the nobles and chiefs of Tirconnell and Fermanagh were 'merry and happy together', drinking their metheglin (a kind of spiced mead) and ale in the hall.[49]

Feasting and coshering also saw Irish women acting as hosts for their guests, as they had been doing for centuries. And what did they serve? Well, alcoholic drinks like beer and ale. Fynes Moryson's 17th-century account of Ireland links Irish women or Old English women closely with drunkenness. He states that aqua vitae or *usquebaugh* was commonly drunk and preferred to others because of 'the mingling of raisins, fennel-seed, and other things mitigating the heat'.[50] Apparently this was consumed in great measures, especially at feasts, so that – gasp – gentlewomen get drunk! In fact, they get *so* drunk:

> Not to speak of the wives of Irish lords or to refer it to the due place, who often drink till they be drunken, or, at least, till they void urine in full assemblies of men. I cannot (though unwillingly) but note the Irish women more especially with this fault, which I have observed in no other part to be a woman's vice, but only in Bohemia.[51]

Further, he observes that the Old English 'drink not English beer made of malt and hops, but ale'.[52] The horror of it all.

Writing in 1619, William Lithgow describes the Irish thusly:

> The alehouse is their church, the Irish priests their conforts; their auditors be, Fill and fetch more; their text Spanish sack, their prayers carousing, their singing of psalms whiffing of tobacco, their last blessing aqua vitae, and all their doctrine found drunkenness.[53]

We really can't trust Lithgow, though, as he also says Irish women have breasts that are half a yard long so that they can feed their infants behind their backs.[54]

In contrast, writing in 1620, Luke Gernon is perhaps a little less biased than other authors, declaring that the Irishman 'is no canniball to eate you up no no lowsy Jack to offend you'.[55] Gernon paints a delightful picture of an Irish castle with small, narrow stairs built for security. Up and up we climb to the uppermost room, where Gernon warns us to behave ourselves:

> I have instructed you before how to accost them. Salutations paste, you shall be presented with all the drinkes in the house, first the ordinary beere, then aquavitae, then sacke, then olde-ale, the lady tastes it, you must not refuse it. The fyre is prepared in the middle of the hall, where you may sollace yourselfe till supper time, you shall not want sacke and tobacco.[56]

He goes on to wax poetic about all the delicious kinds of foods you can find at an Irish feast, including mutton, bacon, deer and pasty, all while being serenaded by the harpist. And when you wake up in the morning? Whiskey!

> The aquavitae or usquebath of Ireland is not such an extraction, as is made in England, but farre more qualifyed, and sweetened with licorissh. It is made potable, and is of the colour of Muscadine. It is a very wholsome drinke, and naturall to digest the crudityes of the Irish feeding. You may drink a knaggin without offence, that is the fourth parte of a pynte.

Start chugging the *usquebaugh* as soon as you wake up and it will all be good, as it's a wholesome drink.

William Brereton also found alcohol to be an important part of hosting when visiting the castle of Clenmoullen, the seat of Sir Morgan Kavanagh and his wife, who he describes as good people but recusants, meaning they didn't go to the Church of England and therefore were rebels of some description in the eyes of crown. However, they did apparently serve 'good beer, sack and claret'.[57] Brereton does remark on a poorly made beer, however. He goes to the house of an Irishman and makes some scathing remarks about his wife, who did not know 'how to carve, look, entertain or demean herself'.[58] What's more, this house had something called charter beer, which he refused to drink because it apparently didn't look particularly appetising; he said it was thick and muddy.[59]

As we can see, many English writers had much to say about the Irish, and most of it wasn't particularly pleasant. They accused them of all sorts, including being cannibals, behaving in uncouth ways and cheating their customers. This went along with the wars being fought for the control of Ireland. This violence would eventually spill over into one of the most controversial events in Irish history: the 1641 Rebellion.

On 22 October 1641, Lord Connor Maguire, the second Baron of Enniskillen, had a meeting with fellow conspirators at the Golden Lion, a tavern on, you guessed it, Winetavern Street.[60] This was one of many such places that lined the sides of the road, places like the Golden Eagle and the Three Cups.[61] It was here that they gathered to formulate a plot to take Dublin Castle as part of a larger uprising of Irish people against colonial English rule.

Unfortunately for Maguire, he chose to trust the wrong person, Owen O'Connolly, who promptly betrayed him to the Lord Justice. While the story of Maguire's planning certainly involves our rather infamous drinking street, so does his capture.

Charles Kinsalagh had a house on this very street, where he was rudely awakened at 6 a.m. the following morning by a banging on his door. He rose from his bed and found none other than Tirlagh O'Connor, servant of Lord Maguire, at his door demanding ale. Kinsalagh replied he had nothing except small beer, which would not do at all, so he sent his boy off to buy four pennies' worth of the requested ale.[62] Kinsalagh left O'Connor to drink the ale with Edmund McMahon, another one of Lord Maguire's servants, while he tried to sneak Lord Maguire out of the city under the noses of the English by dressing him in women's clothing. This proved unsuccessful and Maguire was captured and later executed for treason.[63]

In the story of Maguire's conspiracy and capture, beer (or perhaps more precisely, ale) plays the role of the supporting cast – something in the background at key moments but nothing particularly central to the plot. Maguire's foiled capture of the castle would have been one of the first blows of the 1641 Rebellion, when the Irish people rose up against the colonising English forces, beginning the Eleven Years' War.

This period of history has been examined by countless experts over the years, including Aidan Clarke, Nicholas Canny and Jane Ohlmeyer.[64] The reasons for the rebellion and subsequent war are many and complex. Some of the key themes were the desire for Irish self-governance; that Catholics wanted to end the discrimination against them, as laws had been passed banning them from holding public office or serving in the army; and that they also wanted their lands returned to them from the colonialist plantation system that had seen the influx of thousands of settlers from England and Scotland – a system which, by the outbreak of the 1641 Rebellion, held 40% or thereabouts of profitable land, according to Pádraig Lenihan.[65] We aren't talking about just a small bit of land. James I seized over 3.8 million acres in Ulster alone, and by 1618 some 40,000 Scottish colonisers had settled there.[66] It wasn't like they could buy it back either, as laws were passed banning Catholics from buying land from Scots or English people.[67]

Ohlmeyer contends that the rebellion wasn't popular among Irish peers initially, with only Lord Maguire being involved. This changed, she argues, as it became clear to these Catholic lords that they needed to be involved if they wanted to maintain their positions and power.[68] In the first days, the gentry, with leaders like Sir Phelim O'Neill in Ulster, wanted to keep things under control with minimal violence. He even directed his men not to attack Scots.[69] According to Nicholas Canny, these initial attacks took the form more of stealing and beating and less outright murder; the rebels wanted to help themselves financially, and death usually only occurred when people resisted.[70] This changed as time wore on, though.

I cannot stress enough how much of this background is only skimming the surface of the contested nature of life in late 16th- and 17th-century Ireland, which was an incredibly controversial point in history. Entire academic careers have been built solely on this period of time, so I can't do it justice in a few paragraphs. Nevertheless, we know all these details about where Maguire was drinking and what ale his servants preferred because of a series of documents, the *1641 Depositions,* designed to ascertain the effects of this rebellion on the people who lived through it, particularly the Protestants. It is here that we find Kinsalagh's examination, and while ale is a background character in this particular series of events, in other examples it plays the lead.

In total, there are around 8,000 of these depositions, all of which have been digitised by Trinity College Dublin. Most of them represent witness statements by the Protestant English or Scottish colonisers, though there are also some from Catholics, and they represent people from all social categories, rich and poor alike.

The depositions themselves are incredibly biased and politically controversial, both in their own time and even now. In fact, these documents, like the events they describe, are one of the most, if not *the* most, contested historical sources for Ireland, according to the Trinity College website.[71] For one thing, they are only one side of the story. We don't have a matching set of documents from the other side of this conflict. As Jonathan Bardon states, they were also collected for a specific political purpose – to justify removing land from Catholics – so he found, as many other scholars have also argued, that many of these accounts are exaggerated or even merely hearsay.[72] On the other hand, Bardon argues, some of the stories can be factually verified.[73]

Ohlmeyer echoes these problems, noting that having so many sources from only one side of all this violence creates serious problems, but like others she acknowledges the importance of their study. Canny also recognises the many biases of these accounts, including the intention to portray Irish Catholics poorly, but he believes this material should not be ignored, as there is information to be gleaned within these pages.[74] To reiterate, these are only one side of the story, and a very biased one at that, deliberately designed to paint the Irish in the worst possible light. But there's still much to be learned from these documents. And for our central topic, we can find quite a bit about beer.

Elizabeth Griffith gave her deposition to the Commission for the Despoiled Subject on 6 January 1642. Griffith was a refugee from Tandragee, Co. Armagh, who spoke to the commissioners in Dublin, headed by Henry Jones, Dean of Kilmore, and seven other Church of Ireland clergymen. Griffith recalled her harrowing ordeal alongside her husband, Reynold, to the assembled men. On 23 October 1641, she and her husband were robbed by Irish rebels who made off with a variety of their worldly goods, including their malt. But it was the violence that followed that haunted her. After robbing them, these rebels attacked Reynold, wounding him grievously and leaving him for dead. He was able to flee, but they pursued him for 16 miles before he was finally able to escape.

Elizabeth was not so lucky. They captured her and detained her for three weeks alongside her children. Most horrifying of all, Griffith's 14-year-old son was drowned in a bog pit, held down before her at sword point until he died. This is a terrible story of a mother losing her child in an unspeakable manner and her husband almost being murdered, leaving her, along with her surviving children, traumatised from their ordeal. She also revealed that during her time in captivity, these rebels forced her to brew for them.[75]

Griffith was part of the multitude of Protestants who appeared before the Commission in 1642, and then later again in the 1650s, to talk about their experiences during the 1641 Rebellion in Ireland. Many told stories of theft, murder and utter terror. Mixed in with all these accounts, though, are stories of beer, ale and brewing, which can reveal to us the role these beverages played during this tumultuous period in Irish history.

Griffith wasn't the only one who found herself forced to brew. Sir Baptist Staples was kept prisoner for six months by the 'rebels' along with the widow of a man called Andrew Younge, who they had lately killed. Staples was forced to both brew beer and make aqua vitae, which they then made Andrew Young's widow sell for them.[76]

The combatants on every side of these wars ran on beer. It was central to these war machines, as it had been for centuries. Thomas Lee, writing to Queen Elizabeth about military life in Ireland, states:

> {*Water is now their drinke which breedeth many deseases in our Englishmen.*} After this manner may the souldiors be vittayled with wholesome vittayles and drinke, which is at all tymes verie scarse. For havinge mault they will get it to be brewed at their owne charge, which heretofore hath bene chargable to her Majestie.[77]

The depositions themselves echo such sentiment, with accounts from many men stating the importance of bread and beer to the English military might. Notably, centuries after Hildegarde von Bingen wrote about water and disease, we can see here that the liquid was viewed less favourably than beer for the armies, even though people would continue to drink it throughout this time. Richard Ashbould's account also stresses the importance of beer and bread to the military machine as an essential part of stocking a fort.[78] A letter from William Smyth declares that he did not have beer and bread to supply the fort for the English king.[79] Walter Esmund, John Holland, Peter Hooper and Thomas Fleminge also echo the importance of beer and bread to soldiers. These armies quite clearly ran in part on beer. But it wasn't just the English.

George Devenish stated that in his house in Santry, there were times when the Irish rebels were there under the command of 'Luke Netyerfeild and Collonell ffleming', and according to Devenish, his wife sent the rebels 'a carr load of provisions of severall sortes of victuals and Beere'.[80] Throughout the depositions, one of the common cries made by these 'rebels' was the demand for beer, bread and fresh water. And if they couldn't get it by other means, they were certainly stealing it.

William Free had his beer stolen, as did Richard Oburne, both by rebels who drank it.[81] Hugh Madden had a barrel and a half of strong beer worth 20 shillings stolen.[82] Phillipa Hendra, a widow, had a brewing furnace and other brewing vessels worth some 10 pounds, 10 barrels of barley worth five pounds and beer in her cellar worth five pounds stolen.[83] If the rebels couldn't steal the final product, they would make off with the equipment to make it themselves, or at least sell it on to make some money.

Helenor Adshed had several brewing vessels stolen.[84] Jane Steward went to the house of a widow named Ellein Trimble who had a brewing pan, which the Irish and rebels used to cook their dinner.[85] Margarett Hall, a widow, had brewing vessels stolen.[86] Maudlin Fisher was also a widow and had several brewing vessels stolen from her.[87] Margery Grey also had brewing pans stolen from her.[88] And on and on it goes. Both men and women had brewing equipment taken from their homes.

In total, I found 26 depositions that mention ale, mostly in relation to alehouses. The drink itself is mentioned only seven times, and most of those are in relation to Irish people drinking it or brewing the beverage for them.[89] In contrast, and much different from what we saw in Barnabe Rich's 1610 account, beer is mentioned 76 times in the documents, most often when it's being drunk or stolen. This perhaps suggests that there was, as Rich alludes to, an ethnic line between beer drinkers and ale drinkers to some degree, with the New English favouring the former, while the Irish and Old English preferred the latter.

These 1641 Depositions also reveal these alehouses to be a haunting juxtaposition of hospitality and murder. According to the deposition of Robert Boyle, vicar of Carrickmacross in Co. Monaghan, he, along with his family, was held prisoner in an alehouse for 14 or 15 weeks.[90] In the deposition of Hugh Culme of Leitrim, he reported that he'd heard that a man by the name of Luke Ward was forced into an alehouse, made to get drunk, then taken out back and hanged until dead, with his body dumped in the river.[91] Like our opening story suggests, the devil, it seems, really was in the alehouse.

St Audoen's Church is often overlooked when people think of the medieval history of Dublin. Located on Cornmarket/High Street and Cook Street (where the prior we met in Chapter 4 got his takeaway pies), it's the oldest parish church in Dublin. Originally built by the English soon after their initial invasions in the late 12th century, the church has seen a lot over its years of existence, including the reclamation of the land just below its gate stretching out to the River Liffey. It's here in the parish of St Audoen's in the 1640s where Widow Fitzwilliams, Widow Hanlon and Widow Humphreys all brewed their ale, alongside quite a few men, and we know their names because of the *Dublin City Cess Book of 1647–1649*.

The *Cess Book* contains the payments levied by the Dublin City Assembly for a loan to the English to help support their invading army. This loan was known as the cess, and part of this cess was collected from the creation of ale. In particular, there was a charge for the 'grinding of malt and retailing of ale'.[92]

We don't have all the records, as only a few remain, but they give us a glimpse into who might have been brewing in mid-17th-century Dublin. Among the Cess Records, 84 relate to brewing ale, but none talk about beer. Zero. Of these 84, 14 are for women, five of whom are widows; the other nine would have most likely been single women.[93] The remaining 70 men could have been brewing on their own or alongside their wives as a couple, so the number 14 is a minimum.

Women continued to be an important part of the brewing landscape in Dublin well into the end of the 17th century. A search in what remains of the *Dublin City Water Pipe Accounts 1680–1681* pulls up 31 entries for brewers representing 23 people, six of whom were women. However, before we get too far into investigating these, I need to clarify that they represent a mere fraction of the number of brewers in Dublin. We know this because seven years earlier, in another case of brewers managing to anger the government, we see more than triple this number.

In 1673, beer delivery was destroying the Dublin City pavements. Specifically, the *Dublin Assembly Rolls* tell us that 44 brewers were indicted for carrying their beer upon 'drawes shod with iron' and that this iron tore up the pavements. The brewers were acquitted by the jury in the trial, but because they were afraid that they might be charged again in the future, they decided to pay some reparations for the streets – a yearly fee of 10 shillings sterling for the upkeep of the pavement – as long as they could keep on carrying their beer on these 'drawes shod with iron as hath been done since memorie of man'. This was specific to these 44 brewers, but there were apparently 100 brewers in Dublin using these 'drawes shod with iron'; these 44 just so happened to be the ones who were indicted. Thus, the Assembly concluded that anyone who used this equipment must pay 10 shillings yearly for the privilege of having a license to have their carts and drawes shod with iron.[94]

Not only does this tell us that there were still quite a few breweries operating in Dublin (a minimum of 100), it also shows us that the conditions of the streets were of paramount importance and that efforts were being made to maintain them. Much like we saw in previous chapters, where a tax on malt and ale paid for the city walls throughout English-held Ireland, brewers paid money for licences that paid in part to maintain the city streets. The city brewers vs. the city council would come up again in the 18th century.[95]

From this we know that there were at least 100 breweries in Dublin in 1673, whereas only seven years later, according to the *Dublin City Water Pipe Accounts 1680–1681*, only 31 are to be found. We can ascertain that 69 breweries probably didn't close in the intervening years; it's more likely that these records are incomplete. But that doesn't mean the *Water Pipe Accounts* don't offer a valuable snapshot. Let's look at what they reveal to us.

Of the six women mentioned, all are widows. Widow Malone, Widow Weldon, Widow Surdeville, Widow Toole, Widow Devine and 'Alexander Norton's Widow' are all listed as paying for 'water for ale brewing' of £1,10 shillings, with the exception of Widow Malone, where it appears her chosen heirs or assignees paid 15 shillings in 1681. That they are all widows could tell us a couple of things. First, that brewing after the death of their husbands might have been a way for women to sustain themselves; equally, it could be that they inherited their husband's breweries after their deaths and kept on brewing. The remaining people listed, all men, could have been brewing on their own or, as before, as part of a couple. Some of these men, notably Luke Lowther and Lewis Desminieres, were aldermen, and perhaps, as Rich reported back in 1610, it was their wives who were still responsible for doing the brewing.

In the final years of the century, we can still find women brewing away, and even owning larger commercial operations. By the end of the 1680s, the English army was well established in the Dublin City environs. To say that they weren't always well behaved is an understatement. Apparently some army officers liked to randomly seize horses from brewers for fun. Normally this might not have been a serious concern for the government, but the seizure of these horses seriously hurt His Majesty's bottom line, as it prevented the breweries from selling their beer, which in turn meant he couldn't collect excise. Money, as ever, is a great motivator for the government.

So on 4 September 1689, Richard, Duke of Tirconnell, who was also captain general of the king's forces, set out measures to prevent the commandeering of the horses so that the breweries could conduct their trade unmolested.[96] Specifically, he said that so 'no person may pretend ignorance we have thought it fit to order that the brewers names together with the number of horses allowed them by his majesty for carrying on their brewing trade as aforesaid' be published throughout the city and suburbs. Basically, he was saying, 'Here's a list of breweries, so you can't pretend you don't know about this.'

You can imagine signs posted throughout the city listing all the brewers and how many horses they were allowed to have to transport their beer. The excess, it seems, would be up for grabs. These were common brewers – those who sold their ales and beers on to others to sell in their alehouses and taverns – not those who only sold on their own property. The latter wouldn't have needed horses to transport their goods beyond their premises. To be clear, we aren't talking legions of horses here. Most people were allotted somewhere between one and three, with four men getting six, a widow and another man seven, and a man named John Pearson could have nine.

That said, this list gives us the names and locations of all these brewers in Dublin at the time. There were 69 in total, of which 11 were headed by women, and two of those are a male/female team who might not have been couples; Elizabeth Ashenhors and Liet. Tankersby, and Gowin Skeffe and Katherine Johnson are listed together but both under separate last names. This could mean that they were unmarried and therefore the woman didn't fall under the man's legal charge. Therefore, it's possible, like earlier in the century, that some of the remaining men were brewing alongside their wives, though clearly, some of these men were operating and brewing on their own.

Some of these names appear over and over in the records. There's one name I want you to remember, as we will come back to him in the next chapter: a man by named Giles Mee, who lived in St Katherine's Parish, purchased cistern and water rights near St James's Gate and had the right to have seven horses.

PORTER WARS

BORN IN CO. WESTMEATH IN 1727, Margaret Plunkett was one of her parents' eight children (out of 22 altogether) who survived to adulthood. After the death of her mother, she fled her abusive brother in her teenage years. She arrived in Dublin and took up with a man, Mr Dardis, and soon fell pregnant.

Her story isn't all that unusual at this point. Many girls from the countryside left their towns for the city, whether to escape the hardships at home or simply to try their hand at making it somewhere else. Some succeeded. Others, like Margaret, ended up in bad situations with few options available. Following the death of her child, Margaret found herself thrown out by the man who was keeping her, so she turned to sex work yet again.

But this isn't the end of her story. It's only the beginning.

You see, Margaret Plunkett is none other than the notorious Peg Plunkett, who is probably the most famous 18th-century courtesan in Irish history, let alone the rest of Europe. Anecdotes about her life were reported in newspapers all over Ireland and the UK. People at the time were utterly fascinated by her, following her on dits quite closely. She was a kind of celebrity, at least within a certain set. Between carrying on affairs with elite men the world over, attending lavish events and visiting the theatre, Peg became a bit of a beer snob. She had a particular penchant for Irish porter – Maddocks' Irish Porter, to be exact.

After her years of being a kept woman, Peg eventually went on to set up a brothel. It had various locations before finally settling on Pitt Street in Dublin, on the site where the Westbury Hotel is now. Here Plunkett set up a lavish, extravagant bordello, catering to wealthy clientele including, at some point, Charles Manners, the Duke of Rutland. This cemented her high status as the best brothel-keeper in Dublin.

Peg's good fortune didn't last. In her advanced age, after retiring from sex work, she wrote her memoirs in several volumes to keep herself from the poorhouse after she had lost everything to her accumulated debts. It's from these memoirs that we learn all about her many affairs, and it was during one of Rutland's visits that we learn a bit about her taste in beer. Rutland came to her with two of his aides-de-camp, alongside his 'valiant life guards all drawn up about my door', and remained there through the night. Peg took pity on them and 'properly plied them all night' with 'the pure native and a large portion of Maddocks' Irish porter, than which, not Whitbread's boasted beverage ever excelled, though the produce of the nasty Thames.'[1]

Porter is a difficult beer style to pin down today, with many examples walking the fine line between it and its close, and more famous, companion, stout. It can be hard for many of us to define the differences between the two, though articles all over the internet try. They are closely related, but porter came first. Stout was introduced later as a sort of stronger version of the brew, to completely oversimplify the matter.

Porter became an incredibly popular style in 18th-century Ireland, but it wasn't the only type of beer or ale made. Strong ales, table beers and even pale ales graced the pages of brewers' adverts beckoning customers to try their wares. But Peg's preference for Maddocks' hints at a story that in many ways defined brewing in Ireland in the 18th century: the rivalry between English and Irish breweries and the porter wars that waged between them.

The state of Irish brewing in the 18th century was, in a word, complicated. When we closed our previous chapter in the last decades of the 17th century, brewing in Ireland was doing okay for the most part, minus the egregious horse-stealing episodes. It was a trade that was controlled by breweries in Ireland that sold their beer and ale to local customers.

The 18th-century brewing trade seemed to start off on a similar path. In 1838, Samuel Morewood published *A philosophical and statistical history of the inventions and customs of ancient and modern nations in the manufacture and use of inebriating liquors. With the present practice of distillation, etc.*, which is an incredibly long way to say he looked at the history of alcohol.[2] His consideration of Ireland has been a keystone in the studies on brewing in the 18th century, largely because he provides us with a lot of numbers regarding the amount of beer and ale brewed in the country alongside what was exported and what amount of ale and beer Ireland imported.

Let's start in 1719. That year, Ireland produced 601,457 barrels of ale and beer, of which 6,408 was exported. A small amount – only 299 barrels – was imported.[3] This is for a population, according to Cormac Ó Gráda's estimates, of around 2.9 million people in 1718.[4] That's about 57.6 pints per person per year, if we include everyone, which in reality we wouldn't, as there are teetotallers, people whose preferences lie elsewhere and of course children, who might be drinking tiny amounts. But it does serve to give us a baseline perspective, something we can relate to. Regardless, there is nothing particularly groundbreaking about people drinking 58 pints per year. It's when we compare this to later numbers that things start to take a turn.

Over the course of the 18th century, the population on the island boomed. K.H. Connell argues that this fact, especially in the later part of the century, is 'incontrovertible'.[5] Though scholars may disagree on the precise numbers and why this might have happened, they do agree that the population increased significantly over the century. Which is all well and good, but why do we care?

For that, we need to look at Morewood's numbers for the last decade of the 18th century. In 1790, Ireland was producing only 434,397 barrels of ale and beer, a decrease of more than 150,000 barrels from 1719. Paired with the fact that the population had now reached something around 4.75 million, this means that if we're thinking in terms of pints per person, we're down to 25.92 pints of Irish-made beer.[6] This increase in population coupled with the decrease in production led scholar Caen Harris to argue that Ireland's brewing trade was actually in decline.[7]

Even if we include imports, those numbers are incredibly revealing. In 1790, the amount of beer imported into Ireland (mostly from England) was 109,049 barrels – a huge jump from those meagre 299 barrels in 1719.[8] Even so, imports and local brewing combined still mean the average person consumed only 31.68 pints per year, a difference of 25.92 pints, which, frankly, is a lot. It's an almost 50% decrease in consumption.

These average pints per year are just ballpark figures and should be taken with a grain of salt, as they don't truly represent the state of beer consumption. Yet we can still clearly see from these figures that people were drinking less than they had at the beginning of the century, supporting Harris's argument of an industry in decline. Harris isn't the only one to argue that the industry took a nosedive. Many scholars over the decades have reached similar conclusions. Andrew Malone also argues that in the mid-1700s, and indeed by the 1770s, 'the Dublin brewing industry was as a whole in a very bad state'.[9] This 'bad state' would extend throughout the country for the most part, though like everything, there are always exceptions.

Overall, the brewing trade in Ireland wasn't doing so great over the course of these 100 years, but neither was beer drinking. There are a myriad of reasons why this was the case, but a few big ones stand out, all of which are heavily intertwined. As Harris, Malone and other scholars have found, it wasn't only Irish beer brewing that was hurting. People simply weren't reaching for the beverage full stop. So what were they drinking instead? No prizes for guessing that most famous of intoxicating Irish beverages: whiskey.

Whiskey was the firm fan favourite in Ireland. Irish people in general simply preferred the stuff. Even in Peg Plunkett's hints about brewing in Ireland, she plied those soldiers not only with local Irish beer, but also with Irish whiskey. By and large, the people in the country drank the stronger spirit, which partly fuelled the decline of the beer industry. This worked in tandem with clearly unfavourable restrictions for brewers that discouraged new breweries from starting and deterred those already in existence from growing their businesses.

This preference for whiskey didn't go unnoticed or unchallenged, however. In fact, it was of extreme concern for some moralising middle- and upper-class people who waxed on about the perils of its consumption in those of lower-income status, never mind that people of all walks of life consumed the drink and got drunk. One of the most famous monuments to the debaucheries of the elite is the infamous Dublin Hellfire Club, whose ruins stand atop Montpelier Hill in Dublin. It was a kind of warped fraternity for rich men of the 18th century that now finds itself entwined with many ghost stories and even some tales of the devil himself. The members of the club also appear to have had a decided preference for our beloved scolteen (or scaltheen), which was possibly served during their meetings.[10] Alcoholic overconsumption was not limited by social class in the 18th century, though of course there are always exceptions.

In any event, brewers took this as an opportunity to seek better legal conditions for themselves, especially in the later part of the century. After all, beer was a much more wholesome drink than whiskey, right? At least that's what they told the legislators.

The 1778 committee appointed by the Irish House of Commons to look into the petition of the Dublin Corporation of Brewers revealed that the brewers in the city were in trouble. One of those witnesses was Mr George Thwaites, master of that brewers' corporation, who reported that the number of breweries had dropped from a total of 70 to a mere 30. Thwaites told the committee that one-quarter of those had failed between 1763 and 1773. He attributed this to the competition with English brewers and the increased imports of their beer. Additionally, Thwaites argued that Irish breweries had had to reduce both the malt and the hops in their beer, which put them at a further disadvantage.[11]

Enter Henry Grattan.

A member of Irish parliament, Grattan famously took up the cause against spirituous liquors, and for breweries. In the 1790s, he argued in parliament that the low cost of liquor, as well as the ease with which people acquired licenses to sell it, led to whiskey's alleged reign of destruction. In 1791, he made a famous push for a significant reduction in restrictions on breweries. Grattan wanted to give breweries 'decisive advantages':

> that for this purpose it is necessary that the duties affecting the brewer should be reduced, and the restrictions and regulations whereby he is now restrained, taken off. That it is advisable to take off the whole excise from beer and ale, and in place thereof lay a moderate tax on malt.[12]

Grattan said it was important that breweries 'be encouraged, by taking off every restriction on the brewer, and by lowering duties' by removing the excise on breweries and putting a duty on malt instead. He noted that the number of breweries in Ireland had diminished by one-third in the last 30 years, mirroring Thwaites.[13] Grattan argued this was due to several factors, most importantly because these Irish breweries struggled under these 'severe restrictions and heavy duties' and also had to compete with English breweries. He also argued that 'our malt is worse than that of England, and we have not a sufficiency of hops; these are hardships you cannot remove, restriction and heavy duties you can'.[14] He believed in the 'wisdom of entirely and absolutely repealing the whole excise on beer and ale. The present system cannot be justified. It is expensive in collection, small in production, and in little and vexatious restrictions and penalties, abundant'.[15] He advocated for removing the duty entirely.

At first he got lip service from many of his fellow MPs, who seemed to agree in principle yet lacked the fortitude to get the actual legislation passed. This prompted yet another speech on 19 January 1792, where he noted that they had determined to give breweries the 'decisive advantage, by lowering the duty', but instead Grattan argued:

> the brewer is now taxed and aggrieved. Hear how they have taken off the restrictions by adding to them – they imposed a new restriction affecting the quantity of liquor each brewer is to make; and to exclude the smaller brewer from the trade, they add a new restriction, and they left one of the worst of the old – the division of breweries.[16]

Grattan argued that they had done this intentionally to 'complement' the brewers of London. They did the same with hops, he said, charging twice as much to import hops, among other things, from Flanders as from England, to the point that Grattan found 'however dear, however bad the English hops might prove, you must take them, unless they come to such a price that England cannot export them'. He charged that 'here is the fatal hand of an Irish cabinet legislating against Ireland, to promote its own credit in the court of Great Britain. Thus stands the conduct of the minister':[17]

> He professed to give the brewery decisive encouragement by lowering the duty on beer, he sunk the duty the hundredth part of a farthing a quart; he proposed to leave the brewer free, he left one grievous restriction, and added another: he had professed to agree to permit the import of foreign hops, he fixes the line of permission at an impossible price.[18]

Grattan was eventually successful in the mid-1790s and had the excise charges on beer repealed.

But it wasn't just excise duty that worked against brewers. It could be the very water itself, or more to the point, the control over who the water belonged to.

Picture it: Dublin, 1775. One brewer stands poised at the threshold of violence. Armed only with a pickaxe that he swiped off one of the assailants, he defends his property from destruction. How did it come to this?

Let's rewind a bit.

Water, while an essential ingredient for brewing, was also heavily controlled by the government in the 18th century. In Dublin, there was an entire subcommittee devoted to the watercourses and pipes, and they took their job *very* seriously. In fact, issues with the water pipes are one of the most common places where we find brewers mentioned in the 18th-century legal records. They are everywhere.

Paying for the privilege of using water to brew was enshrined in the laws of the city. For example, in 1663, 'regarding the cess and water distribution and pipes', there were rates that had to be paid by the freemen of the city of Dublin if they brewed:

> a wholesale brewer, if he brewes his beere with the said water, is to pay yearely foure pounds; a brewer of ale or beere to retaile, one pound, tenne shillings, sterling; a malt man making use of said water, two pounds tenne shillings, sterling; a distiller, two pounds, tenne shillings, sterling.[19]

We can see here that there were two different kinds of brewers: those who brewed to sell directly to customers, and those who brewed to sell to people who then sold it on to customers at pubs or taverns. These are the retail vs. wholesale brewers. It should also be noted that further down in this list of people who must pay for the pipes, 'foreigners' had to pay twice whatever the norm was.[20] This Dublin City Water Pipe Committee controlled the water and access to it on behalf of the Dublin City Corporation, interlopers be damned.

In 1772, we find our committee investigating the water pipes and courses between St James's Street and the city basin. St James's Street at this time was the home of many breweries, and in this particular case, three find themselves in the crosshairs.

The committee went out, had a look around and found that things were not as they should be. There were encroachments in many places, people were wasting water and the cistern itself was not up to standard.[21] This cistern had been placed in the middle of three breweries, and these three breweries were availing themselves of the water without permission. They had made three breaches into the cistern and one brewery was also using 'secret sewers'.[22] The most important part of all this, and the reason why the committee cared in the first place, is because they were losing money – people paid for the privilege of using the city water pipes. Naturally, the committee was enraged and sought to rectify this situation immediately, but the problems persisted, at least for one of the three breweries. While you might not be familiar with two of them, Green and Forster, you certainly know the third: Guinness.

We find ourselves in 1775 and Arthur Guinness is now ready to go to war, quite literally. We're talking again about the watercourse on St James's Street and the use of it by the brewers on that road, allegedly illegally (at least according to the committee). This time the dispute is whether a certain watercourse belonged to the city or to the brewer himself.

The committee was really rather smug about the whole matter. They duly informed Arthur Guinness that his watercourse must be destroyed immediately, but allowed him what they believed to be a 'reasonable amount of time'.[23] This went down like a lead balloon, so Arthur chose violence. He replied that the water was his and was prepared to defend it with arms. The committee snarked back: 'Defence by that they were not to be intimidated from the execution of their duty by threats, but would certainly proceed to accomplish it', to which our brewer 'invited them to try how far their strength would prevail'.[24] Basically, feck around and find out.

Things escalated from there. The committee enlisted Sheriff Trulock, who took two of his men and began to destroy the whole thing entirely. In response, Guinness sent a servant to try to stop them, whose efforts to defend the watercourse were quickly abandoned when the sheriff asked if he would like to have a small holiday at Newgate Prison. After this, they went back to destroying the structure until the arrival of Arthur Guinness himself, who 'violently rushed upon them', ripped a pickaxe from one's hands and 'declaring with violent improper language, that they should not proceed'. This is likely code for he cursed them out.

Guinness then positioned himself in front of the course and told them that if they tried to fill it up, he would immediately un-fill it. The sheriff had now become a bit wary of the whole matter and

[141]

> ... declared as his opinion, that in proceeding this far, committee had ascertained the city's right to the water course and city's right, that it would be wrong to proceed further, to which, committee replied, that their instructions were to fill up the whole of that part of the water course which supplied messieurs Cox and Guinness and many others not entitled, that they were now ready to perform their duty, would not act in contradiction to the declared opinion of the Sheriff and so desisted.[25]

At this, Guinness opted for a compromise, whereby on the 22nd of the month he would submit his title to the water for the Water Pipe

Committee to look over. He later produced his argument that he owned it by 'ancient custom', perhaps based on the lease he had.

Remember that man we met in the last pages of the previous chapter, Giles Mee, and his brewery at St James's Gate in the latter half of the 17th century? Well, Mee passed his property on to a series of owners, including the Rainsfords, before it finally fell into the hands of none other than Arthur Guinness. It might have been Mee's original claims that Guinness was referring to when talking about this 'ancient custom'. Regardless, it should be noted that this entire account was written by the assembly that created the committee, so it's a bit biased in their favour.

Following this incident at the watercourse, Guinness proceeded in action again the corporation and was granted an injunction.[26] This was not entirely resolved and crops up again later in 1779, when we are back with *Guinness v. the Water Pipe Committee*, and what a saga it is. This time, Guinness had reached out to try to smooth things over between himself and the city. In that vein, he proposed that he might become a tenant of a kind, where for the watercourse from James's Gate to Echlin's Lane, and specifically, for enough water from a 2-inch bore for the duration of his lease with Mark Rainsford, he proposed an annual rent of £10, which the committee agreed to, but with quite a few caveats. In the end, they both agreed and the crisis appears to have been averted.[27]

Guinness found a loophole where he could retain control of the water and also satisfy the committee somewhat. That was the name of the game in the 18th century: that is, regulation, control and, more importantly, how to get around it.

The issues with those ubiquitous water pipes don't start and end with Arthur Guinness. A quick glance at the *Dublin Assembly Rolls* sees many instances of brewers getting into trouble with the Water Pipe Committee. For example, in 1704 there was a case involving the Earl of Limerick;[28] John Merryman and his brewery ran afoul of them in 1752[29] and again in 1779;[30] in 1772, a Mr Edward Byrne sought more water to brew;[31] and Mr Coppinger did the same in 1776.[32]

Alongside the duty, the preference for whiskey and issues with hop imports, we can also see that, at least in Dublin, there were problems getting water to brew with. But that's not all.

Grattan's arguments in parliament brought up another clear issue for Irish breweries: competition. And not just among Irish breweries, but from further afield in England.

Grattan noted that in the last 30 years, the imports of 'foreign beer' had increased by two-thirds.[33] Returning to Morewood's data, those 109,049 barrels of beer and ale imported into the country largely came from England, especially from London, where their porter beer had made a big splash with Irish palates. But why did Irish palates prefer English beer? Morewood argues that the preference for whiskey might also be in part because Irish beer wasn't all that great, particularly compared to its English counterparts:

> the malt drink made in Ireland was never of strength, flavour, nor purity equal to that manufacture in England. Hence to the warm and exhilarating spirit a preference was given, rather than to the thin, cold, unpalatable beer or ale to be met in shops and taverns of the kingdom.[34]

Of course, Irish breweries didn't just cave in to these incursions from foreign breweries. The rivalry between English and Irish beer in the 18th century was fierce. Fuelled by competition but also large doses of patriotism, in the latter half of the 1700s English and Irish porter were pitted against each other in a battle royale, with each drink meaning more than just personal taste – they also signified political allegiances.

That English beer was better than Irish beer is something that has been argued by contemporaries as well as historians. An article in the *Freeman's Journal* on 2 November 1793 contends that the Right Honourable Mr Beresford had attempted to bolster the breweries in Ireland over and over again by 'obtaining for them every possible encouragement' in order to make sure that the 'laborious part of the people' had a 'substantial and wholesome beverage' so they wouldn't drink those dreaded 'ardent spirits'. However, he is sorely disappointed because 'they converted the opportunity into an object of profit, and have ever since produced their malt liquor considerably worse':

> That now sold by many brewers for porter, is not near so good as the common ale drank in this country a few years ago. In short there is no good well-bodied malt liquor of Irish manufacture any here to be met with. That offered in general to the public is a poor, sour trash, unwholesome and disgusting. Such offensive stuff had given the lower classes an aversion to malt liquor; and the cause of ardent spirits being used amongst them is, from want of a good malt beverage – a matter which claims the attention of the legislature.[35]

Peter Mathias attributes the better English beer in some part to the advanced industrial nature of London breweries compared to their Irish counterparts, arguing that the brewing trade in Ireland in 1790 was like that of England in 1730. He also found that contemporaries believed English beers were made from superior materials and by better brewers.[36]

Irish ingredients weren't necessarily worse, or at least that's what people hoped, and organisations stepped in to promote their use. Irish brewers were encouraged to brew using local ingredients, with the Dublin Society offering prizes for the best versions. In a meeting held on 3 May 1744, 'A premium of 20 pounds was adjudged to Mr. George Thwaites, for making use of the greatest quantity of Irish hops in his brewing, in the year 1743. A premium of ten pounds was also paid to Mr. William Brereton, for using the next greatest quantity.'[37] At this same meeting, the society also issued a new list of premiums for the current year:

> to the person who shall make use of the greatest quantity of
> Irish hops, of the growth of 1744 in his brewings on the first
> of May next, 20 pounds, second place 10 pounds, for the
> best barrel of ale produced in Dublin in bottles or barrels,
> the third Wednesday in March next, six pounds, and second
> best four pounds, for the best barrel of ale produced as
> aforesaid brewed with Irish hops and malt, six pounds and
> for the second best four pounds.[38]

Throughout the century, the Dublin Society held similar competitions with awards for the best beers produced with Irish ingredients.

I want to return here to Peg Plunkett's remarks about Irish beer. She stated that she was serving the soldiers a 'large portion of Maddocks' Irish porter, than which, not Whitbread's boasted beverage ever excelled, though the produce of the nasty Thames'.[39] She is directly pitting Irish and English porter against each other here, and for her the clear winner is the local brew. This sentence, which appears at first to be a small throwaway in the context of the larger, salacious volumes of her memoirs, is actually incredibly telling. Peg's remarks so closely mirror that of some Irish porter brewers or sellers that it begs the question of whether she had a horse in the race.

Ralph Card certainly seemed to be an avid Irish porter fan. On Monday, 21 June 1784, he published an entire affidavit, signed and witnessed, that he would be selling Irish porter and only Irish porter. Card, located on Aungier Street in Dublin, made the following oath 'on the holy evangelists' that from and after the day hereof, for the term of twelve months he (shall) NOT sell or ensure to be sold for him, any malt liquor, commonly called PORTER, except what deponent shall verily believe to have been brewed in IRELAND; and that which required by any person purchasing malt liquor from him, he will truly declare from whom he bought such malt liquor, to the best of his knowledge, and that he will give directions to all those acting under him in the sale of his goods to declare as aforesaid in his absence, and deponent further saith, that for the aforesaid term he will not mix, or cause to be mixed, any other liquor with the malt liquor he shall sell as aforesaid, by way of increase or adulteration; and deponent maketh this affidavit, believing it may be a means of increasing the consumption of IRISH PORTER, and of supplying the public with a better malt liquor than is frequently sold under the denomination English Porter, and that it may in some degree remove prejudices against what deponent verily believes to be a wholesome drink of Irish manufacture.[40]

We can learn a lot from this. Much like Peg's words, Card believes there to be a clear bias in the public against Irish porter and seeks to exalt it above its English counterparts. He believed, like Plunkett did, that Irish porter was in fact superior, so much so that he put his money where his mouth was and swore to sell it, and only it, for a period of one year. We also learn that mixing different porters or adulterating them might have been a problem, but that's a tangent for another day. Card ran his advert, and affidavit, multiple times over the ensuing months, trying to get the maximum amount of exposure for his endeavours in support of the local beverage.

He wasn't the only one. The following year, Samuel Brown let readers of the *Belfast Newsletter* know that he was selling Irish porter, made in fact by brewers lately from London who now were residing in the country. He noted that the beer was 'of a quality equal to any imported, be such as is confidently drank in the city of LONDON':

It is presumed unnecessary to point out the propriety of encouraging the brewing of Porter, in the same manner and of the same kind of that used in London. The want of such Porter brewed in this kingdom, had long been regretted; and the public, by giving that encouragement which this will be found to merit, will have it in its power to establish the brewing of Porter in this Country on as good a footing as it is in England.[41]

You see, some of those allegedly superior London brewers upped sticks and moved to Ireland to ply their trade to an audience of customers who were absolutely delighted to have them. Of course, not all the Irish porter brewers were from England. Some were certainly born and raised in Ireland.

Adverts like this by Irish brewers can be found throughout the last 30-odd years of the 18th century. John Magee, brewer to Alderman Warren at No. 6 Mill Street, posted one such advert in the *Dublin Evening Post* on Thursday, 15 July 1779, for his 'Irish Porter, of the Finest Quality', which he sold for 5 shillings and 3 pence per dozen with the bottles included, or 3 shillings and 3 pence if the bottles were returned immediately. The ad goes on to state, 'As this liquor was Brewed by HIMSELF and from the best materials, he is well convinced it will give satisfaction; and hopes for a Preference from the generous Public.'[42] Similarly, on Monday, 4 November 1776, an advert for Irish porter taken out by Philip Woods at Cork-bridge in *Saunders's News-Letter* advertised that he 'continues to be supplied as usual, with a large Quantity of the so much esteemed Irish Porter, in Wood and Bottles'.[43]

These appeared over and over again throughout the following months and even years. In an earlier ad for the same Irish porter on Friday, 18 August 1775, Woods took an even stronger stand to support local beer:

> Philip Woods, at his Ware-house, in Meath-street, has now for Sale a large Quantity of IRISH PORTER, in Bottles, in prime Order to Drinking, which by the best Judges is allowed far superior to any London Porter ever imported, not only from its peculiar Flavour and Mellowness, but because it never afflicts the Stomach with Wind, nor causes the Head to ache, (the constant complaints against London bottled Porter). The Price is 3 shillings 3d per dozen exclusive of bottles.[44]

William Shaw of Lurgan also advertised Irish porter 'of a quality equal to any imported' that was also brewed by a 'Company of Brewers from London', now local.[45]

Drinking Irish porter and supporting its manufacture became a matter not only of local pride, but perhaps also patriotic duty, or at least according to Magees and Callwell of No. 10 Bridge Street in Belfast. They ran an advert that appeared several times in the *Belfast Newsletter* in 1785, where they declared:

> It must give particular pleasure to those who admire and
> consume that salutary liquor- PORTER- to find it is now
> brought to that state of excellence in IRELAND, which
> equals, if not exceeds, any that can be imported from
> Britain; - 'Tis the duty of those who are PATIOT [sic] in
> DEED, and not in NAME only- to protect and consume
> those products which their country in perfection yields...[46]

They go on to tell readers that they have for sale Irish porter made by one of the first brewers in Ireland at 3 shillings 6 pence for 12 bottles, alongside London porter, which they are selling for 4 shillings for 12 bottles.

Porter brewing had certainly become a battleground of sorts. A letter in the *Freeman's Journal* on 2 September 1779 really hammers this idea home. Directed to the 'Committee for conducting Free-Press' and signed from 'A Native', this letter congratulates the committee on their efforts to get people drinking Irish porter. However, the author notes:

> your patriotic sentiments are, at length, almost everywhere
> adopted, and there are not now in the whole city, over half
> a dozen houses of any note, that continue to sell English
> porter, and they too (being only frequented by Englishmen,
> or those connected with the interest of the porter merchant)
> must very soon fall in with the rest, or else, by obstinately
> persisting to oppose the laudable wish and intentions of the
> publick, become neglected and despoiled.[47]

The letter-writer goes on to tell the gentlemen:

> it is with secret pleasure I remark the chearful satisfied
> countenance each consumer of this wholesome beverage
> displays, when he calls for a pot of Irish Porter: The inward
> gratification he feels, while drinking the produce of his
> native soil ... is happy expressed in his face, and nothing but
> mirth harmony and friendship are every where found to be
> the attendant effects of it.

He also notes that it has 'rendered a material saving to the laborious class of people, by being so much cheaper, and from its healthful and enlivening qualities inspiring a universal lover and fellowship that is evident on every occasion' and that it's important that these Irish porter brewers keep brewing.[48]

Speaking of Irish breweries, what of Maddocks' that Peg Plunkett mentioned? I have searched high and low to find a Maddock's Irish porter operating in the 18th century and have come up with absolutely nothing.

There are no records whatsoever in any source I have come across so far. It's possible this was a brewery that wasn't mentioned often or perhaps it was quite small. But given that she had enough to ply all the guards with it, this would have been a commercial brewery. This leads me to conclude that perhaps this was a mistake in the publication or a deliberate use of a pseudonym in her handwritten notes, because while Maddocks' doesn't seem to have existed, Madder's did.

Known as the Phoenix Porter Brewing Company, Samuel Madder (who, incidentally, had been a London brewer) started the operation in 1778. The brewery would go on to be purchased by the son of Daniel O'Connell, The Liberator himself, and would eventually become the second largest brewery in Dublin. Nothing in Peg Plunkett's memoirs indicate any kind of rendezvous with Madder, but who knows, they could have been friends. Or she might have been a fan. Nevertheless, her championing of Irish porter over English porter does seem to indicate either a particular fervour for local beer or a friendship with Irish brewers.

The Usher Street brewery owned by Samuel Madder and Co. ran an advert in 1785 stating that they

> are ready to supply customers with such Porter as is equal to any imported from London. They hope it will be considered a national Object, So as to be encouraged and supported throughout the Kingdom, and the Proprietors will make it their Study to deserve such an Establishment, by the Goodness of the Commodity.[49]

However, it wasn't just porter where a political proxy war was played out; it was brewing itself.

We've learned about the British colonisation of Ireland since the medieval period. In the previous chapter we learned about the reconquest of Ireland, the 1641 Rebellion and how beer played a role in the Irish struggle for independence in the face of increasingly worse conditions. We learned of the plantation system and how Catholic Irish people had their lands and rights stripped from them in favour of English and Scottish colonisers.

This overall pattern continued into the 18th century with the Protestant Ascendancy, in which the economic and political power was concentrated in members of the Church of England from the 17th century onward. One of the things they introduced to further disenfranchise the Irish people were the Penal Laws, a series of legal measures designed to discriminate against Irish Catholics and anyone else who didn't support the Ascendency. This included banning Catholics from most public offices; prohibiting intermarriage between Catholics and Protestants, which was only repealed in 1778; barring Catholics from joining the military (repealed in 1793); banning Catholics from membership in the Irish or English Parliament until 1829; barring Catholics from voting until 1793; Catholics couldn't attend Trinity College Dublin until 1793; and Catholics couldn't be teachers until 1782. Specifically, for economic purposes Catholics couldn't inherit land from Protestants, couldn't buy land with a lease of more than 31 years and couldn't own a horse worth more than 5 pounds.

Naturally, this led to a largely impoverished native population with much less power than their Protestant colonist counterparts, which was further exacerbated by clear and direct policies of discrimination and abuse set out by the British ruling elites. Of course, some Irish Catholics found a way around these laws designed to keep them out of power. Amidst all this, there was at least one place where the Catholic Irish were still allowed to participate and make money: brewing.

On the River Liffey, along the south quays overlooking O'Connell Bridge, a large, originally Georgian building boasting hanging baskets and signs beckons punters to venture in to sample their various adult beverages. Now called J.R. Mahon's, in recent years the pub went by another name, J.W. Sweetman's.

The Sweetman family has had a long and inspiring influence on brewing history in Dublin. Members of the family have been brewing in locations throughout the city from at least the 17th century, when the cess records from 1647 list a James Sweetman who paid £2 and 2 shillings for the 'impost for grinding of malt and retailing of ale'.[50]

If we leave the old city walls around what was at one point the Cornmarket on Thomas Street (the site we learned about just a bit ago that played host to the awards for the best brews made with Irish ingredients) and turn down Francis Street, we can meander down to what was once home to the Iveagh Markets, a purpose-built indoor space created so that local traders could have a place to sell their goods out of the rain. It was founded in part by the 1st Baron of Iveagh, a member of the Guinness family. It now lies derelict, as it has for many years, though recent efforts to revitalise the space will hopefully soon be successful.

Before the Iveagh Markets were even a glimmer in anyone's eye, way before the period we're discussing in this chapter, the space on Francis

Street was once the medieval city's fairgrounds, a place where people went to enjoy the festivities and maybe quaff some local ales. In the centuries between the medieval fairs and the creation of the 19th-century markets, many buildings would be constructed alongside what was once the open green, including on the site of the markets themselves. Here, in the 18th and 19th centuries, a brewery stood belonging to none other than the Sweetman family. This was just one of the five to seven breweries in Dublin belonging to the Sweetman family in the 18th century.

Seán Magee wrote a compelling study on the Sweetman family and notes that while the Penal Laws banned Roman Catholic families in Ireland from holding down many types of businesses or accessing many parts of life, brewing was an avenue that was still available to them.[51] Magee argues that there was a strong solidarity in the brewing trade and with the Roman Catholic business community at this time.[52]

Involvement in brewing came from three family lines: James Sweetman in James's Street; John Sweetman on Aston Quay; and Patrick Sweetman on St Stephen's Green.[53] While the men of the family can take credit for undertaking a lot of the physical labour of brewing itself, their legacy continued through the women. For example, in 1738, Henry Sweetman, brewer and oldest son of Mary Sweetman, married Mary Callan, eldest daughter of Patrick Callan, Dublin brewer.[54] This was not limited to the Sweetman or even the Callan families. Just like aristocratic families married each other to solidify alliances or grow their power, so did our brewing families. Daughters brought with them in their dowries breweries or portions of breweries; husbands left their entire trade to their wives upon their demise; and widows even left their breweries to their daughters.

Alice Ford, widow of Thomas Ford, a Dublin brewer, was likely left the operations on his death. On 24 March 1727, she entered into a lease with Richard Williams, also a Dublin brewer. She granted to him a dwelling house as well as a brewhouse and malthouse on Church Street for 31 years at the yearly rental of 17 pounds sterling to be payable half-yearly.[55]

Women didn't necessarily need to inherit land to own a brewhouse; some just bought them outright. This was the case for Lettice Crow, a widow who in 1725 bought a mortgage for a plot on Capel Street from William Crawford, a merchant, and George Overend, a pewterer. On this property there were, among other things, tenements, a dwelling house, stables and a brewhouse, all for 200 pounds.[56]

This didn't only happen in Dublin. Cork had quite a few brewhouses too. On 17 July 1716, Thomas Roland leased to Lewis Genest, both gentlemen, a property that included a brewhouse, malthouse, cistern and tenements or house.[57] A few years later, in 1720, Genest filed a mortgage between himself and a Mrs Ann Bateman, a widow, for the lands he had acquired from Roland at the fee of 100 pounds plus interest for a term of 60 years.[58] But Ann didn't hold this property for long. Just two years later, on 10 November 1722, she submitted a deed of assignment to Moves Deane, who paid her 116 pounds sterling, 13 shillings and four pence for the privilege of those properties for the rest of the term of the original lease.[59]

Keep in mind that the women who were leasing and owning these properties were of a certain social status. These are not the successors of medieval alewives making ale in their houses and selling extra to their neighbours to boost their household income. These women were from the landlord class, and some of them were astonishingly wealthy by any standard. All this is to say that women owned the brewhouses. They leased them out, inherited them and passed them down the family lines. Through their marriages, they served to consolidate the power of their brewing families and/or to act as landladies for various brewing tenants. While many of these women likely did not brew for profit themselves using their properties, they gained ownership of breweries through inheritance and passed them down the family lines.

Of the breweries that the Sweetman family managed to acquire over the years, one was also once owned by a woman. Her name was Maria O'Reilly, and she was a brewer at 235 Francis Street, according to the *Treble Almanack of 1794*.[60] Maria eventually sold her premises to John Sweetman and Co. for the sum of 1,500 pounds.

While many women appear in brewing history from the 18th century onwards as middle (wo)men in the brewing world, either bringing it with them in marriage or leasing the premises to male brewers, some women, like Maria O'Reilly, also still brewed commercially, or at least owned and operated commercial breweries, often taking over the trade after the death of their husbands. O'Reilly wasn't the only one.

These women appear in the *Dublin Directory* throughout the latter half of the century, albeit in much smaller numbers than their male counterparts. Though to be fair, breweries themselves appear in much smaller numbers too, as we saw earlier. Some years there aren't any women to be found. For example, in the 1766 edition of *Wilson's Dublin Directory*, I found a total of 35 brewers listed and all were apparently men. This changed a mere two years later – the 1768 directory lists 34 brewers, which includes a total of six women: William Clinch and Widow Clinch together at James's Street; Widow Edwards on Little Green; Widow Ennis on James's Street; Widow Fegan on Usher's Quay; Widow Hamill on Newmarket, The Coombe; and finally, another woman by the illustrious name of Margaret Plunkett who ran her brewery on Ann Street in Oxmantown.[61]

Notably, many of these women were widows who had inherited the breweries from their husbands after their deaths and continued the trade themselves. Margaret Plunkett was the widow of Barnaby Plunkett, a brewer on Ann Street.[62] Widow Clinch later married Ambrose Cox, described as an 'eminent merchant', sometime before 12 January 1768.[63] It appears Ambrose took over the brewing in some capacity, as he is listed as a brewer in 1780 and still was in 1794, the same year he also apparently died.[64] Widow Hamill might have eventually got out of the trade when she remarried, but she is listed as still brewing in Newmarket in the 1780 directory (a Widow Hamill of Cole Alley, located very close to the Coombe, is listed as marrying a Mr James Baker of Crane Lane in 1782; Baker does not appear to have taken up brewing and Hamill does not appear again).[65] In that 1780 directory, Hamill appears alongside only one other woman, Lady Sarah Taylor at Cork Bridge.[66]

Lady Sarah Taylor was the widow of Alderman Samuel Taylor, who ran a commercial brewery on Ardee Street with an output of some 300 barrels. By 1768, Taylor's brewery was the largest in Dublin.[67, 68] Like our other widows, Lady Sarah took over the brewery operations after her husband's death and was still listed as proprietor of the brewery in 1783. This brewery was eventually sold to the Watkins family and will appear quite prominently in that regard in our next chapter.

Ardee Street, and indeed the area that had once been the Liberties themselves, was the central location for breweries in Dublin. The land that had once been the Abbey of St Thomas of tolboll fame was now home to a large amount of the city's brewing trade. Most of the largest breweries in the city operated here, and indeed the majority of all the breweries in Dublin did. Francis Street, Thomas Street, James's Street, Ardee Street and their adjoining roads from the old city walls to The Coombe were all prime brewery locations in the 18th century, with dozens of such set-ups operating there. The Coombe itself was home to breweries like Patrick McCann, Joseph Andrews and Patrick Lawless (Lawless is another surname we were introduced to earlier on in this book, when Agnes Laweles left her daughter her mash tun). Lady Sarah's brewery was one of the many large commercial breweries that made their homes in the surrounding area. She wasn't the only woman who brewed there, or even on that street itself.

On 8 April 1784, *Saunder's News-Letter* advertised for a brewery to let on Usher's Quay that was currently occupied by a Mr Edmond Byrne but had formerly been under the control of a Mrs Fagan.[69, 70] Byrne's brewery, originally on Usher's Quay, would at one point be relocated to Crooked Staff, a street that would eventually be aptly renamed Brynes Hill but is now known as Ardee Street. Edmond died, and by 1798 his widow, Magdelene Byrne, had taken over. According to *Wilson's Dublin Directory* of 1800, a Magdelene Byrne is listed as the only female brewer in Dublin, located on Byrne's-hill, The Coombe.[71] She was running the brewery as early as 1793, when her name appears on a map of the site.[72]

Women also continued to brew at their own alehouses, where you could only purchase the beer on the premises. On 24 March 1761, the *Belfast Newsletter* ran an article by Mary Shaw and her son John Shaw, who state that even though their 'ancient Inn', called the Black Bull, had been run by her recently deceased husband, she and her son are writing to 'assure the public' that they will still be carrying out business as usual, including 'to be particularly careful to preserve the good character they have obtained for making fine, strong, and well flavoured malt liquor', which is a strong kind of ale or beer. Basically, they wanted to assure their customers that everything would still be carrying on as usual under their new ownership and to please continue patronising their establishment.[73]

Similarly, the *Belfast Newsletter* ran an advert on 10 July 1753 for a rental, namely, the home of Mrs Agnew, an innkeeper who ran the Sign of the Swan on Movilla Street in Newtown, Co. Down. The house was apparently quite 'spacious' and had, among other things, a large cellar, a brewhouse, well water and an adjacent river close to the brewhouse. This all seems to imply that brewing was happening at the Sign of the Swan, and as the innkeeper, one would venture that Mrs Agnew was either doing it herself or closely monitoring the situation.

Of course, brewing for sale wasn't the only way to brew. People still brewed, as they had for centuries past, for their own households, albeit in a slightly different manner than previously.

Apparently, she had been asleep at the brew. Quite literally.

Mrs Heap, a housekeeper for Bishop Edward Synge at his Roscommon estate, was in charge of the beer production for the household. Synge, in a letter to his daughter, Alicia, in Dublin dated 11 July 1749, ranted about his ale cellar, noting 'the mortification to find that there is a multitude of drink, but not one drop good'.[74] Mrs Heap had dropped that ball, it seems, as instead of supervising the brewing like she was meant to, she was off having a nice rest and left those making the beer to their own devices. The resultant brews were quite horrible, Synge reported to his daughter.

Mrs Heap hadn't kept track of when the brews had taken place or in what amount; she hadn't even recorded when the malts had been delivered. Synge told Alicia that not a single drop of the drinks was clear and fit for consumption; all of it was 'scarce drinkable' and 'bitter beyond sufferance'. Mrs Heap in turn blamed the whole affair on the poor quality of the malt that had been delivered to her, which Synge refuted, as it was his very own malt. He was left with only his own small beer, he said, which was some comfort in the midst of all the bad brews.[75]

Even if the beer wasn't clear, the meaning behind the letter certainly is. Brewing was taking place in the rural estates of wealthy households in Ireland, and this was at least maintained by women to some degree, as it had been for centuries. Mrs Heap was supervising the process, which means she had a direct knowledge of how to brew. She was familiar with the malts and she knew what was meant to occur during a brew day. She was in charge, after all, even if she did a poor job of it.

More to the point, Synge's daughter Alicia, who he was writing to, must have also had some understanding of brewing because his letter explains in detail what had possibly gone wrong to a reader who would clearly understand his woes. And understand them she did. In a later letter from Synge to Alicia on 11 September 1750, he goes on about household issues in Dublin, notably the brewer that was serving her there. He asks her if she is happy with what the brewer has been producing, because if not, he would see fit to fire the man. If this was all fine, he was going to prevail upon the brewer to make him some ale, the kind Alicia knows he likes, 'pale, soft, smooth, and not too bitter'. Synge left her in charge of telling the brewer precisely what to make for this ale and to also make him some small beer.[76] So Alicia, like Mrs Heap, is in charge of overseeing the brewing in her household, making sure that everything was created to Synge's specifications. Perhaps unlike Mrs Heap, Alicia was a bit better at her endeavour.

Historian Tara McConnell is an expert in beer production in 18th-century elite households like that of Bishop Synge, who she studied. McConnell argues that, like we saw in previous centuries, ale and beer were an essential part of nutrition for all people in such households, from the homeowners themselves to the servants. She believes that beer itself was a significant part of the diet for people from all walks of life, except for perhaps the poorest among them.[77]

However, brewing in the Irish home faced a significant number of roadblocks, unlike our neighbours in England. Here in Ireland, regulations forced many homebrewers out of the practice altogether. According to Charles Abbot's tour of the country in 1792, the regulations on brewing on top of the already high rates of duty made it so difficult to brew for domestic use that 'even in great families it is rarely attempted'.[78] James Kelly found that what added to this was the fact that Revenue actively and aggressively pursued those who brewed without a license, even for private consumption.[79] Yet brewing in homes continued, as we can see with the Synge household.

McConnell found that in Ireland, elite rural households were brewing for their own use in the 18th century, noting that the Marquis of Kildare employed a steward at his country estate who supervised the brewing to some degree, though unlike our Mrs Heap, this steward was decidedly male.[80] Madeline Shanahan is an archaeologist and historian who has studied the exchange of recipes between women during the late 17th and 19th centuries and found that the fourth most popular category of recipe exchange she encountered was for kinds of alcohol. This included things like mead, metheglin and wines as well as types of ales. This led her to conclude that brewing was still happening in elite households in Ireland during the 18th century.[81]

Even when brewing itself isn't mentioned directly, there are hints that women who lived in these wealthy homes would have had some knowledge of the process, or at least easy access to it. *A Book of Cookery for dressing of Several Dishes of Meat and making of Several Sauces and Seasonings for Meat or Fowel* hints at Ireland's brewing past. Written by Hannah Alexander with some additional recipes by her daughter, also called Hannah, the book was composed in the 1680s. According to Jennifer Nuttall, who wrote the introduction to the edited volume of their recipes, Hannah Alexander and her husband lived on Great Ship Street in Dublin. Her daughter, referred to by Nuttall as Hannah Dorothea, lived for a time on Aungier Street. This is important because it tells us that even in urban environments, women would have had a knowledge of and practical applications for brewing.[82]

Interestingly, when her food recipes use some kind of alcohol, they typically call for sack or wine, not, as is so often the case, ale. Though that doesn't mean that ale doesn't feature. Ale, or at least ale yeast, features prominently in her recipes for cakes, many calling for a 'pinte of good ale barme'.[83] Her caraway cake, 'good woodstreet cakes' and saffron cakes all call for this ingredient.[84]

She also wrote many recipes for various alcoholic drinks, including a 'rare secret for cider', which she tells readers was to scald whatever containers you were using in boiling water with cow dung and hay, then right before adding your cider to the bottles, you smoke it out with sulphur, then add a 'sprig' of clary sage. She also says it's important not to let the cider sit in a beer cellar. This also points to a knowledge of brewing and making alcoholic beverages because it's assumed that the reader knows how to make cider, as this is merely a tip. Further, her references to the beer cellar also seem to indicate that the person reading this would at a minimum have beer available to them in the household, even if they weren't brewing it themselves.

We can see other hints that both Hannah and the reader would be familiar with brewing. She includes many recipes for wines, including a cowslip version, which is much closer to a ginger or herb beer than a wine. The ingredients call for sugar and ginger, which need to cool 'and it being as cold as wort finally is', before you add ale yeast to it and then the cowslips. All this suggests that both the reader and the writer would be familiar with brewing to some degree.

If all that doesn't quite convince you, her medicinal recipes just might. These contain multiple instances where ale or beer feature as the base for medical cures, including the illustrious snail water, which involves adding snails, among other things, to a gallon of the best strong ale, or another drink that was good for scurvy and dropsy that also had a base of ale. One that Alexander says was a particularly excellent remedy for scurvy involved adding water trefoil to eight gallons of wort instead of adding hops, or as she says, the same added to small ale or the wort made for that, and that the patient was to use it for their 'ordinary drinking'. This example, perhaps above all the others, solidifies that Alexander and the reader would have had a strong knowledge of brewing and were likely doing it themselves.[85]

In most of these texts, the basic instructions for brewing are missing. This makes sense when you consider that it was something many women would have grown up knowing how to do. They would have seen their mothers doing the task and learned by watching, or in the case of upper-class women, they would have learned by observing servants or brewers as part of their household management duties taught by their own mothers. Just as you might not write down instructions on how to boil an egg, the basics of brewing wouldn't necessarily be written down in a book either. Instead, specialty beers or ales, or hints, like we can clearly see in Alexander's book, reveal the ubiquitous nature of this task.

Similarly, Mary Cannon's *Commonplace Book*, written in the 1700s, also reveals much about brewing history in Ireland. Here she has recipes for a fine cider as well as elder, sage, birch and cowslip wine, which are likely a bit more similar to ale or beer. She also has multiple recipes for metheglin and mead and a recipe for a black cherry beer.[86]

Our final example was written by Sophia Blundon in the later years of the 18th century. Blundon was born around 1760 to Sir John Blundon and Lucinda Cuffe at Castle Blundon in Ballytobin or Ballaghtobin, Co. Kilkenny. Sophia married Abraham Whyte Baker around 1778 and thus became Mrs A.W. Baker, the author of an extensive and exemplary book of receipts. Baker's recipe collection contains all sorts of foods, including, importantly for our purposes, how to make all kinds of wine, such as the perennial favourite, gooseberry (in my research into the history of alcohol recipes in the 18th century, I have located approximately 10,000 recipes for gooseberry wine, so we're sorted if that's something you like).

In her 2016 PhD thesis, Dorothy Cashman carefully examined Baker's collection and outlined all the ingredients that appear in them.[87] It wasn't just gooseberry or raspberry wine. Baker had recipes for barm (that is, yeast), those including hops and recipes calling for ale. One recipe for small beer had been given to her by a Mr Brabazon of the Brabazon brewing family. This led Monica Nevin, who had actually found and later donated this notebook of recipes to the National Library, to conclude that homebrewing might have been done at her estate.[88] I think we can go a step further and say without a shadow of a doubt that homebrewing was happening at some wealthy rural estates in Ireland, and was often either done by household female servants or supervised by the acting lady of the house or housekeeper while a hired brewer, likely male, undertook the actual onerous task of brewing for the household.

Brewing at home came with its own set of perils, notwithstanding the massive issues that the strict regulations put on homebrewers. The wealthiest among them could either afford or circumvent the regulations, but that was perhaps not possible for members of other echelons of the socio-economic ladder. Even for the wealthy households it could become quite difficult to produce given the hefty regulations and the stringency with which they were enforced.

Irish beer production was down over the course of the century, a by-product of the preference for whiskey or English porter in addition to unfavourable regulations for commercial producers. This was on top of the political landscape that defined the century, culminating in the 1798 Rebellion. Melesina Trench was an 18th-century writer, though her works didn't gain any acclaim until after her son published them following her death. On 11 August 1801, she wrote a memorandum about her visit to her uncle by marriage, Mr Alcock, who lived in Enniscorthy. Here she notes that in the years following the 1798 Rebellion, 'the servants have been unmanageable, the horses restive, the beer sour.'[89]

And with that we will venture forth into the 19th century to see whether the state of Irish beer saw any improvement from Trench's early indictment.

OF TEA KETTLE BREWS AND COTTAGE-SIZED COPPERS

1800–1900

ONE OF THE MOST QUINTESSENTIAL THINGS in a household is the tea kettle. For decades, tea has been deeply intertwined with Irish culture. We've been brewing the stuff daily for caffeine and for comfort. We make cups for our friends, when we have meetings, after a long day or at the beginning of a new one. The rituals surrounding the drink are the stuff of legend, invading just about every bit of pop culture. It's almost sacrilege to even refuse a cup – cue *Father Ted*'s Mrs Doyle: 'Go on, go on, go on, go on...'

For most of us, even those who don't drink tea, the newer electric version of the kettle sits in pride of place on our counters. It's one of the first things you acquire in a new home and it's one of the handiest gadgets in the kitchen, whether it's to make a cuppa or boil water for ramen. Maybe even beer. It's a great way to heat up some water for your homebrews, adding a bit here and there to your mash to raise the temperature to get it to that perfect window for maximum saccharification. But what if you could brew your whole beer conveniently in your tea kettle?

Inscribed only with *Book of Recipes 1811* on its frontispiece, this collection likely came from Co. Limerick. It was written in approximately 1811–1831 and is home to our tea kettle ale.[1] Dorothy Cashman, a culinary historian who studied the recipes, calls it 'The Cholera

'Manuscript' because it records the aftermath of the initial breakouts of the disease and the attempts to create medicinal cures to combat its spread.[2] The medicines in the book are abundant. It should go without saying, but do not try any of these at home. Ever.

The recipes are illuminating and, as elsewhere, filled with malt. One recipe for a 'gargle to be used three or four times a day' is made from barley water, honey or roses, and '40 drops of spirit of sea salt'. Another, to cure the 'bite of a mad dog', calls for two quarts of strong ale among its ingredients.

The book is home to a wonderful array of foods and beverages, like our earlier examples from the previous century. Recipes include lamb cutlets with cucumber sauce, pickled oysters, sausages and red cabbage, anchovy toast, curry, and apple fritters, which manage to find their way into practically every recipe collection I read and every book I write. Instead of using ale, like the ones I made in my book on women brewers in the UK,[3] this one has you soaking the fritters in white wine and sugar for two hours before dunking them in a batter made from eggs, flour, cream and combined with a white wine and sugar mixture. Fry it all in lard, sift more sugar over them and heat them a bit again to melt, and *voilà*! Apple fritters.[4]

In any event, the collection has recipes for things like barm, raisin wine, gooseberry wine, ginger beer, lemon wine and parsnip wine. There's also a recipe for a 'pleasant cheap ale' that calls for readers to 'boil four ounces of best farmhouse hops and ten pounds of treacle or brown sugar in twelve gallons or more of water, boil them ten minutes; work with yeast as in the common method of brewing with malt; tap the same in the ten days when the beverage be fit for drinking'.

But it's the tea kettle ale that caught my eye. Here is the recipe in full:

> To Brew Ale on a Small Scale
>
> Put a handful of malt into a tea kettle, fill it with water,
> rather under boiling heat – when it has stood some
> time, pour it off & fill it up again, but with boiling water
> – continue pouring it off & filling it up till the malt is
> tasteless – then boil the liquor with a few hops in it & when
> lukewarm, add a little yeast to ferment it – one peck of malt
> and 4 ounces of hops will produce 10 quarts of Ale, *much
> better than porter.*[5]

Once again we are wading into the porter debate that defined the 18th century, though in this case, we are making a superior beer altogether, or at least better than porter. Allegedly. The process is a slow, steady kind of mini brew. A handful of malt for a tea kettle, assuming a regular kettle is around 1 litre, is still a small amount, though it depends on precisely whose hands are doing the measuring.[6] It would probably end up making a kind of small ale, or a weak one certainly, since there wouldn't be much malt sugars to turn into alcohol.

We shouldn't assume that this practice of homebrewing was particularly widespread. The number of women who brewed at home wasn't even close to the number who brewed in the late medieval period and 16th century. As had been the case in the 1700s, regulations and taxation on private brewing were a burden not many families could afford. Over the course of the 1800s, homebrewing fell even further in popularity, happening rarely except in a minority of the elite households or, perhaps, in these small brews evident in the *Book of Recipes 1811*. The book itself is anonymous, but I would argue that based on all the collections we have worked with so far, it was most likely written by a woman. Specifically, Cashman contends that it's the work of a 'less grand' or 'minor' household in Ireland,[7] though they would have still been wealthy, especially compared to most people in Ireland.

Ireland in the 19th century was highly stratified, with the haves and the have nots very much divided. The rich were incredibly rich and the poor were absolutely destitute. Those who could brew for their own homes would have generally been those of wealthier status, given the costs in taxes and regulations. Of course, there's always room for exceptions, like people who circumvented the laws and brewed illegally. Even our receipt writer, while making recipes for economical foods like cheap ale and tea kettle brews, who may have been from a 'minor' household, as Cashman notes, was nonetheless wealthy, especially compared to those of lower economic status.

To look more into this beer and brewing gap, let's turn to a series of studies undertaken on behalf of the Royal Dublin Society in the early years of the 19th century. This series of *Statistical Observations* often includes a specific section dedicated to the consumption of beer and spirits by those of lower economic status, especially labourers. From these, we can learn that many people simply did not have the money to buy beer, let alone the time or finances to brew it. They were entirely too poor.

William Tighe, author of the *Statistical Observations* from Co. Kilkenny, notes a decrease in the number of malthouses, i.e. those places where you could purchase and consume beers and ales. In Kilkenny, the number had decreased from 60 in 1795 to 23 in 1799, perhaps reflecting the shift away from the labouring people being able to even afford to drink.[8] Tighe's work includes a section on the 'State of the Poor in Kilkenny' by Mr J. Robertson, who tells readers that 'the condition of the labouring poor here, appears to me, from the observations I have had an opportunity of making, to be wretched in the extreme'.[9] In fact, Robertson did a breakdown of expenses compared to yearly pay and found that even the best-paid labourers and their families were left with an excess of only around 10 shillings a year after all rent, food, fuel and various other necessary items had been paid for.[10] To put this in perspective, the price of a quart of ale was anywhere between 2 pence and 3.5 pence and whiskey was 5 to 8 shillings per gallon.[11]

The food these labourers and their families were eating was mostly potatoes and milk, if they could even get milk, and sometimes herring, though that was a bit of a treat.[12] Tighe agrees with Robertson's findings, noting that 'potatoes alone are the food of the poorest, generally but not always with salt, sometimes a herring, and often buttermilk or milk'.[13] Beer or ale was a rarity.

To be clear, the author of this particular book was an incredibly classist man. His writing about the poor Irish labourers barely able to eke out a living sounds like something Scrooge himself would say. While reading it, I was practically waiting for Jacob Marley to make his way into the text, chains clanking about, to warn our fair author of his follies and the upcoming ghostly visitors. In any event, we can glean a few things of value, minus his prejudice, from this text as it relates to people and beer. Suffice it to say that the poor in Kilkenny simply weren't drinking it, at least not often. The author concedes that people would drink during events like wakes, fairs, weddings, christenings and similar occasions, but otherwise they simply couldn't afford it.[14]

Kilkenny doesn't appear to be alone in this regard. Elsewhere in Co. Clare (which in many ways may have been much more similar to what life might have been like in Co. Limerick, where our tea kettle beer was made), people weren't drinking much beer either. This statistical observation was written by a significantly more sympathetic author, Hely Dutton, who often remarks about the strength and kindness of the labouring people. He notes that here, too, people of lower economic status mostly survived on potatoes and milk. Those closer to the Atlantic supplemented their food with fishing, though this could be difficult because they didn't have the money for the proper equipment.[15] Their wages and living conditions were roughly the same as people in Kilkenny, again with very little beer. Dutton also found that the 'poorer classes' couldn't spare much money, so whiskey was generally beyond their reach.[16]

He also notes that the breweries had disappeared in Co. Clare. There used to be two breweries in the county, but 'only one petty brewery remains'.[17] That's not all Dutton has to say about brewing in the county, and in Ireland: 'The beer or ale of this county is a most abominable compound, indeed not worse than the trash made in almost every part of Ireland; it is astonishing how those of better rank can taste it, but habit will lower the palate down to any standard of depravity'.[18]

This is a stunning indictment on the state of brewing in the country that reminds me of Sedulius from Chapter 1, minus the whole eternal torments thing. Dutton then tells readers that 'happily the brewers are gradually receiving their just punishment, in the increasing use of water at the table in preference to their poisonous mixtures'.[19] Dutton describes beer in Ireland as not being brewed like in former times – 'pale ale with hops and malt alone'. Instead, he accuses brewers of adding all sorts of 'drugs' to the mixture. He writes, 'I suppose they have lost the art', as they have so long forgotten the proper way to brew. Like our cheap ale and tea kettle version from our Limerick collection, perhaps certain people could homebrew. Unfortunately, they didn't really do that either. Dutton remarks that it was 'extraordinary' that more people didn't brew because not only would it provide them with beer, but also barm used for making good bread.[20]

Dutton also conducted one of these statistical observations on Co. Galway, and like in Co. Clare and Co. Kilkenny, found labourers to generally be living in not the best of conditions, to make a sweeping understatement. This work was written 16 years after his book on Co. Clare and conditions had largely remained the same. He takes aim at landlords and their unwillingness to provide for the comforts of their tenants and their unskilled agents who ran their farms in their absence, noting that the general stances of these men was 'what the devil do I care about how they live, so long as they come to work when I want them and pay me my rent'.[21] Dutton has a lot to say about all this and how it might be improved, but that is beyond the scope of this book. I want to include this bit here simply because I think many of us can relate to his words, written over 200 years ago, to the current state of the rental and job markets today.

In any event, like their neighbours in Co. Clare, the labouring classes in Galway were mostly subsisting on potatoes. However, they appear to have had a slightly better quality of life than those in Co. Clare or Kilkenny, especially those in Connemara, who 'are superior in person and dress than any other part of this county', so much so that Dutton argues that they 'look like another race of people'. These men, women and children from Connemara, he writes, lived on potatoes, but they also had cows, and whereas on the coast many had two or three cows, those in Connemara may have had as many as eight to twelve.[22] Of course, there was fish and seafood to be had as well, and most importantly for our purposes, beer.

In 1824, when Dutton wrote this book, his stance on the brews offered in the county seems to be slightly more positive, and more people did seem to be consuming the stuff. That didn't stop him from having opinions on the beers available, however, which still weren't particularly great:

> and if beer or ale could be had of pure quality, brewed
> from malt and hops only, the use would still increase; but
> the brewers have been so long in the habit of using drugs
> of various kinds, that all idea of drinking such wholesome
> pale ale as we were used to in the days of yore has long been
> abandoned.[23]

Again, he tells readers that the brewers are using 'drugs' in their beers, adulterating them with all sorts of things. Dutton once again turns to homebrewing, though of course here, as before, he means people of a higher socio-economic status than those poor labourers.

> I am at a loss to know what every private house does not
> brew as formerly, when even small farmers brewed; the
> reason generally given by many are, that they do not wish
> to be liable to the visits of guagers [sic: gaugers] at all hours,
> and that they cannot get good malt to buy.[24]

This might give us some insight into why our homebrewer in Limerick was making cheap ale and tea kettle ale with very little malt. Dutton reveals that the people were afraid of gaugers, here meaning the excise and customs officials charged with ensuring that the government was getting their fair tax. Further, he suggests building a sort of community malthouse, with its use split between several families, which might also host a brewer who brews for them too.[25] Again, this would mean people of a certain wealth level, perhaps even someone like our tea kettle ale household.

Galway was home to quite a few breweries at this time, including a large one at Newcastle that brewed English pale ale, two in Ballinasloe, one in Tuam, two in Loughrea, one in Gort, which was held in particular esteem, and one in Oranmore.[26] In some ways, the 19th century was defined by the increasing commercialisation, expansion and eventual consolidation of brewing on a scale heretofore not seen in the country. The advent of these massive industrial breweries, which had begun to take shape in the previous century, would shoot to new heights in this one.

While our writer of the Limerick recipe collection was most likely female, it wasn't just at home where women took the reins of brewing. The 19th century also saw women, but mostly men, at the helm of commercial breweries. Women largely disappear from the annals of breweries by the end of this century, but not entirely. As in the centuries before, brewing was never just about the beer.

In recent years, more attention is paid to how breweries conduct their business. Beer consumers in particular are drawn to establishments whose politics match their own. Many of us want to frequent breweries that demonstrate their commitment to inclusive environments where the diversity of our human experience is celebrated and acknowledged. Many breweries have responded in kind, supporting causes and charitable organisations that align with those stated goals. So this quotation about breweries being political institutions might feel like a given to us:

> Breweries are in all parts of Ireland, more or less, *political institutions;* and we think it conducive to peace and justice that the business connected with them should be regulated by right principles.[27]

We also know that breweries should be holding themselves accountable, operating in a way that sees them as welcoming spaces for all. We see it in fundraisers, collaborations or blogs. It's clear in how breweries present themselves and their goals and how they treat their workers. We can even see it in beer festivals, with codes of conduct and panel talks, in academic articles, on walking tours – basically, in just about everything to do with beer. With the critical push by breweries and activists alike to ensure beer is open and welcoming to everyone, we can clearly see that breweries are political in many ways.

Contrary to what you might have guessed, the above quotation isn't a social media post by a favoured beer writer. It dates from 23 October 1833 and appears in an article in the *Waterford Mail*. Like the quote suggests, breweries in 19th-century Ireland were intricately tied to politics, with many directly linked with certain politicians. Nothing underscores this idea like naming your beer after The Liberator himself, Daniel O'Connell. O'Connell was one of the most important figures in the cause for Irish Catholic emancipation in the 19th century. Called O'Connell's Dublin Ale, the beer was brewed first at Phoenix Brewery on James's Street, which had been famously acquired by Daniel O'Connell Jr. The brewery traded on this fact, even changing its name temporarily to O'Connell Brewery for a time in the 1830s.[28] However, by 1832, Daniel O'Connell Sr was forced to state that he wasn't a patron of the brewing trade or his son's company, in part because of O'Connell Sr's rivalry with Guinness.

Tensions didn't end there. The article our quotation comes from in the *Waterford Mail* also tells readers that anonymous letters had been circulating about the Daniel O'Connell brewery, ostensibly not in support but 'to give a character to it'. However, this doesn't seem to have worked out quite how the letter-writers thought it might. Instead, the writer notes that:

> ...and if a concern be fading away from public attention, the most effectual mode of reviving its notoriety, and attending sympathy towards it, is to raise a persecution. Were beer as dead and spiritless as Nebuchadnezzar, a crown of martyrdom, more sharp than super-carbonate of soda, would give it freshness and the froth of immortal youth.[29]

Instead of putting people off, the letters served to remind the 'porter-drinking public, just at the commencement of porter-drinking season, that Daniel O'Connell the younger, son of Daniel O'Connell the elder, is a brewer of strong drink'. This was 'an important service' that allowed 'patriotic grocers a fair occasion to come forward in the very nick of time, when the tribute was looking flatter than any beer, and with "candied tongues" to celebrate the claims of Daniel O'Connell the elder; thus proving themselves friends of the family from generation to generation'.

Support for Daniel O'Connell from breweries did not begin and end with the one owned by his son. This was a national concern.

On Friday, 2 January 1829, the *Newry Telegraph* published an article from a man going by the name of Paul Pry, who wrote about the Dublin 'weeklies' (those who supported Daniel O'Connell) meeting at a tavern and about the goings-on therein.[30] Importantly, the men called to their waiter that he had in fact 'forgot to bring us some malt', to which the waiter replied, 'Whose will you have Gentlemen- Popery- Pro-popery, or Anti-popery- Orange or Green?' One man, known as Warder, threatens to throw oyster shells at the man's head for being a 'rascal' and asks what do they care about the politics of the brewery, so long as the brewing 'be not deleterious'. In the end they insisted that both the Protestant porter and the Catholic porter be served.[31] Perhaps not everyone wanted to acknowledge the ties between brewing and politics, but despite the best efforts of these 'weeklies', these links persisted.

In fact, the divide along religious and political lines could be disastrous for some breweries, because just as people supported those whose politics they liked, they boycotted those they didn't. John Alley, son of a previous mayor and brewer also named John Alley, wrote to Charles Grant, the chief secretary, in 1819, stating that his brewing business had completely collapsed after it was boycotted because of his father, whose stance on taxes, especially the window tax, were incredibly unpopular. Therefore, he needed employment and requested work in the revenue department.[32] J. Wilkinson of Co. Limerick wrote to the chief secretary's office in Dublin Castle to get her husband a job. Apparently he had invested her entire fortune, some £12,000, in a brewery in Limerick, which worked out fine for a time, until there was an 'unfortunate contest' between an Independent party and Lord Gort, after which 'the trades refused to drink his Porter' and he went bankrupt.[33]

Boycotts were also enacted along religious lines. Major Thomas Powell, Inspector General, wrote to Henry Goulburn about a local Catholic priest in Mountmellick, Co. Laois, who was barring his flock of parishioners from dealing with any Protestant brewers like Mr Kenny and Mr Pim. The priest, Doughan, defended his actions against these Protestant brewers as appropriate.[34] Apparently, there were serious problems with the Orange Party there making illegal processions and displaying orange flags throughout the town. These increasing tensions between Catholic and Protestant workers in breweries even led 27 manufacturers in Mountmellick, including brewers James Pim and Co., to sign a document stating that they would not 'give employment hereafter to any person, or persons, who shall presume to act contrary to the Law by acting abusive to those of the opposing faith'.[35] They were hoping to try to circumvent these boycotts by committing to these rules of employment.

These are just a few examples of how the political landscape of 19th-century Ireland was deeply intertwined with the brewing trade. It impacted the entire country, and most breweries leaned one way or the other – or if not, they had to combat the perceptions that they did by working to demonstrate that they were on the side of 'fairness'. This wasn't limited to breweries, of course; that's just the business we're discussing in this book. Ireland in the 19th century was awash with political change – and hope. Many Catholics believed that they would finally see their rights restored and their freedom ensured.

One brewery that entwined its existence with the cause of Daniel O'Connell was Deasy and Co. On 25 March 1806, the Earl of Shannon granted to Reverend Horatio Townsend premises in Clonakilty, which he promptly turned around and leased to Reverend William Stewart and Rickard Deasy. For the period of 999 years, the pair would be able to use the property to found what was known as the 'new brewery'. Rickard and William quickly got to work making that famous beverage from the previous chapter: porter. When William died, his portion would go to his heir, Henry Stewart. Rickard would also bring his heir, Thomas Deasy, into the mix. Things continued this way for a while, all fairly standard and uncomplicated.[36]

Then Rickard up and died, leaving his portion of the brewery to Thomas. Thomas Deasy was a key supporter of Daniel O'Connell and worked to collect the O'Connell Tribute, a public fund by which Daniel O'Connell paid his expenses in his quest for Catholic emancipation.[37] On 19 June 1843, a letter he'd signed appeared in the *Cork Examiner*, entitled 'Repeal! Repeal! Repeal!', which told readers that 'The Liberator of your Country, the beloved son of Erin', aka Daniel O'Connell, would be coming their way in order to garner support for his endeavours:

> ...in the cause of your persecuted Country and suffering People, and of receiving your co-operation is the noble struggle by moral and peaceable means to raise her from her present prostrate position to the rank of Independence and Prosperity, we therefore call upon you, without distinction of Creed or Class, to MEET to PETITION Parliament for a REPEAL of the odious Act of Union, - pour forth your Tens, your Hundreds, and your Thousands, and in peaceful and Constitutional attitude of Freemen, humbly, respectfully, but firmly demand your Independence and your Rights.[38]

Simply put, Deasy was a huge proponent of O'Connell, the cause of Catholic Emancipation and repealing the Act of Union.

By 1831, Deasy and Co. was one of 215 breweries dotted across the country.[39] These breweries were mostly concentrated in towns and cities. In 1837, Samuel Lewis published *A Topographical Dictionary of Ireland*, where we can learn more about some of these urban breweries. Newtown-

Ardes, for example, a town of 11,000 including its surrounds, boasted a brewery that produced more than 7,000 barrels of beer annually and was home to its own maltings.[40] These 7,000 barrels are a sharp contrast to the 300 brewed in the previous century at the biggest brewery in Dublin, Phoenix. This clearly illustrates just how much breweries were growing in this century.

Lewis recorded many breweries in his *Topographical Dictionary*. One in Donaghmore, Co. Tyrone, which brewed the 'celebrated' Donaghmore ale, produced 10,500 barrels a year. In Templemore just outside of Derry, a brewery there made 5,300 barrels of beer annually. There were seven breweries in Limerick City, brewing what Lewis calls porter, ale and beer (which also tells us precisely how they categorised various kinds of malt beverages, or at least how Lewis did). These breweries, he tells us, mainly sell their product to those locally. In contrast, Strabane, Co. Tyrone, had a brewery that sent its beer to Derry, Coleraine, Donegal and other places. Magherafelt, which had a population of 1,436 in the town itself, had a large ale and beer brewery, as did Newcastle in Co. Limerick, with a population of 2,908 in the town. New Ross in Co. Wexford had three breweries and Co. Armagh was home to many as well, as beer was in high demand, apparently.[41] And on and on it goes.

Beer was reaching a level of popularity it hadn't had in the 18th century. Overall, scholar Andy Bielenberg argues that in the first half of the century in Ireland, beer was 'the preserve of the inhabitants of larger towns', noting that big breweries were mostly concentrated in larger towns and that the transportation structure at that time did not yet support a wide influx of big breweries' beers into small rural concerns.[42] By 1846, there were apparently 118 breweries in Ireland. This is a marked decrease from the 215 breweries in 1831, but this wasn't because the industry was struggling – it was because the breweries were expanding, buying each other out and consolidating.[43]

An Gorta Mór, or the Great Hunger, lasted from 1845 to 1852, killing roughly 1 million people and causing the mass emigration of millions. We saw earlier in the accounts of the *Statistical Observations* precisely just how important the potato was to the diet of the Irish labourer – in many cases, it made up the entirety of what they ate, alongside milk. Its loss from the blight that destroyed the crop was immense. The Famine brought a myriad of diseases with it, especially typhus, which preyed on those weakened by starvation. By 1851, 25% of the population was gone, either dead or because they had fled the country.[44] In 2024, Ireland has still not reached pre-Famine population levels.

Why the Famine happened has been a matter of great debate in the decades since it occurred. An excellent resource on this topic is *The Atlas of the Great Irish Famine*, one of the most important academic works to come out of the country in recent memory.[45] In this book, the actions, and inactions, of the British government, the failure of their famine relief policies, the wanton disregard that many of the English elite had for the plight of the Irish and how all these impacted the onset and subsequent years of the Famine are considered.

William J. Smyth, one of the book's editors, argues that the London government was primarily responsible for the failures of the Famine efforts. While he agrees with Mary Daly's assertion that landlords, grain traders and others could have done more, the ultimate responsibility lies with the government.[46] Author Peter Gray argues that Robert Peel, who was the British prime minister for the first bit of the Famine, did have some effective policies that stopped widespread mortality, but these were unpopular with his cohorts and led to the end of his political career.[47] The subsequent administration under Lord John Russell adopted a policy of 'self-help', a sort of obsession with the idea of free markets and a total reluctance to interfere in said markets.[48] Smyth contends that these policy failures and neglect were also fuelled by xenophobic anti-Irish sentiment that had its roots in the colonial system and the fact that the Irish people were not represented in their government.[49] Ultimately, Smyth found that the English turned their backs on the Irish.[50]

In the same book, an article by David Nally explores the deep-seated impact that colonialism had on the Famine, tracing its roots back to the plantation system we learned about in Chapter 6.[51] Nally, like others, argues that the Irish were especially vulnerable to starvation and famine because of colonialism, essentially due to the fact that by the 18th century, only 5% of Irish land was held by Irish people. This, combined with the Penal Laws as well as the criminal way in which these colonisers treated the native population, meant that the Irish in Ireland found themselves in the hands of a hostile foreign government that wasn't particularly concerned with their welfare.[52] Absentee landlords and the reliance of labourers on the potato were the products of this colonial system, he found, and these factors contributed greatly to the Famine.[53]

A detailed examination of this atrocity is beyond the scope of this book, but what I *will* do is show you what brewing looked like in its wake. The second half of the 19th century saw exponential growth for the brewing industry in Ireland. Whiskey became less popular and the railway system expanded into smaller towns, which meant breweries could get their products to previously unavailable customers. Output rose from 617,000 barrels in 1847 to 3,149,000 in 1901.[54] Keep in mind that the population of the country had dramatically decreased following the Famine, both from people dying and emigrating.

Authors Patrick Lynch and John Vaizey argue that the government's relief measures, lacking as they were, changed the face of the rural economy, which switched to a money-based system from what had been subsistence.[55] They base this argument on post-Famine sales of Guinness, which grew dramatically, leading them to conclude that the Irish brewing market increased after the Famine, especially in rural areas.[56]

However, following on from Lynch and Vaizey's research, J. Lee argues that Guinness's brewing stats are not representative of the larger brewing trends.[57] Lee found that the increase in beer consumption in the 1850s was likely linked to the changes in tax on spirits.[58] Lee challenges Vaizey and Lynch's assertions that beer sales rose during the Famine, when this is perhaps only representative of Guinness.[59]

The output for Guinness did fall during the Famine, dropping from 1,017,000 barrels to 500,000 barrels in 1845.[60] During the Famine itself, some 150 small breweries shut their doors between 1838 and 1852.[61] Lynch and Vaizey respond directly to Lee's assertions about their arguments regarding the Famine's impact on brewing in Ireland, arguing that the brewing industry grew after the Famine.[62] For some breweries in the country, the latter half of the century was a period of prosperity; for others, it was a time to sell the premises to competitors and move on to other pastures; and for a select few, it was a period of consolidation. For that, we need to return to Deasy and Co.

On Friday, 16 November 1849, amidst the Famine, Thomas Deasy died.

> Mr. Thomas Deasy, brewer of Clonakilty, County Cork, while superintending the workmen in the brewery, accidently fell into a deep vat, and when extricated life was quite extinct.[63]

In a further article, it is stated that 'every effort was made by Drs O'Hea and Ffolliott to restore animation, but in vain'. The article goes on to say, 'In him society has lost one of its most useful members, and the poor of this district, to whom his purse was freely opened during the late visitation, will never cease to remember him with feelings of the deepest thankfulness and gratitude.'[64]

His portion of the brewery was left to his wife Jane, with the brewery then becoming Jane Deasy and Co. Jane ran it for several years until her own death in 1872. She was one of a few women who retained control of a brewery in the late 19th century, as were her daughters, who inherited her portion of the business after her death.

Jane and Thomas had four unmarried daughters: Mary Jane, Kate, Ellen and Honoria (though Honoria later married an English navy commander). Let me briefly remind you here that Thomas did not own the brewery outright – he was in a partnership with another family, now called the Travers.

Each Deasy daughter was willed a stake in their portion of the brewery, effectively each getting one-quarter of their family's controlled portion of the brewing concern. The Travers family still maintained control of their portion. The deeds are very clear that after Jane's death, Kate stepped up to the plate and ran the brewery in partnership with Rev. Henry Travers, and that when he died in 1874, he left his concerns to his wife Deana August Stewart. Kate took over the management of the entire brewery on behalf of both the Deasy and Travers families and everything went great. For a while.

After Deana's death, things got rather confusing on the Travers side of the family as to who owned what and how. I'll spare you all the details – what you need to know is that eventually, Robert Travers,[65] and ostensibly the rest of his family who also held ownership portions, wanted to buy the Deasy family out. But the Deasys didn't want to go. So Travers filed a bill of complaint against them in the Irish Chancery Court to dissolve the partnership and wind down operations on 12 September 1877.

Kate and her family eventually lost the case and the court ordered the brewery, also known as Clonakilty Brewery, to be sold. And wouldn't you know who bought the whole thing? Robert Travers. He bought out the Deasys for £8,000, not a small sum at the time, then proceeded to buy out the rest of his family, getting them to sign their inheritance in the brewery over to him and a Thomas William Wright. That was the end of Kate Deasy owning and operating the brewery.

But that wasn't the end of brewing for the Deasy family. Today, the legacy of Kate and Jane lives on in descendants at Canvas Brewery in Co. Tipperary. Dedicated to small-batch farmhouse ale, using malt grains grown on site and local ingredients, Canvas Brewery makes creative brews that are a fitting tribute to the long family tradition.

I don't necessarily want to paint the Travers family in a bad light. There are many legitimate reasons one might have to force an end to a partnership, details that we aren't privy to. But the end result was the same. For better or worse, yet another woman was removed from the brewing industry in the 19th century, a trade which they had once wholly dominated.

Kate wasn't the only woman to own and operate a brewery in the latter half of the 19th century. Much like the previous case with the Deasy family, Catherine Fitzgerald of Garryowen, Limerick, also found herself running afoul of powerful men. Specifically, bankers.

In a memorial of a deed poll or letter of deposit from 19 October 1874, Fitzgerald is listed as both a widow and, importantly, a brewer. She must have been somewhat wealthy, and her brewery, called Garryowen, must have been successful, at least at some point, because this agreement between her and Munster Bank was to have an overdraft of some £4,000 sterling, which is equivalent to over €600,000 today – not something to sneeze at. Ostensibly her brewery must have been doing okay, or at least it had been previously, to be granted such an amount. In any event, she put the brewery itself up as collateral for repayment of the overdraft. This did not end well.

Over the ensuing years, Catherine Fitzgerald had multiple dealings with the bank, which paint a picture of a woman trying to save herself from drowning financially. Unfortunately for her, she couldn't keep up and on 17 January 1885, she had to sign over Garryowen brewery and everything inside it – machinery, utensils, vats – to Munster Bank with a proviso for redemption upon repayment of monies owed.[66] On 6 April 1885, Catherine lost the brewery entirely.

Johanna Hurley of Bandon in Co. Cork also had issues with finances. She owned a brewery called Hurley and Co., also known as Clancoole Brewery, that she seems to have acquired through her widow's portion from her husband, John Hurley. Unfortunately, she, too, found herself on the wrong end of the Court of Bankruptcy and Insolvency in Ireland, and as such, much like Catherine Fitzgerald, she had to make deals with Munster Bank to keep herself afloat. Like Catherine, she lost the brewery and malthouse that she had inherited from her husband.[67] In this instance, though, she and her daughters, who all held an interest in the brewery, ended up signing over their interests to their brother, Francis Hurley, who was acting as the brewer at the time. Francis then took over the venture from the family, but he did have to buy out his sisters Elizabeth and Mary.[68]

It's not all doom and gloom when it comes to women in breweries, nor is it only women who had problems with banks. Francis Hurley, son of Johanna and brother to Elizabeth and Mary, soon had his own issues when Munster Bank filed a bill against him in the Court of Chancery.[69] Kate Deasy had been happily running Deasy and Co. for some time, and had been running it well, ensuring that the beers were being produced competently for their customers, so much so that the brewery was worth some £16,000 when she was forced out.

Another woman-led brewery run by Eliza Alley, or Elizabeth Alley, made history. Eliza Alley & Sons was a brewery based on Townsend Street in Dublin. Eliza had inherited the brewery from her husband William following his demise in 1836. Remember Mary Shaw of the Black Bull, who we learned about in Chapter 7? Mary took out an advertisement in 1761 after her husband's death to assure her customers that she, alongside her son, would still be brewing malt liquor to the highest quality. Eliza did the same, employing much the same language:

> Eliza Alley, Widow of the Late WILLIAM ALLEY, impressed with a deep sense of gratitude to her numerous friends and patrons, who, by their kind feeling and warm support have marked their approbation of her exertions, and encouraged her to persevere in the arduous undertaking in which she engaged, for the advancement of her numerous family, begs to return them her most sincere and heartfelt thanks, and to assure them that her unceasing efforts shall be directed, and her best attention given, to merit a continuance of that patronage which she with pride and gratitude acknowledges. In soliciting the orders of those who have not already honored her with their support, she confidently assures them that the MALT DRINK manufactured in her Establishment is of the *very best* quality.[70]

She appears to have convinced them. To end on a high note here, according to Liam K., expert in Irish beer history at his aptly named blog, *IrishBeerHistory*, Eliza Alley & Sons was the first brewery to make India pale ale (IPA) in Ireland.[71] Liam studied the brewery in detail and concludes that they were likely the first to make the beverage on Irish soil in 1842 by tracing the brewery's advertisements.[72] Thus, we can end our study of women owning breweries with the creation of the first Irish IPA.

Another place we can see women in the beer business in this century is in public houses, as owners, operators and landladies. The census from 1901 includes well over 2,000 women who gave their occupation as publicans.

Women like Margaret Boal of Antrim, who at 42 years old was a widow and the head of her household; or Agnes Casey, aged 66 years, a widow and also head of her family.[73] The list goes on. Most of these women didn't start their businesses in 1901, so we can infer that they had been hard at work in their premises long before the turn of the century.

In fact, many of the women who worked as publicans were the widowed or unmarried heads of their families. Still others were married, possibly to husbands who also worked as publicans. In the census, even more women declared themselves to be retired publicans or publicans' assistants, while others stated that they were specifically licensed publicans. A further group, identified as daughters or wives of publicans, might have also found themselves working in their establishments. In total, nearly 3,000 women were connected to work in pubs in some way. Throughout Ireland at the end of the 19th century and into the 20th, women were hard at work in the pub trade.

Women also worked as grocers, selling beer and ale alongside the other foodstuffs and goods one would typically expect at such an establishment. This could go hand in hand with being a publican. Julia Hogan, for example, was one of many women in the 1901 census who listed her occupation as being both a grocer and a publican in Co. Tipperary.[74] Like many others, she was not married and was the head of her household.

Let's not forget the women who frequented such establishments. The stories of snugs (those small, private spaces where women could drink without being seen) and spirit grocers (a grocers that could sell spirits) are interconnected with women's history. In fact, over the next 100 years, women fought for their right to be served pints of beer in pubs throughout the country without discrimination based on their gender. This is all an important story of its own. It's related to brewing, of course, but it deserves its own separate investigation elsewhere.

Suffice it to say that like the women centuries before who sold ale out of their homes to their neighbours and passers-by, women continued to do much the same in the 19th century. However, unlike those women living in medieval times, most publicans weren't brewing their own beer on their own premises, as they had done even a century before. Now, more often than not, their beer was provided by commercial breweries, large industrial affairs that kept getting bigger, using modern machines and becoming global enterprises. We don't need to guess what these types of establishments looked like and how they operated. For that, we can turn to a man called Alfred Barnard.

෨෮

One brewery had a copper – that is, a vessel used for boiling the wort with hops – so large that it could fit a couple of Irish cabins, or even a one-storey cottage, in it. When it was built, 'over thirty persons partook of refreshments therein'.[75] Another brewery was home to a storage vat so large 'if an army of 700,000 men were encamped around the largest vat, and its contents divided among them, the soldiers would get one pint each- this is a fact'.[76] This firm also had its own railway, a fleet of small boats, rows of stables and purpose-built villages for workers. These breweries were massive, on a scale that would have been unheard of just 150 years previously, let alone in the medieval past. We are a long way from a 17th-century brewer being allotted only three horses or the tolboll of one and a half gallons of the best ale being too large a burden to bear.

Brewing in Ireland had reached an industrial scale, with premises taking up huge amounts of space in the landscape. The smaller of these breweries measured 3 acres, with the largest premises measuring upwards of 42 – to put that in perspective, that's the size of over 20 Premier League football fields. These breweries also boasted steam engines, refrigeration systems, their own maltings and more. But let's not get too far ahead of ourselves before we dive more into these details. Just how do we know all this?

Alfred Barnard was a late-19th-century English historian and writer. He had a particular interest in alcoholic beverages, first writing *The Whisky Distilleries of the United Kingdom* after touring 162 of them in England, Scotland and Ireland. Following this, he wrote a similar work, *The Notable Breweries of Great Britain and Ireland*, where over the course of three years he toured brewing establishments all over these areas, providing readers with in-depth details about everything from the size of their mash tuns to their refrigeration techniques. A lot of Barnard's accounts sound like something you could find on a beer blogger's brewery tour written in 2024. He gave detailed descriptions of the brewing process, the final product and everything in between. What we have now, over 100 years later, is a serious guide on what brewing looked like in Ireland (as well as Great Britain) around the last decade of the 19th century.

In total, Barnard toured 10 Irish breweries: Phoenix Porter Brewery on James Street, Dublin; Lady's Well Brewery (J. Murphy & Co. Ltd), Cork; Beamish & Crawford, aka Cork Porter Brewery, Cork; Ardee Street Brewery, proprietors J. Watkins & Co., Dublin; Anchor Brewery, Usher Street, Dublin, proprietors Matthew Peter D'Arcy A.P. and D.L.;

Mountjoy Brewery, proprietors Findlater & Co. Ltd, Dublin; North Anne Street Brewery, Dublin, proprietors Jameson, Pim & Co.; St James's Gate Brewery, Arthur Guinness, Son & Co. Ltd, Dublin; South Gate Brewery Ltd, proprietors Lane & Co. Ltd, Cork; and finally, J. Arnott & Co. Ltd, Cork.

The size of these premises varied greatly. Phoenix Porter Brewery was the one that covered only 3 acres, whereas, surprise, surprise, Guinness was the one that had a sprawling campus of 42 acres.[77] It was also Guinness that boasted that massive 700,000-pint storage vat, their own railway, a fleet of boats, stables and two purpose-built worker villages, Bellevue and Rialto.[78, 79] Most breweries fell somewhere between these, though generally below 10 acres. J. Arnott & Co. in Cork covered 7 acres,[80] while Cork Porter Brewery, Mountjoy Brewery and Ardee Street Brewery each covered about 5 acres.[81] In contrast, only one half of Anchor Street Brewery, the south side of their Usher Street location in Dublin, covered 5 acres, with large areas vaulted underground.[82]

Barnard's findings were incredibly intricate and written over four volumes, but I'll give you some of the highlights here. Let's start with the basics: what were they brewing? Most of the breweries he toured made at least porter and stout. The clue for some is right there in the name: Phoenix Porter Brewery and Cork Porter Brewery. However, they weren't only making porter. Cork Porter Brewery, also known as Beamish & Crawford, was also hard at work making ale, and while the porter was also exported, the ale was drunk in Ireland only and was sold in both bottles and casks.[83] They also made a pale ale that was said to have used their well water, which was similar in character to 'the famous water of Burton', which perhaps gives us an idea of the flavour profile of this likely bitter brew.[84] Guinness was making a single stout or plain porter, and a double stout.[85] We're told that North Anne Street Brewery produced both ale and porter, but they also made stout for export.[86]

To make these brews, the breweries in question used engines to power their machines – a far cry from our tea kettle ale. Ground malt was sent off to mash tuns where hot water was added to the malt to create saccharification, where the malt releases sugars that will then be converted to alcohol by the yeast during the fermentation process. These mash tuns could be huge. Lady's Well Brewery had two large mash tuns made of metal. The first could mash in up to 500 barrels and the second 300 barrels.[87] North Anne Street Brewery had four mash tuns in the New Brewery, as Barnard calls it, with copper coverings and containing the automatic stirring and sparging equipment. These were capable of mashing 330 barrels altogether.[88]

In a similar vein, the Anchor Brewery No. 4 mash tun was 25 feet in diameter and 7 feet deep, with a total capacity for 300 barrels. This mash tun contained Steel's mashing machine and had within it a 'sparging apparatus and internal mashing gear driven by steam'.[89] You don't need to know all the details about what Steel's mashing machine was; I mention it simply because we are now in the period of steam, as Barnard notes, and machine-operated brewing equipment, and its use was quite ordinary. In fact, Steel's mashing machine was a common denominator in these breweries and was used by most of them in their mashing equipment.[90] The bottom of Anchor Brewery's mash tun was false to facilitate sparging, that is, adding more water to the malt while the wort is being drained in order to get the most from your mash.

After mashing in was complete, the wort (the liquid that's produced after the mash) was sent over to coppers, where it was boiled with hops. Anchor Brewery is the one that had a copper that was so large it could fit some cottages or a one-storey house inside.[91] Other breweries also boasted large vessels. Cork Porter Brewery had four coppers that altogether could hold up to 1,560 barrels and each vessel cost £2,000.

From these coppers, the now-hopped wort was sent off to the coolers, another place where we can really see the advances in technology, because now we are using refrigerators – and a variety of refrigerators at that. Many of the breweries, like Anchor Brewery, were utilising open coolers, which were shallow and designed to allow the wort to cool faster. This was helped along by the use of these refrigerators. Anchor specifically had four made by Morton & Co., which was a common brand of refrigerator used in Irish breweries in this period, which were capable of cooling 50 barrels per hour.[92, 93] Lady's Well Brewery also had a large cooling room with two open coolers, each holding 650 barrels, and five Morton refrigerators.[94] A final example, Mountjoy Brewery, had a large cooling room with open coolers made of pine and used a large fan to speed up the cooling process. Morton refrigerators were also placed in this room, and Barnard tells us they were the first to use this piece of kit in Dublin.[95]

Brine was often employed in coils and pipes to cool rooms or keep the beer itself cool, because brine doesn't freeze at the same temperature that water does and so can be kept cooler and therefore reduce the temperatures further and faster.[96] Phoenix Brewery used brine to keep the vat houses cool.[97] At Guinness, the air in the fermenting tun rooms was kept cold by attemperators made from pipes through which cold brine was passed through from the freezing machines. According to

Barnard, even on the hottest summer days, these pipes would be coated with ice.[98] Brine was also employed to help cool the yeast.[99]

From here, the now-cooled wort was sent off to the fermenting tuns, where yeast was added and left to work its magic, converting the sugars into alcohol. Yeast was an important product, one that these breweries produced and sold on to distillers to use. Spent hops were also sold off to farmers.

At North Anne Street Brewery, Barnard tells us that they had 14 fermenting tuns, all of which had attemperators that had hot or cold water running through them – whatever they needed to keep the correct temperatures.[100, 101]

After fermentation was complete, the beer was sent off to skimmers, which were designed to remove the yeast from the finished beer and were kept cool. At North Anne Street Brewery, for example, in the No. 1 cleansing and skimming house there were six large skimming tanks, two made of timber and four made of metal into which the porter was pumped after it finished fermenting.[102]

Finally, the beer was sent off to storage vats, where it waited to be bottled, kegged, or casked. Like everything else, some of these storage vats were massive, like that Guinness vat that held those 700,000 pints.[103]

Before it was sold, beer could be bottled or distributed in casks. Many breweries had their own cooperage departments at their disposal. The cooperage at North Anne Street Brewery was particularly impressive and their casks were highly regarded. When they were sent to the Manchester Exhibition, Barnard tells us that their casks were 'noted for the neatness and lightness'.[104]

Very little remains of many of these late-19th-century industrial breweries. Often a building here or there still stands as a testament to their existence, while others have almost entirely disappeared, at least above ground, victims of growth and industry. Like Winetavern Street, we can find clues if we look close enough. Near Croke Park in Dublin, for example, a range of two- and three-storey buildings remain that once belonged to Mountjoy Brewery. Meanwhile, the residence and office for the brewers of Watkins Brewery still stand at Number 10 Ardee Street. We can still find traces, even if they aren't evident at first glance.

The last thing to consider from Barnard's tours is that these breweries had in-house maltings. Every single one of the breweries that Barnard toured had their own. For example, Anchor Brewing had one machine specifically designed for the 'the delicate operation of roasting malt for porter'.[105] While these firms certainly made their own specialty roasts, many also supplemented with outside malts as needed. And where might they get their outside malt? Plunkett Brothers Maltings, of course, which is also where we find women again in our story of beer.

Like many of our breweries, Plunkett Brothers Maltings had its roots in the cause of Irish emancipation. According to Barnard, the founder of the business participated in the Rebellion of 1798 when he was a mere 20 years old, marching on Wexford, where he found himself wounded and on the run from the king's troops. He was eventually nursed back to health by the woman who would become his wife, and later went on to found the maltings, marrying his love of chemistry and beer to create roasted malts for porters. He brought his son, Randal, into the business and it prospered under his leadership.

After Randal's death in May 1856, his widow, Eliza, took over the maltings. Described by Barnard as 'a lady of great energy and spirit', Eliza Plunkett expanded the business, opening a roasting house in London that eventually had to be shut following severe mismanagement by the gentlemen in charge. At the time of his visit, however, Eliza had passed on and the business had been inherited by her two sons, Oliver and J. Randal Plunkett.[106]

When we look at the history of beer and brewing in Ireland in the 19th century, and indeed throughout this book, we have to consider the industries that are adjacent to brewing. Plunkett Brothers Maltings, like Deasy and Co., passed into women's hands through inheritance, and just the same, it passed out of them.

We can also see women in another of the key ingredients in beer: hops.

A September 1865 article in the *Taunton Courier and Western Advertiser* tells the story of Margaret Moore, described as 'an Irish hop picker' who had allegedly set fire to stacks of hay, beans and wheat among other things at a farm belonging to Mr Hill near the borders of Herefordshire and Worcestershire. The fire quickly spread, engulfing much of the farming equipment and destroying the property. Moore apparently set the fires because she was 'dissatisfied with her treatment by Mrs Hill'.[107]

Another case from that same year features Julia Bennett, a woman described as an Irish hop picker who, like Moore, had found herself under arrest. Bennett was charged with stealing two aprons and a knife and fork from the Chapter Arms public house at Chartham in Kent while she pretended to be there to get some beer.[108]

We often find stories like these because these women ran afoul of the law; it wasn't that hop-picking Irish women were particularly prone to the behaviour. Articles about well-behaved workers not doing much of anything exciting aren't going to make the news.

Irish people were key workers in hop-picking in the 19th century. Many lived in cities like London and ventured out during the season to pick hops alongside other urban labourers in places like Kent. On 5 October 1862, the *Weekly Dispatch*, a London newspaper, reported that a group of 1,000 of these Irish hop pickers came to blows while returning to London at the end of the picking season, where, at Maidstone Railway Station in Kent, the parties divided into groups, with one side laying claim to Tonbridge Road and the other to the station yard. Women hurled stones and men bludgeoned each other with their shillelaghs and bagging hooks. As a result, many ended up injured, some quite severely, including a small child.[109]

In my book *The Devil's in the Draught Lines* I explore what conditions would have been like for these hop pickers on 19th-century farms.[110] Suffice it to say that the environment would have been rough. Diseases spread frequently and shelter was often subpar, with many working for long hours in the cold and damp. The work was often done in this period by working-class or poorer labourers who travelled to the rural hop farms from their urban homes to earn extra income, and women, along with their own children, frequently worked as pickers. Entire families would pick hops together to earn money. And so it's also in hops that we can still find Irish women in the history of beer, long after female brewers were the norm.

At the end of the 19th century, and even into the one beyond, we can still find glimpses of women in the brewing industry, although men had come to dominate the trade. I'm not going to venture too far into the 20th century here, as that is a subject for a different book – an in-depth history of the brewing industry in that period would be better suited to interviews with the people who worked then, many of whom are still very much alive. Suffice it to say that women were still there.

For example, in the 1901 census, Bridget Tobin of Eccles Street in Dublin was working as a brewer as a 51-year-old single woman.[111] Ten years later, the 1911 census lists Margaret J. Cousins of Wexford, a single woman aged 21, as a brewer, while Mary Tew of Harrington Street in Dublin, also a single woman, aged 20, was working as a brewer's clerk.[112] A look through Guinness's digital archives also yields results for women working in the brewery in the late 19th and early 20th centuries. During the first half of the 20th century, Guinness employed hundreds of women in their premises. You can browse over 25,000 personnel files online that are available to the public to look for your ancestors, but this is also an incredibly important resource for the history of Irish women.[113]

In the first half of the 20th century, women worked as clerks or most often as cleaners, making sure the brewery was kept to exacting specifications. As anyone who has ever brewed knows, keeping the actual equipment and the area in general sparkling clean is critical to keeping contaminants out of the beer. Cleaning is an important part of brewery work, so women were a crucial part of the brewing industry.

There is no point in Irish history where we can't find women hard at work in the brewing trade if we look close enough. In the second half of the 20th century, women returned to work in breweries as scientists, clerks, administrative staff, marketing executives, social media managers, quality control officers and brewers. The craft beer revolution in particular has seen women taking the helm at many breweries. But that's a story for a different book.

CONCLUSION

 It's difficult to sum up a book in a few paragraphs, especially one that spans centuries and that explores not only at different people, but also entirely separate cultures.

We started by examining Ireland before the invasions, a time of saints and kings, goddesses and law makers, in the Late Iron Age and early medieval period, when brewers were hard at work adhering to the Brehon Laws lest they be found wanting and fined heavily for their errors.

From there, we looked at two invasions: the Vikings, who brought with them a remarkably similar culture as it pertains to beer, and the English, who actually invaded at least twice, since the first time didn't work out the way they'd initially envisioned. We saw how beer was woven within these stories of conquest, violence and colonisation.

We learned about cheating alewives and ducking stools, about cannibalism, human sacrifice and, of course, the zombies.

We explored how beer was used in war as a way to maintain armies and build walls to keep enemies out.

We moved forward in time to the 17th century, where we learned that in contrast to places in England, women in Ireland were by and large still dominating the brewing industry, especially in Dublin. These 'filthy queens' were responsible for brewing almost the entirety of the city's beer and ale supply and doing it, perhaps, in ways that were viewed as somewhat shocking to the new English invaders.

In the 18th century, through the eyes of one of the most famous sex workers to ever exist, we learned about the state of the brewing industry and the porter wars, with Ireland and England vying for supremacy in the Irish beer world, a proxy war in many ways for the very real tensions of colonisation.

The next 100 years saw a revival for Irish beer, a trade that ended with large commercial enterprises pushing out smaller firms, leaving only a few breweries remaining to see in the 20th century.

The pages of this book have been filled with stories of our ghosts, spirits of the past that have left echoes in our modern brewing world. While we have only scratched the surface of these tales, they can shed some light on the world of our forebears. They reveal that while our love of Irish beer hasn't always remained steady throughout the ages – as we have seen, there were times when it fell to the wayside in preference for things like whiskey or foreign imports – it's always had an important place in our history.

As in the centuries before, we have clung to beer as a way to mark our occasions. What we now bring out for birthdays or celebrations was used similarly by those before us for victories or feasts. While that may seem to be quite a different reasoning, the closer look we have taken reveals that at its core, we still use beer in much the same ways: to celebrate, to commiserate, to mark the special and the mundane days of our lives. In many ways, beer is a way to view the past through a lens that we can quickly understand. Its uses haven't changed all that much, even if its recipes have. We can easily relate to its language. Modern brewers can find themselves in the stories of medieval alewives fighting for their rights to brew without too much government oversight. Homebrewers might see themselves in the pages of 18th-century recipe books, finding common ground with the women who inscribed the ingredients on their pages with our own trials and errors. And all of us might see ourselves within the walls of an alehouse, swapping stories with mates while enjoying our pints.

Beer is a medium through which we can view the past not as a foreign place, but as something familiar, close and altogether relatable. We can see ourselves in these ghosts, in these stories of people long gone from this world, but perhaps not forgotten. And we can remember them, and honour them, whenever we raise our pints: to those brewers who came before us, to those beer lovers who drank just like we do and to all those who made our modern trade possible. *Sláinte*!

NOTES

INTRODUCTION

1 Isabella Travers Steward, *The Interdict*, Vol. I (London: T.W. Boone, 1840), p. 67.
2 Joseph Stirling Coyne and N.P. Willis, *The Scenery and Antiquities of Ireland*, Vol. I (London: George Virtue, 1842), p. 62.
3 Steward, *The Interdict*, Vol. I, p. 14.
4 See, for example, Beyond 2022: Ireland's Virtual Record Treasury, which has made incredible strides to recreate what has been lost.
5 I've made my own version of scolteen, which you can find on my blog, *Braciatrix*. <https://braciatrix.com/2022/07/26/scolteen-an-irish-hot-whiskey-and-beer-cocktail/>

CHAPTER ONE

1 Whitley Stokes (ed. and trans.), 'On the Life of Saint Brigit', in *Three Middle-Irish Homilies on the Lives of Saints Patrick, Brigit and Columba* (Calcutta, 1877), p. 65.
2 Whitley Stokes (trans.), *Annals of Tigernach* (Felinfach, 1993); William M. Hennessy (ed. and trans.), *Chronicum Scotorum: A Chronicle of Irish Affairs from the Earliest Times to AD 1135: with Supplement, Containing Events from 1141–1150* (London, 1866).
3 Laurance Maney, 'Date and Provenance of Vita Prima Sanctae Brigitae', *Proceedings of the Harvard Celtic Colloquium*, 23 (2003), pp. 200–18, p. 200, 204.
4 Maney, 'Date and Provenance', p. 204.
5 Ibid., p. 218.

6 Lisa M. Bitel, 'St. Brigit of Ireland: From Virgin Saint to Fertility Goddess', presented at Fordham University, February 2001.

7 Stokes, 'On the Life of Saint Brigit', pp. 65–7.

8 Ibid., p. 67.

9 Ibid., pp. 65–7.

10 Donnchadh Ó hAodha (ed. and trans.), *Bethu Brigte* (Dublin: Dublin Institute for Advanced Studies, 1978), p. 26.

11 Ó hAodha, *Bethu Brigte*, p. 8.

12 Sean Connolly and J-M. Picard, 'Cogitosus's "Life of St Brigit" Content and Value', *Journal of the Royal Society of Antiquaries of Ireland*, 117 (1987), pp. 16–17.

13 Richard W. Unger, *Beer in the Middle Ages and the Renaissance* (Philadelphia: University of Pennsylvania Press, 2013).

14 Mick Monk and Orla Power, 'More Than a Grain of Truth Emerges from a Rash of Corn-Drying Kilns?', *Archaeology Ireland*, 26/2, Special 100th Issue (Summer 2012), p. 38.

15 Lorcan Harney, 'Fasting and Feasting on Irish Church Sites: The Archaeological and Historical Evidence', *Ulster Journal of Archaeology Third Series*, 73 (2015–16), pp. 182–97, p. 184.

16 Tracy Collins, *Female Monasticism in Medieval Ireland: An Archaeology* (Cork: Cork University Press, 2021), p. 180, p. 341.

17 Collins, *Female Monasticism*, p. 180.

18 Fiona Fitzsimons, 'Tudor Fiants', *History Ireland*, 23/4 (July/August 2015). <https://www.historyireland.com/tudor-fiants/>

19 Collins, *Female Monasticism*, p. 341.

20 Hildegard Von Bingen, Priscilla Throop (trans.), *Hildegarde Von Bingen's Physica: The Complete English Translation of Her Classic Work on Health and Healing* (Rochester: Healing Arts Press, 1998), p. 85.

21 Von Bingen, *Physica*, p. 88.

22 Ibid., p. 16.

23 Ibid., p. 100.

24 Ibid., p. 36.

25 G.G. Coulton and Eileen Power (eds.), Caesarius of Heisterbach, *The Dialogue on Miracles*, Vol. I (New York: Harcourt, Brace & Co., 1929), pp. 377–80.

26 Caesarius, *Dialogue*, p. 379.

27 Monk Jonas of Bobbio, 'Life of St. Columban', in *Translations and Reprints from the Original Sources of European History*, Vol. II (Philadelphia: University of Pennsylvania Press, 1897–1907), pp. 31–2.

28 Jonas, 'Life of St. Columban', pp. 25–6.

29 Ibid., pp. 26–7.

30 Whitley Stokes (ed. and trans.), 'On the Life of Saint Patrick', in *Three Middle-Irish Homilies on the Lives of Saints Patrick, Brigit and Columba* (Calcutta, 1877), p. 25.

31 Stokes, 'On the Life of Saint Patrick', p. 25.

32 James O'Leary (ed.), 'Tripartite Life of Saint Patrick', in *The Most Ancient Lives of Saint Patrick; including The Life by Jocelin, Hitherto Unpublished in America, and His Extant Writings* (New York: P.J. Kenedy, 1880), pp. 510–1184, Part III.

33 Jocelin, 'The Life and Acts of Saint Patrick', in James O'Leary (ed.), *The Most Ancient Lives of Saint Patrick; including The Life by Jocelin, Hitherto Unpublished in America, and His Extant Writings* (New York: P.J. Kenedy, 1880), Chapter LXXI.

34 For further reading, see Anthony Thomas Lucas, 'The Plundering and Burning of Churches in Ireland, 7th to 16th Century', in E. Rynne (ed.), *North Munster Studies: Essays in Commemoration of Monsignor Michael Moloney* (Limerick: North Munster Studies, 1967); and Liz FitzPatrick, 'Raiding and Warring in Monastic Ireland', *History Ireland*, 1/3 (1993).

35 Stokes, *Annals of Tigernach*, p. 260.

36 Michael Richter, *Medieval Ireland: The Enduring Tradition* (Dublin: Gill & Macmillan, 2005), p. 158.

37 Richter, *Medieval Ireland*, p. 160.

38 Ibid., p. 161.

39 Ibid.

40 Ibid.

41 Columban, *Monks' Rules*, in G.S.M. Walker (ed. and trans.), *Sancti Columbani Opera II, Scriptores Latini Hiberniae* (Dublin: Dublin Institute for Advanced Studies, 1957), p. 147.

42 Columban, *Monks' Rules*, p. 147.

43 Ibid., p. 125.

44 Max Nelson, *The Barbarian's Beverage: A History of Beer in Ancient Europe* (London and New York: Routledge, 2005), p. 110.

45 A full translation of Sedulius' work in prose can be found in Nelson, *The Barbarian's Beverage*, p. 111.

CHAPTER TWO

1 George Henderson (ed.), *Fled Bricrend: The Feast of Bricriu* (London: Irish Texts Society, David Nutt, 1899).

2 H. Wagner, 'Studies in the Origins of Early Celtic Traditions', *Èriu*, 26 (1975), p. 12.

3 Henderson, *The Feast of Bricriu*, pp. 75–9.

4 Ibid., pp. 93–5.

5 Ibid.

6 Bettina Arnold, '"Drinking the Feast": Alcohol and the Legitimation of Power in Celtic Europe', *Cambridge Archaeological Journal*, 9/1 (1999), p. 71, p. 75.

7 Arnold, 'Drinking the Feast', p. 81.

8 Michael Enright, *Lady with the Mead Cup: Ritual, Prophecy and Lordship in the European Warband from La Tène to the Viking Age* (Dublin: Four Courts Press, 1995), p. 10.

N O T E S

9 See, for example, Enright, *Lady with the Mead Cup*, pp. 8–10; Arnold, 'Drinking the Feast', pp. 71–5.

10 Myles Dillon (ed. and trans.), '*Baile in Scail*', in *The Cycle of the Kings* (Oxford: Oxford University Press, 1946).

11 See, for example, Enright, *Lady with the Mead Cup*, p. 2 and p. 6; Arnold, 'Drinking the Feast', pp. 81–2; Wagner, 'Studies', p. 11.

12 Wagner, 'Studies', pp. 11–12.

13 'Deirdre or the Exile of the Sons of Usench', in Richard Irvine Best, Osborn Bergin, M.A. O'Brien and Anne Sullivan (eds.), *The Book of Leinster formerly Lebar na Núachongbála*, 6 vols (Dublin: Dublin Institute for Advanced Studies, 1954–1983). An accessible translation can be found here: http://www.maryjones.us/ctexts/usnech.html

14 Enright, *Lady with the Mead Cup*, p. 2 and pp. 6–10, pp. 146–7.

15 Henderson, *The Feast of Bricriu*, pp. 19–23.

16 Ibid., p. 23.

17 Ibid., p. 25.

18 Ibid., p. 27.

19 Ibid.

20 Ibid., p. 29.

21 Enright, *Lady with the Mead Cup*, p. 2 and pp. 6–10.

22 Ciaran Carson (ed. and trans.), *The Táin: A New Translation of the Táin Bó Cúailnge* (London: Penguin Classics, 2007), p. 157.

23 Charles Doherty, 'Exchange and Trade in Early Medieval Ireland', *Journal of the Royal Society of Ireland*, 110 (1980), p. 67.

24 Doherty, 'Exchange and Trade', p. 73.

25 Ibid.

26 Arnold, 'Drinking the Feast', p. 78.

27 Miles Dillon (ed. and trans.), *Lebor na Cert* (Dublin: Irish Texts Society, 1962), p. 83.

28 Dillon, *Lebor na Cert*, p. 91.

29 Ibid., p. 5.

30 Ibid.

31 Arnold, 'Drinking the Feast', p. 83; D.A. Binchy, *Scéla Cano meic Gartnáin* (Dublin: Dublin Institute for Advanced Studies, 1963; repr. 1975), p. 462.

32 Doherty, 'Exchange and Trade', p. 74.

33 E.J. Gwynn, 'The Three Drinking-Horns of Cormac úa Cuinn [from the *Liber Flavus Fergusiorum*]', *Ériu*, 2 (1905), pp. 186–8.

34 Gwynn, 'The Three Drinking-Horns', pp. 187–8.

35 Ibid.

36 Ibid.

37 Ibid.

38 Nancy Edwards, *The Archaeology of Early Medieval Ireland* (London: Routledge, 1996), p. 86.

39 Edwards, *The Archaeology of Early Medieval Ireland*, p. 86.

40 Maire MacDermott, 'Terminal Mounting of a Drinking Horn from Lismore, Co. Waterford', *Journal of the Royal Society of Ireland*, 80/2 (July 1950), p. 262.
41 Anne Sassin, 'Feasting and Subsistence in Early Medieval Ireland and Wales: An Examination of the Literary and Archaeological Evidence', in *Food and Archaeology I* (Devon: Prospect Books, 2008), p. 125.
42 Sassin, 'Feasting and Subsistence', p. 123.
43 Catherine Marie O'Sullivan, *Hospitality in Medieval Ireland, 900–1500* (Dublin: Four Courts Press, 2004), p. 88.
44 Dillon, *Lebor na Cert*, p. 74.
45 Ibid., p. 77.
46 Kuno Meyer (ed. and trans.), *The Triads of Ireland* (Dublin: Hodges, Figgis & Co., 1906), p. 13.
47 Arnold, 'Drinking the Feast', p. 76.
48 Meyer, *The Triads*, p. 33.
49 Riitta Latvio, 'Status and Exchange in Early Irish Laws', *Studia Celtica Fennica II* (2005), p. 69.
50 Katherine Simms, 'Guesting and Feasting in Gaelic Ireland', *Journal of Royal Society of Ireland*, 108 (1978), p. 68.
51 W. Neilson Hancock, Thaddeus O'Mahony, Alexander George Richey and Robert Atkinson (eds. and trans.), *Ancient Laws of Ireland: Uraicecht Becc and Other Selected Brehon Law Tracts*, Vol. 5 (Dublin: Stationery Office, 1901), p. 77.
52 Hancock et al., *Ancient Laws of Ireland*, p. 79.
53 Edel Bhreathnach, 'The *Tech Midchúarta*, "The House of the Mead-circuit": Feasting, Royal Circuits and the King's Court in Early Ireland', *Archaeology Ireland*, 12/4 (1998), p. 20, p. 21.
54 Bhreathnach, 'The *Tech Midchúarta*', p. 20.
55 'Liadin and Curithir' in Kuno Meyer (ed. and trans.), *Selections from Ancient Irish Poetry* (London: Constable, 1911), p. 65.
56 D.A. Binchy, 'The Fair of Tailtiu and the Feast of Tara', *Ériu*, 18 (1958), p. 135.
57 Binchy, 'The Fair of Tailtiu', p. 134.
58 William M. Hennessy (ed.), *Mesca Ulad or The Intoxication of the Ultonians*, Royal Irish Academy Todd Lecture Series, Vol. 1, Part I (Dublin: Royal Irish Academy, 1889), p. 3.
59 Hennessy, *Mesca Ulad*, p. 9.
60 Arnold, 'Drinking the Feast', p. 79.
61 Hennessy, *Mesca Ulad*, p. 9.
62 Lorcan Harney, 'Fasting and Feasting on Irish Church Sites: The Archaeological and Historical Evidence', *Ulster Journal of Archaeology Third Series*, 73 (2015–16), p. 189.
63 Harney, 'Fasting and Feasting', p. 189.
64 Ibid.
65 Sassin, 'Feasting and Subsistence', p. 126.

66 Ibid.
67 Richard Warner, 'The Irish Early Medieval Feasting House and its Iron Age Origin', *Ulster Journal of Archaeology*, 74 (2018), p. 33.
68 Warner, 'Feasting House', p. 45.
69 Breathnach, 'The *Tech Midchúarta*', p. 22.
70 Hennessy, *Mesca Ulad*, p. 9.
71 Meyer, *Triads of Ireland*, p. 29.
72 Ibid., p. 35.
73 Kuno Meyer, *The Instructions of King Cormac Mac Airt: Tecosca Cormaic*, in Todd Lecture Series (Royal Irish Academy), Vol. 15 (Dublin: Hodges Figgis & Co., 1909), p. 12.
74 Meyer, *Tecosca Cormaic*, p. 21.
75 Fergus Kelly, *Early Irish Farming: A Study Based Mainly on the Law-texts of the 7th and 8th Centuries AD* (Dublin: Dublin Institute of Advanced Studies, 1997), p. 332.
76 Meyer, *Tecosca Cormaic*, p. 9 and p. 5.
77 Ibid., p. 13.
78 The Fear, if you aren't familiar, is that feeling of anxiety you wake up with after a night out, also known as hangxiety.
79 Meyer, *Triads of Ireland*, p. 13.
80 Meyer, *Tecosca Cormaic*, p. 31.
81 Meyer, *Triads of Ireland*, p. 35.
82 Kelly, *Early Irish Farming*, p. 350.
83 Ibid., p. 154.
84 D.A. Binchy, 'Brewing in Eighth-Century Ireland', in B.G. Scott (ed.), *Studies on Early Ireland: Essays in Honour of M.V. Duignan* (Belfast, 1982), p. 5.
85 Kelly, *Early Irish Farming*, p. 334.
86 Kuno Meyer, 'The Lament of the Old Woman of Beare', in *Selections from Ancient Irish Poetry* (London: Constable, 1911), p. 91.
87 Dillon, *Lebor na Cert*, p. 125.
88 Ibid., p. 133.
89 Myles Dillon, 'The Taboos of the Kings of Ireland', *Proceedings of the Royal Society of Ireland: Archaeology, Culture, History, Literature*, 54 (1951/1952), p. 13.
90 Dillon, 'Taboos', p. 17.
91 Eugene O'Curry with W. K. Sullivan (ed.), *On the Manners and Customs of the Ancient Irish: A Series of Lectures*, 3 vols, Vol. 2: Lectures, Vol. 1 (London, 1873), pp. cclxxiv–cclxxv citing MS., H. 2. 16., TCD, col. 786.
92 O'Curry, *On the Manners and Customs of the Ancient Irish*, Vol. 1, pp. cclxxiv–cclxxv.
93 Binchy, *Scéla Cano meic Gartnáin*, p. xxvi.
94 O'Curry, *On the Manners and Customs of the Ancient Irish*, p. cclxxvi.
95 For more on unhopped ales in the medieval period, see Tofi Kerthjalfadsson, 'Recreating Medieval English Ales: A Recreation of Late

13th–14th c Unhopped English Ales', Carnegie Mellon University (23 September to 28 December 1998) <https://www.cs.cmu.edu/~pwp/tofi/medieval_english_ale.html>. I used these recipes to create a medieval English small ale. See also Martyn Cornell, *Amber, Gold and Black: The History of Britain's Great Beers* (Cheltenham: The History Press, 2010).

96   O'Curry, *On the Manners and Customs of the Ancient Irish*, p. ccclxxiv.

97   Susan Lyons, 'Food Plants, Fruits and Foreign Foodstuffs: The Archaeological Evidence from Urban Medieval Ireland', *Proceedings of the Royal Irish Academy: Archaeology, Culture, History, Literature*, 115C (2015), p. 157.

98   Lyons, 'Food Plants', p. 157.

99   Kuno Meyer, 'King and Hermit', in *Selections from Ancient Irish Poetry* (London: Constable, 1911), p. 49.

100   Binchy, 'Brewing', p. 3.

101   See page 55 of this book.

102   Binchy, 'Brewing', p. 3.

103   O'Curry, *On the Manners and Customs of the Ancient Irish*, p. cclxxii.

104   Kuno Meyer (trans.), 'The Wooing of Emer by Cú Chulainn', *Archaeological Review*, 1 (1888), p. 69.

105   O'Curry, *On the Manners and Customs of the Ancient Irish*, p. ccclxxii.

106   Ibid., p. ccclxxii.

107   Ibid.

108   Cherie N. Peters, 'Legal Position and Living Conditions of Peasants and Commoners in Early Medieval Ireland, c.680–c.1170', PhD thesis (Trinity College Dublin, 2014).

109   D.A. Binchy, 'Bretha Déin Chécht', *Ériu*, 20 (1966), p. 23.

110   Binchy, 'Bretha', p. 23. All statuses defined as in *Críth Gablach*.

111   Martyn Cornell, 'Pea Beer', 16 October 2012, *Zythophile* [website]. <https://zythophile.co.uk/2012/10/16/pea-beer/>

112   Cornell, 'Pea Beer', *Zythophile*.

113   Ibid.

114   Harney, 'Fasting and Feasting', p. 185.

115   *Senchus Mor, Vol. II* in Dr O'Donovan and Professor O'Curry (trans.), *Hiberniae Leges Et Institutiones Antiquae or Ancient Laws and Institutions of Ireland* (Dublin, 1869), p. 243.

116   Peters, 'Legal Position', p. 95.

117   Binchy, 'Brewing', p. 4.

118   O'Donovan and O'Curry, *Senchus Mor, Vol. II*, pp. 243–5.

119   Binchy, 'Brewing', p. 5.

120   O'Curry, *On the Manners and Customs of the Ancient Irish*, Vol. 2, p. ccclxxvi.

121   Binchy, 'Brewing', p. 5.

122   Aidan O'Sullivan and Triona Nicholl, 'Early Medieval Settlement Enclosures in Ireland: Dwellings, Daily Life and Social Identity', *Proceedings of the Royal Irish Academy: Archaeology, Culture, History, Literature*, 111C (2011), pp. 72–3.

123 O'Sullivan and Nicholl, 'Early Medieval Settlement', p. 79.
124 Ibid.
125 Ibid., p. 80.

CHAPTER THREE

1 Henry Adams Bellows (ed. and trans.), 'Athlakvitha En Grönlenzka: The Greenland Lay of Atli', in *Poetic Edda* (New York: The American-Scandinavian Foundation, 1923), pp. 480–535.

2 See *Jordanes: The Origins and Deeds of the Goths*, Charles C. Mierow (ed. and trans.), part of the PhD thesis at Princeton University (1908).

3 *Atlamál in grönlenzku*, Ch. 82, translation my own:
   hausa veizt þú þeira
   hafða at ölskálum,
   drýgða ek þér svá drykkju,
   dreyra blett ek þeira.

4 *Vǫlundarkvioa*, translation my own.

5 *Gylfaginning*, Ch. 36, translation my own: *eru þær aðrar, er þjóna skulu í Valhöll, bera drykkju ok gæta borðbúnaðar ok ölgagna.*

6 *Grímnismál*, Ch. 36, translation my own from:
   Hrist ok Mist vil ek, at mér horn beri,
   Skeggjöld ok Skögul, Hildr ok Þrúðr,
   Hlökk ok Herfjötur, Göll ok Geirönul,
   Randgríðr ok Ráðgríðr ok Reginleif,
   þær bera Einherjum öl.

7 *Njál's Saga*, Ch. 34, translation my own.

8 *Egil's Saga*, Ch. 7, translation my own: *En er þeir höfðu afklædzt ok tekit upp yfirhafnir, þá lét Högni bera inn skapker ok mungát. Hildiríðr bóndadóttir bar öl gestum.*

9 William Morris and Eiríkr Magnússon (ed. and trans. 1892), *The Saga of the Heath Slayings* on the Icelandic Saga Database, Ch. 11. <https://www.sagadb.org/heidarviga_saga.en>

10 Harold Mytum, 'The Vikings and Ireland: Ethnicity, Identity, and Culture Change', in James H. Barrett (ed.), *Contact, Continuity and Collapse* (Turnhout: Brepols, 2005), p. 115.

11 See, for example, Christina Wade, 'Gendered Symbolism as a Medium to Negotiate Power as Evidenced in the Furnished Viking Burials of Ireland', PhD thesis (Trinity College Dublin, 2017).

12 'Deirdre or the Exile of the Sons of Usench', in Richard Irvine Best, Osborn Bergin, M.A. O'Brien and Anne Sullivan (eds.), *The Book of Leinster formerly Lebar na Núachongbála*, 6 vols (Dublin: Dublin Institute for Advanced Studies, 1954–1983). An accessible translation can be found here: http://www.maryjones.us/ctexts/usnech.html

13 George Henderson (ed.), *Fled Bricrend: The Feast of Bricriu* (London: Irish Texts Society, David Nutt, 1899), p. 67.

14 Stephen Harrison and Raghnall Ó Floinn, 'Viking Graves and Grave-Goods In Ireland', *Medieval Dublin Excavations 1962–81*, Series B, Vol. 11

(Dublin: National Museum of Ireland, 2014), pp. 595–604; Stephen Harrison, 'Furnished Insular Scandinavian Burial: Artefacts and Landscape in the Early Viking Age', PhD thesis (Trinity College Dublin, 2008), p. 519. See also Christina Wade, 'Gendered Symbolism', p. 369.

15 Shelia Raven, 'The Scandinavian Bowls', in Rupert Leo Scott Bruce-Mit-ford, *The Corpus of Late Celtic Hanging-bowls with an Account of the Bowls found in Scandinavia* (Oxford: Oxford University Press, 2005), p. 43.

16 Ibid.

17 Harrison, 'Furnished Insular Scandinavian Burial', p. 517; Harrison and Ó Floinn, 'Viking Graves', p. 615.

18 Jenny Jochens, *Women in Old Norse Society* (Ithaca: Cornell University Press, 1998), p. 131.

19 Aina Margrethe Heen-Pettersen, 'Feasting, Friendship, and Alliances: The Socio-Political Use of Insular Vessels in Viking-Age Norway', in Hanne Lovise Aannestad, Unn Pedersen, Marianne Moen, Elise Naumann and Heidi Lund Berg (eds.), *Vikings Across Boundaries: Viking-Age Transforma-tions*, Vol. II (New York: Routledge, 2021), p. 12.

20 Peter Harbison, 'The Derrynaflan Ladle: Some Parallels Illustrated', *Journal of Irish Archaeology*, 3 (1985/1986), p. 55.

21 Merryn Dineley and Graham Dineley, 'Where Did the Vikings Make Their Ale?', *Orkney Archaeological Society Newsletter*, 10 (November 2013), p. 1.

22 Dineley and Dineley, 'Where Did the Vikings Make Their Ale?', pp. 1–2.

23 Joan Elisabeth Rosa Brusin, 'Brewing and Drinking Ale in Late Iron Age Scandinavia: An Interdisciplinary Investigation on Drinking Customs with a Female Perspective', MA thesis (University of Oslo, 2021), p. 54.

24 Brusin, 'Brewing and Drinking', p. 54.

25 Henry Adams Bellows (ed. and trans), 'Hymiskvitha or The Lay of Hymir', in *Poetic Edda* (New York: The American-Scandinavian Foundation, 1923), p. 139.

26 Bellows, 'Hymiskvitha', p. 140.

27 Ibid., p. 141.

28 Ibid., p. 144.

29 Lars Marius Garshol, *Historical Brewing Techniques: The Lost Art of Farmhouse Brewing* (Boulder: Brewers Publications, 2020), ebook.

30 Garshol, *Historical Brewing Techniques*.

31 Geir Grønnesby, 'Hot Rocks! Beer Brewing on Viking and Medieval Age Farms in Trøndelag', in Frode Iversen and Håkan Petersson (eds.), *The Agrarian Life of the North 2000 BC–AD 1000: Studies in Rural Settlement and Farming in Norway* (Cappelen Damm Akademisk).

32 Dineley and Dineley, 'Where Did the Vikings Make Their Ale?', p. 1.

33 Alan Hawkes, 'Medieval *Fulachtai Fia* in Ireland? An Archaeological Assessment', *Journal of Irish Archaeology*, 20 (2011), p. 77.

34 Hawkes, 'Medieval *Fulachtai Fia*', p. 77.

35 Declan Moore and Billy Quinn, 'Ale, Brewing and *Fulacht Fiadh*: Archaeology Ireland' on MooreGroup.ie, 08 October 2007. <http://www.mooregroup.ie/2007/10/the-archaeology-ireland-article/>

36 Ibid., p. 82.
37 Ibid., p. 86.
38 Hawkes, 'Medieval *Fulachtai Fia*', p. 78.
39 Ibid.
40 John Locke, 'The Heath-beer of the Ancient Scandinavians', *Ulster Archaeology*, 7 (1859), p. 219.
41 Ibid., p. 222.
42 Ibid.
43 Ibid.
44 bid.
45 D.A. Binchy, 'Brewing in Eighth-Century Ireland', in B.G. Scott (ed.), *Studies on Early Ireland: Essays in Honour of M.V. Duignan* (Belfast, 1982), p. 3.
46 Eugene O'Curry with W. K. Sullivan (ed.), *On the Manners and Customs of the Ancient Irish: A Series of Lectures*, 3 vols, vol. 2: Lectures, vol. 1 (London, 1873), p. ccclxxviii.
47 The Moore Group, 'How to Make a "Viking" Ale in 4 Easy Steps', MooreGroup.ie, 27 September 2010. <http://www.mooregroup.ie/2010/09/how-to-make-a-viking-ale-in-4-easy-steps/>
48 Henry Adams Bellows (ed. and trans.), 'Alvíssmál', in *Poetic Edda* (New York: The American-Scandinavian Foundation, 1923), p. 193.
49 Bellows, 'Alvíssmál', p. 193.
50 Jesus Fernando Guerrero Rodriguez, 'Old Norse Drinking Culture', PhD thesis (University of York, 2007), p. 93.
51 Guerrero Rodriguez, 'Old Norse Drinking Culture', p. 93.
52 Christie L. Ward, 'Norse Drinking Traditions' in Alexandrian Company Symposium on Food and Festival in the Middle Ages (2001), p. 2.
53 Ibid., p. 95.
54 Ibid.
55 Ibid., p. 36.
56 Brusin, 'Brewing and Drinking', p. 60.
57 See, for example, Siobhán Geraghty, *Viking Dublin: Botanical Evidence from Fishamble Street* (Dublin: Royal Irish Academy, 1996).
58 Geraghty, *Viking Dublin*, pp. 48–9.
59 Mary A. Valente, 'Taxation, Tolls, and Tribute: The Language of Economics and Trade in Viking-Age Ireland', *Proceedings of the Harvard Celtic Colloquium*, 18/19 (1998/1999), p. 252.
60 Valente, 'Taxation', p. 252.
61 Ibid. p. 249.
62 Ibid., p. 247.
63 Ibid., p. 245.
64 Ibid., p. 246.
65 Locke, 'Heath-beer', p. 223.
66 Ward, 'Norse Drinking Customs', p. 3.
67 Dineley and Dineley, 'Where Did the Vikings Make Their Ale?', p. 1.

68 Else Roesdahl, *The Vikings* (London: Penguin Books, 1998), pp. 119–20.

69 Bellows, 'Hymiskvitha', p. 142.

70 Peter Tunstall (trans.), 'The Saga of Half and His Heroes' (2005), available on the Internet Archive Wayback Machine. <https://web.archive.org/web/20100908082818/http://www.oe.eclipse.co.uk/nom/Half.htm>

71 Additionally, this may also suggest that the Norse were fermenting ale using saliva. This isn't a radical or unique way to brew. For example, in medieval Peru, the Wari and Incan women chewed corn as part of the brewing process for creating chicha, a corn-based beer, which as a byproduct might have imbued the beer with yeast. In Japan, young women came together to chew rice to make a type of saki known as 'beautiful woman saki'. In a time when humans didn't know exactly how ale fermented, using saliva, which would be rich in natural yeasts and bacteria, was an ingenious way of fermenting ale, and one that has been used all over the world.

72 *Egil's Saga*, Ch. 31, translation my own.

73 Ibid., Ch. 61.

74 Ward, 'Norse Drinking Customs', p. 3.

75 William Morris and Eiríkr Magnússon (ed. and trans. 1892), 'Eyrbyggja Saga', on the Icelandic Saga Database, Ch. 54. <https://www.sagadb.org/eyrbyggja_saga.en>

76 See translations in Bernard Mees, 'Further Thoughts on the Tune Memorial', *Norsk Lingvistisk Tidsskrift*, Vol. 33 (2015), p. 49; Bernard Mees, 'Weaving Words: Law and Performance in Early Nordic Tradition', in Guus Kroonen, Erika Langbroek, Arend Quak and Annelies Roeleveld (eds.), *Amsterdamer Beiträge zur Älteren Germanistik*. Band 70 (Amsterdam, 2013), p. 136; and also translation by Terje Spurkland, *I begynnelsen var Futhark* (Oslo: Cappelen akademisk forlag, 2001). For more information on the stone, see Frans-Arne Stylegar, 'The Tune Stone and Its Archaeological Context'.

77 Mees, 'Weaving Words', p. 136.

78 Olof Sundquist, *An Arena for Higher Powers: Ceremonial Buildings and Religious Strategies for Rulership in Late Iron Age Scandinavia* (Leiden: Brill Academic Publishers, 2016), p. 482, translating and quoting Gulathingslov NGL 1, 14: '*er men verda dauder, oc vill ervingi ol efter gera*'. 'Men' in this case can also be translated as 'people'.

79 Muriel A.C. Press (1880 trans.), 'Laxdaela Saga', on Icelandic Saga Database, Ch. 4 <https://sagadb.org/laxdaela_saga.en>; George W. DaSent (1861 trans.), 'Njál's Saga', on Icelandic Saga Database, Ch. 107 <https://sagadb.org/brennu-njals_saga.en> For more information on bragafulls, minni and toasting rituals, see Charles Riseley, 'Ceremonial Drinking in the Viking Age', master's thesis (University of Oslo, 2014).

80 Sarah Semple, Alexandra Sanmark, Frode Iversen and Natascha Mehler, *Negotiating the North: Meeting-Places in the Middle Ages in the North Sea Zone*, The Society for Medieval Archaeology Monograph 41 (London: Routledge, 2020), p. 256.

81 Semple et al., *Negotiating the North*, p. 256.

82 Natascha Mehler, 'Þingvellir: A Place of Assembly and a Market', *Debating the Thing in the North: The Assembly Project II Journal of the North Atlantic*, Special Volume 8 (2015), p. 69.

83 Mehler, 'Þingvellir', p. 69 and p. 72.

84 '*Orms þáttr Stórólfssonar*' in Guðni Jónsson (ed.), *Íslendinga þættir* (Reykjavík: Sigurður Kristjánsson, 1935).

85 Mehler, 'Þingvellir', p. 72.

86 William Sayers, 'Serial Defamation in Two Medieval Tales: The Icelandic Ölkofra Þáttr and the Irish Scéla Mucce Meic Dathó', *Oral Tradition*, 6/1 (1991), p. 38.

87 Sayers, 'Serial Defamation', p. 46.

88 George A. Little, 'The Thingmote', *Dublin Historical Record*, 13/3–4 (1953), p. 66.

89 Semple et al., *Negotiating the North*, p. 257.

90 Clare Downham, 'The Viking Slave Trade: Entrepreneurs or Heathen Slavers', *History Ireland*, 17/3 (May–June 2009), p. 15.

91 Downham, 'Viking Slave Trade', p. 16.

92 Laurence M. Larson (trans.), *The Earliest Norwegian Laws: Being the Gulathing Law and the Frostathing Law* (New York: Columbia University Press, 1935), p. 335.

93 For more, see Christina Wade, 'Contextualising Gormlaith: Portrayals and Perceptions of Medieval Irish Queen', MPhil thesis (Trinity College Dublin, 2012).

94 James Henthorn Todd (ed., intro. and trans.), *Cogadh Gaedhel re Gallaibh = The war of the Gaedhil with the Gaill, or, The invasions of Ireland by the Danes and other Norsemen* (London, 1867), p. 226.

95 Neil Price, 'Bodylore and the Archaeology of Embedded Religion: Dramatic Licence in the Funerals of the Vikings', in David S. Whitley and Kelley Hays-Gilpin (eds.), *Belief in the Past: Theoretical Approaches to the Archaeology of Religion* (New York: Routledge, 2008), p. 147.

96 Neil Price, T*he Viking Way: Religion and War in Late Iron Age Scandinavia* (Uppsala: Uppsala University, Department of Archaeology and Ancient History, 2002), p. 64.

97 Anders Andrén, 'Behind Heathendom: Archaeological Studies of Old Norse Religion', *Scottish Archaeological Journal*, 27/2 (2005), p. 113.

98 Wade, 'Gendered Symbolism', pp. 167–8.

99 Ibid.

100 Translation is this author's own from '*Eiðsivaþingslov* I:24' in R. Keyser and P.A. Munch (eds.), *Norges gamle Love indtil* 1387 (Christiania, 1846), p. 383.

101 Ibid, pp. 168–9.

102 Ibid.

103 Arnold, 'Drinking the Feast', p. 87.

104 Price, *The Viking Way*, p. 347.

105   Michael Winkelman, 'Cross-cultural and Biogenetic Perspectives on the Origins of Shamanism', in David S. Whitley and Kelley Hays-Gilpin (eds.), *Belief in the Past: Theoretical Approaches to the Archaeology of Religion* (London: Routledge, 2008), pp. 43–66.

106   William Frazer, 'Description of a Great Sepulchral Mound at Aylesbury Road, near Donnybrook, in the County of Dublin, Containing Human and Animal Remains, as well as Some Objects of Antiquarian Interest, Referable to the Tenth or Eleventh Centuries', *Proceedings of the Royal Irish Academy: Polite Literature and Antiquities*, 2 (1879–1888), pp. 29–55.

107   Frazer, 'Description', pp. 32–3.

108   Ibid., p. 33 and pp. 48–9.

109   R.A. Hall, 'A Viking-age Grave at Donnybrook, County Dublin', *Medieval Archaeology*, 22/1 (1978), p. 64.

110   Paul Lunde and Caroline Stone (intro. and trans.), 'Introduction', in *Ibn Fadlan and the Land of Darkness: Arab Travellers in the Far North* (London: Penguin Classics, 2012), p. xiii.

111   Ibn Fadlan, 'Ibn Fadlan' in Paul Lund and Caroline Stone (intro. and trans.), *Ibn Fadlan and the Land of Darkness: Arab Travellers in the Far North* (London: Penguin Classics, 2012), p. 51.

112   Ibn Fadlan, 'Ibn Fadlan', p. 51.

113   Ibid., p. 53.

114   Ibid.

115   Ibid., p. 65.

116   Ibid.

117   Ibid.

118   Ibid., p. 67.

CHAPTER FOUR

1   If you aren't familiar with the phrase 'the Brits are at it again', see Colm Mac Gearailt, '"They're At It Again": The "English" in Irish Textbooks', *Public History Weekly*, 11 (2003), p. 5.

2   J.T. Gilbert, *Calendar of Ancient Records of Dublin, in the Possession of the Municipal Corporation of That City*, Vol. I (Dublin: J. Dollard, 1889), p. 166.

3   Henry F. Berry, 'Proceedings in the Matter of the Custom Called the Tolboll, 1308 and 1385 St. Thomas' Abbey v. Some Early Dublin Brewers', *Proceedings of the Royal Irish Academy: Archaeology, Culture, History, Literature*, 28 (1910), p. 172.

4   CIRCLE 6/8/1/49, 'Patent Roll 8 Richard II (1384–1385), Item 49', accessed on Virtual Record Treasury of Ireland. <https://virtualtreasury.ie/item/CIRCLE-6-8-1-49> Repository: CIRCLE: A Calendar of Irish Chancery Letters, 1244–1509.

5   CIRCLE 6/10/1/42, 'Patent Roll 10 Richard II (1386–1387), Item 42', accessed on Virtual Record Treasury of Ireland. <https://virtualtreasury.ie/item/CIRCLE-6-10-1-42> Repository: CIRCLE: A Calendar of Irish Chancery Letters, 1244–1509.

6 Paul Dryburgh and Brendan Smith (eds.), *Handbook and Select Calendar of Sources for Medieval Ireland in the National Archives of the United Kingdom* (Dublin: Four Courts Press, 2005), p. 260.

7 Berry, 'The Custom Called the Tolboll', p. 172.

8 Gilbert, *Calendar of Ancient Records of Dublin*, Vol. I, p. 181.

9 Ibid.

10 Berry, 'The Custom Called the Tolboll', p. 173.

11 Mary McMahon, Vincent G. Butler and J. Collins, 'Archaeological Excavations at Bridge Street Lower, Dublin', *Proceedings of the Royal Irish Academy: Archaeology, Culture, History, Literature*, 91C (1991), p. 42.

12 Gilbert, *Calendar of Ancient Records of Dublin*, Vol. I, p. 223.

13 Breandán Ó Ríordáin, 'Excavations at High Street and Winetavern Street, Dublin', *Medieval Archaeology*, 15 (1971), p. 75.

14 Ó Ríordáin, 'Excavations', p. 77.

15 Ibid., p. 78.

16 James Wright, *Historic Building Mythbusting: Uncovering Folklore, History, and Archaeology* (Cheltenham: The History Press, 2024).

17 Timothy Dawson, 'The Brazen Head Re-Visited', *Dublin Historical Record*, 26/2 (1973), p. 46.

18 Dawson, 'The Brazen Head Re-Visited', p. 43.

19 Henry F. Berry, 'House and Shop Signs in Dublin in the Seventeenth and Eighteenth Centuries', *Journal of the Royal Society of Antiquaries of Ireland*, 40/2 (1910), p. 86.

20 McMahon et al., 'Bridge Street', p. 42.

21 Ibid., p. 44.

22 Howard Clarke, *Medieval Dublin, c. 840–1540: The Medieval Town in the Modern City* (cartographic material), The Irish Historic Towns Atlas (Dublin: Royal Irish Academy, 2002).

23 McMahon et al., 'Bridge Street', p. 56.

24 Ibid.

25 Ibid., p. 62.

26 Ibid., p. 65.

27 Peter Clark, 'The Alehouse and Social Integration in English Towns (1500–1700)', in Maurice Garden and Yves Lequin (eds.), *Habiter La Ville* (Lyon: Presses Universitaires de Lyon, 1984), p. 225.

28 Clark, 'The Alehouse', pp. 226–7.

29 Ibid., p. 227.

30 Ibid., p. 225.

31 John Hare, 'Inns, Innkeepers, and the Society of Later Medieval England, 1350–1600', *Journal of Medieval History*, 39/4 (2013), pp. 480–1.

32 Hare, 'Inns', pp. 481–2.

33 'Satire' in Angela M. Lucas (ed.), *Anglo-Irish Poems of the Middle Ages: The Kildare Poems* (Dublin: The Columba Press, 1995).

34 H. Cameron Gillies (ed.), *Regimen Sanitatis: The Rule of Health, A Gaelic medical Manuscript of the early sixteenth Century or perhaps older from the Vade Mecum of the famous Macbeaths, physicians to the Lords of the Isles and*

the Kings of Scotland for several centuries (Glasgow: University Press, 1911), p. 35.

35 Gillies, *Regimen Sanitatis*, p. 35.

36 Ibid.

37 'Satire', in Lucas, *Anglo-Irish Poems of the Middle Ages*.

38 See, for example, Judith Bennett, *Ale, Beer, and Brewsters in England: Women's Work in a Changing World 1300–1600* (Oxford: Oxford University Press, 1996), especially Ch. 7; James Davis, *Medieval Market Morality: Life, Law and Ethics in the English Marketplace 1200–1500* (Cambridge: Cambridge University Press, 2011); and Christina Wade, *The Devil's in the Draught Lines: 1,000 Years of Women in Britain's Beer History* (St Albans: CAMRA Books, 2024).

39 'Satire', in Lucas, *Anglo-Irish Poems of the Middle Ages*.

40 Gilbert, *Calendar of Ancient Records of Dublin*, Vol. I, p. 224.

41 Ibid., p. 222.

42 Ibid., p. 220.

43 James Mills (ed), *Calendar of the Justiciary Rolls or the Proceedings of the Court of the Justiciar of Ireland, Preserved in the Public Record Office of Ireland*, Edward I, Part 2, Vol. 2 (Dublin, Alex Thom & Co., 1914).

44 Ibid., p. 134.

45 J.T. Graves, 'Ancient Corporation By-Laws', *Transactions of the Kilkenny Archaeological Society*, 1 (1849), p. 49.

46 Gillian Kenny, 'Anglo-Irish and Gaelic Women in Ireland c. 1277–1534: A Study of the Conditions and Rights of Single Women, Wives, Widows and Nuns in Late Medieval Ireland', PhD thesis (Trinity College Dublin, 2005), p. 86.

47 Ibid., pp. 86–7.

48 See Michelle M. Sauer, *Gender in Medieval Culture* (London: Bloomsbury, 2015); and Bennett, *Ale, Beer, and Brewsters in England*.

49 See Matthew Frank Stevens, 'Women Brewers in Fourteenth-Century Ruthin', *Denbighshire Historical Society Transactions*, 55 (2006).

50 Wade, *The Devil's in the Draught Lines*.

51 Berry, 'The Custom Called the Tolboll', p. 173.

52 James Mills (ed.), *Account Roll of the Priory of the Holy Trinity, Dublin, 1337–1346, With the Middle English Moral Play "The Pride of Life" from the Original in the Christ Church Collection in the Public Record Office* (Dublin: Royal Society of Antiquaries, 1891), p. 82.

53 Clarke, *Medieval Dublin*, map.

54 Kenny, 'Anglo-Irish and Gaelic Women in Ireland', p. 216.

55 Mills, *Account Roll*.

56 Ibid., p. xiv.

57 Ibid., p. 54, p. 82.

58 See, for example, https://www.sizes.com/units/crannock.htm, especially citations from John T. Gilbert, *Historic and Municipal Documents of Ireland, A.D. 1172–1320, from the Archives of the City of Dublin, etc.* (London: Longmans, Green & Co., 1870), pp. xxxiv–xxxv.

59 Mills, *Account Roll*, p. 62.

60 Ibid.

61 Ibid., p. 86.

62 Herbert Wood, Albert E. Langman and Margaret Griffith, *Calendar of the Justiciary Rolls or Proceedings in the Court of the Justiciar of Ireland I to VII Years of Edward II* (Dublin: Stationery Office, 1905), p. 86.

63 Wood et al., *Justiciary Rolls*, p. 383.

64 Mills, *Account Roll*, p. 70.

65 Ibid., p. 71.

66 Ibid., p. 74.

67 William Sayers, 'Brewing Ale in Walter of Bibbesworth's 13th C. French Treatise for English Housewives', *Studia Etymologica Cracoviensia*, 14 (2009), pp. 255–66.

68 See Martyn Cornell, 'How to Brew Like a Medieval Knight', 29 April 2021, *Zythophile*. <https://zythophile.co.uk/2021/04/29/how-to-brew-like-a-medieval-knight/>

69 Tofi Kerthjalfadsson, 'Recreating Medieval English Ales', 23 September to 28 December 1998, Carnegie Mellon University. <https://www.cs.cmu.edu/~pwp/tofi/medieval_english_ale.html>

70 Bennett, *Ale, Beer, and Brewsters in England*, p. 18 and p. 21.

71 Don't add any of these to anything, it will kill you!

72 Micheál Ó Conchubhair (ed. and trans.), *Materia Medica* (2018) on CELT: Corpus of Electronic Texts Edition, p. 535. <http://research.ucc.ie/celt/document/G600005>

73 Ibid., p. 498.

74 Ibid., p. 527.

75 Ibid., p. 501.

76 Ibid., p. 537.

77 Ibid., p. 567.

78 Ibid., p. 362.

79 Ibid., p. 826.

80 See Martyn Cornell, 'Herb and Flavoured Ales', in *Amber, Gold and Black: The History of Britain's Great Beers* (Cheltenham: The History Press, 2010), pp. 235–62.

81 Cornell, 'Herb and Flavoured Ales', p. 242.

82 Martyn Cornell, *Amber, Gold and Black: The History of Britain's Great Beers* (Cheltenham: The History Press, 2010), p. 238.

83 Translation is the author's own from the Latin in John Clyn and Thady Dowling, *The Annals of Ireland*, Richard Butler (ed.) (Dublin: Irish Archaeological Society, 1849), p. 37.

84 Bernadette Williams, 'The Annals of Friar John Clyn: Provenance and Bias', *Archivium Hibernicum*, 47 (1993), pp. 66–7.

85 Author's own translation of the Latin '*Videtur quod Author hic obit*' from Clyn and Dowling, *The Annals of Ireland*, p. 37, though some scholars like Williams believe it is possible he might have died later; see Williams, 'Clyn', pp. 71–2.

[201]

86 Clyn and Dowling, *The Annals of Ireland*, p. 36.
87 Maria Kelly, *A History of the Black Death in Ireland* (Stroud: Tempus, 2004), p. 35.
88 Translation author's own after: Geoffrey Le Baker and E. Maude Thompson (eds), *Chronicon Galfridi le Baker de Swynebroke* (London: Henry Frowde, 1889), p. 100.
89 Kelly, *Black Death*, p. 45, p. 42.
90 Ibid., p. 42, p. 33.
91 Ibid., p. 33.
92 Maria Kelly, '"Unheard-of Mortality"....The Black Death in Ireland', *History Ireland*, 9/4 (Winter 2001). <https://www.historyireland.com/unheard-of-mortality-the-black-death-in-ireland/>
93 See Sauer, *Gender in Medieval Culture*; and Kristen Burton, 'The Citie Calls for Beere: The Introduction of Hops and the Foundation of Industrial Brewing in London 1200–1700', MA thesis (Oklahoma State University, 2010).
94 Bennett, *Ale, Beer, and Brewsters in England*.
95 I wrote about this extensively in my book *The Devil's in The Draught Lines* if you want more details.
96 Kelly, 'Unheard-of Mortality'.
97 Ibid.
98 Ibid.

Chapter Five

1 H.F. Berry, *Register of Wills and Inventories of the Diocese of Dublin in the Time of Archbishops Tregury and Walton, 1457–1483: From the Original Manuscript in the Library of Trinity College, Dublin* (Dublin: University Press for the Royal Society of Antiquaries of Ireland, 1898), pp. 133–5.
2 J.T. Gilbert, *Calendar of Ancient Records of Dublin, in the Possession of the Municipal Corporation of That City*, Vol. I (Dublin: J. Dollard, 1889), p. 220.
3 Gilbert, *Calendar of Ancient Records of Dublin*, Vol. I, p. 288.
4 Ibid., p. 342, and see also further decrees on pp. 360, 364, 460.
5 See Judith Bennett, *Ale, Beer, and Brewsters in England: Women's Work in a Changing World 1300–1600* (New York: Oxford University Press, 1996), p. 47, p. 137, p. 147. See also Christina Wade, 'Rules, Regulations, and How to Blithely Ignore Them', in *The Devil's in the Draught Lines: 1,000 Years of Women in Britain's Beer History* (St Albans: CAMRA Books, 2024).
6 Ibid.
7 Gilbert, *Calendar of Ancient Records of Dublin*, Vol. I, p. 360.
8 Ibid.
9 Ibid.
10 Edmund Curtis (ed.), *Calendar of Ormond Deeds*, Vol. III: 1413–1509 AD (Dublin: Stationery Office, 1932): 'Council there Received from Johanna Gower 50 gallons (lagena) of ale; price of each gallon 1½ 5 shilling and 9

pence; Robert Talbot 54 gallons of ale; 1 pence the gallon; the same 54
ditto, at 1½ the gallon for 6 shillings and 3 pence; Isabella 51 gallons ditto
at 1½ for 5 shillings 9 pence. Matilda Lybbe 26 gallons of ale 1½ pence the
gallon. For a total of 3 shillings. John Lumbardc 44 gallons of ale 1½ 5
shillings and 6 pence.'

11 Berry, *Register of Wills and Inventories of the Diocese of Dublin*, p. 156.
12 Ibid., pp. 157–8.
13 Ibid., p. 64.
14 Ibid., p. 48.
15 Ibid., p. 206.
16 Owen Connellan, Esq. (trans. and ed.) (annot.), Philip Mac Dermott,
   Annals of Ireland, Translation from the Original Irish of the Four Masters
   (Dublin: Bryan Geraghty, 1846), p. 208.
17 Connellan, *Four Masters*, p. 103.
18 James Hardiman, Conor Thomond, Edmund Grace, Donogh O'Daly,
   Hugh O'Davoren, Hugh O'Finne, Nehemias O'Davoren and Donald Mac
   Gernasdir, 'Ancient Irish Deeds and Writings, Chiefly Relating to Landed
   Property, from the Twelfth to the Seventeenth Century, with Translations,
   Notes, and a Preliminary Essay', *The Transactions of the Royal Irish Academy*,
   15 (1828), p. 80.
19 Berry, *Register of Wills and Inventories of the Diocese of Dublin*, p. 103.
20 Ibid., p. 56.
21 Ibid., p. 5.
22 Greer Ramsey, 'A Breath of Fresh Air: Rectal Music in Gaelic Ireland',
   Archaeology Ireland, 16/1 (Spring 2002), pp. 22–3.
23 Ramsey, 'A Breath of Fresh Air', p. 22.
24 Sparky Booker, *Cultural Exchange and Identity in Late Medieval Ireland:
   The English and Irish of the Four Obedient Shires*, Cambridge Studies in
   Medieval Life and Thought 109 (Cambridge: Cambridge University Press,
   2018), p. 179.
25 Booker, *Cultural Exchange*, p. 179.
26 K.W. Nicholls, *Gaelic and Gaelicized Ireland in the Middle Ages* (Dublin:
   Lilliput Press, 2003), ebook.
27 Nicholls, *Gaelic Ireland*.
28 Booker, *Cultural Exchange*, p. 180, p. 182.
29 Katharine Simms, 'Guesting and Feasting in Gaelic Ireland', *Journal of the
   Royal Society of Antiquaries*, 108 (1978), p. 67.
30 Simms, 'Guesting', pp. 67–8.
31 Nicholls, *Gaelic Ireland*.
32 Ibid.
33 Simms, 'Guesting', p. 79.
34 Ibid., p. 80.
35 Ibid.
36 Nicholls, *Gaelic Ireland*.
37 Booker, *Cultural Exchange*, pp. 180–1.

38 Simms, 'Guesting', p. 71.
39 Laurent Vital (ed.), Dorothy Convery, *Archduke Ferdinand's Visit to Kinsale in Ireland, an Extract from Le Premier Voyage de Charles-Quint en Espagne, de 1517 à 1518* (Cork: CELT Project, 2012), p. 284. <https://celt.ucc.ie/published/T500000-001.html>
40 Jean Froissart, *The Chronicles of Froissart* (London: Macmillan, 1968), p. 410.
41 Froissart, *Chronicles*, p. 410.
42 Ibid.
43 CIRCLE 5/32/1/158, 'Patent Roll 32 Edward III (1358–1359), Item 158', accessed on Virtual Record Treasury of Ireland. <https://virtualtreasury.ie/item/CIRCLE-5-32-1-158> Repository: CIRCLE: A Calendar of Irish Chancery Letters, 1244–1509.
44 CIRCLE 3/31/1/100, 'Patent Roll 31 Edward I (1302–1303), Item 100', accessed on Virtual Record Treasury of Ireland. <https://virtualtreasury.ie/item/CIRCLE-3-31-1-100> Repository: CIRCLE: A Calendar of Irish Chancery Letters, 1244–1509.
45 CIRCLE 4/4/1/132, 'Patent Roll 4 Edward II (1310–1311), Item 132', accessed on Virtual Record Treasury of Ireland. <https://virtualtreasury.ie/item/CIRCLE-4-4-1-132> Repository: CIRCLE: A Calendar of Irish Chancery Letters, 1244–1509.
46 CIRCLE 4/4/1/132, 'Patent Roll 4 Edward II (1310–1311), Item 132'.
47 CIRCLE 5/49/1/257, 'Patent Roll 49 Edward III (1375–1376), Item 257', accessed on Virtual Record Treasury of Ireland. <https://virtualtreasury.ie/item/CIRCLE-5-49-1-257> Repository: CIRCLE: A Calendar of Irish Chancery Letters, 1244–1509.
48 See, for example, CIRCLE 5/49/1/259, 'Patent Roll 49 Edward III (1375–1376), Item 259', accessed on Virtual Record Treasury of Ireland. <https://virtualtreasury.ie/item/CIRCLE-5-49-1-259> Repository: CIRCLE: A Calendar of Irish Chancery Letters, 1244–1509.
49 CIRCLE 5/49/1/258, 'Patent Roll 49 Edward III (1375–1376), Item 258', accessed on Virtual Record Treasury of Ireland. <https://virtualtreasury.ie/item/CIRCLE-5-49-1-258> Repository: CIRCLE: A Calendar of Irish Chancery Letters, 1244–1509.
50 CIRCLE 6/17/1/1, 'Patent Roll 17 Richard II (1393–1394), Item 1', accessed on Virtual Record Treasury of Ireland. <https://virtualtreasury.ie/item/CIRCLE-6-17-1-1> Repository: CIRCLE: A Calendar of Irish Chancery Letters, 1244–1509.
51 CIRCLE 6/18/2/41, 'Close Roll 18 Richard II (1394–1395), Item 41', accessed on Virtual Record Treasury of Ireland. <https://virtualtreasury.ie/item/CIRCLE-6-18-2-41> Repository: CIRCLE: A Calendar of Irish Chancery Letters, 1244–1509.
52 CIRCLE 6/5/1/220, 'Patent Roll 5 Richard II (1381–1382), Item 220', accessed on Virtual Record Treasury of Ireland. <https://virtualtreasury.ie/item/CIRCLE-6-5-1-220> Repository: CIRCLE: A Calendar of Irish Chancery Letters, 1244–1509.

53 CIRCLE 7/9/1/28, 'Patent Roll 9 Henry IV (1407–1408), Item 28', accessed on Virtual Record Treasury of Ireland. <https://virtualtreasury.ie/item/CIRCLE-7-9-1-28> Repository: CIRCLE: A Calendar of Irish Chancery Letters, 1244–1509.

54 Curtis, *Calendar of Ormond Deeds*, Vol. III, p. 119.

55 CIRCLE 7/11/1/99, 'Patent Roll 11 Henry IV (1409–1410), Item 99', accessed on Virtual Record Treasury of Ireland. <https://virtualtreasury.ie/item/CIRCLE-7-11-1-99> Repository: CIRCLE: A Calendar of Irish Chancery Letters, 1244–1509.

56 CIRCLE 7/11/1/99, 'Patent Roll 11 Henry IV (1409–1410), Item 99'.

57 CIRCLE 6/15/1/14, 'Patent Roll 15 Richard II (1391–1392), Item 14', accessed on Virtual Record Treasury of Ireland. <https://virtualtreasury.ie/item/CIRCLE-6-15-1-14> Repository: CIRCLE: A Calendar of Irish Chancery Letters, 1244–1509.

58 Christine Casey, *Dublin: The City within the Grand and Royal Canals and the Circular Road with the Phoenix Park* (New Haven and London: Yale University Press, 2005), p. 348.

59 Charlie Taverner, and Susan Flavin, 'Food and Power in Sixteenth-Century Ireland: Studying Household Accounts from Dublin Castle', *The Historical Journal*, 66/1 (2023), online version.

60 Susan Flavin, Marc Meltonville, Charlie Taverner, Joshua Reid, Stephen Lawrence, Carlos Belloch-Molina and John Morrissey, 'Understanding Early Modern Beer: An Interdisciplinary Case-Study', *The Historical Journal*, 66/3 (2023) cf (citation from) Raymond Gillespie (ed.), *A History of Christ Church Dublin: The Proctor's Accounts of Peter Lewis 1564–1565* (Dublin: Four Courts Press, 1996).

61 William G. Neeley, *Kilkenny: An Urban History, 1391–1843* (Belfast: Institute of Irish Studies, Queen's University, 1989), p. 79.

62 Anon, 'Famous Kilkenny Pub Launches Its Own Locally-Brewed Beer!', *Kilkenny People*, 3 July 2023. <https://www.kilkennypeople.ie>

63 Andrew Sneddon, 'Witchcraft Belief and Trials in Early Modern Ireland', *Irish Economic and Social History*, 39 (2012), p. 1.

64 St John D. Seymour, *Irish Witchcraft and Demonology* (Dublin: Hodges, Figgis & Co., 1913), p. 4.

65 Seymour, *Irish Witchcraft*, p. 4.

66 Ibid., p. 78.

67 George Sinclair, *Satan's Invisible World Discovered, or, A choice collection of modern relations proving evidently against the saducees and atheists of this present age, that there are devils, spirits, witches, and apparitions, from authentick records, attestations of famous witnesses and undoubted verity: to all which is added, that marvellous history of Major Weir, and his sister: with two relations of apparitions at Edinburgh / by Georg Sinclar* (Edinburgh: Thomas George Stevenson, 1685), p. 261.

68 Sinclair, *Satan's Invisible World*, p. 261.

69 Ibid., p. 262.

70 Berry, *Register of Wills and Inventories of the Diocese of Dublin*, p. 86.
71 Ibid., pp. 148–9.
72 Sic: thee
73 Berry, *Register of Wills and Inventories of the Diocese of Dublin*, p. 218.
74 Katty Dalton and Willie Crowe, 'No title', dúchas.ie: The Schools' Collection, Volume 0903, page 099.

CHAPTER SIX

1 St John D. Seymour, *Irish Witchcraft and Demonology* (Dublin: Hodges, Figgis & Co., 1913), p. 100.
2 Seymour, *Irish Witchcraft*, p. 101.
3 Ibid., p. 102.
4 Ibid.
5 Ibid., p. 103.
6 Ibid.
7 Ibid.
8 Ibid., p. 104.
9 Ibid., pp. 100–1.
10 Barnabe Rich, *A new description of Ireland wherein is described the disposition of the Irish whereunto they are inclined. No lesse admirable to be perused then credible to be beleeved: neither unprofitable nor unpleasant to bee read and understood, by those worthy cittizens of London that be now undertakers in Ireland: by Barnabe Rich, Gent* (London: William Jaggard for Thomas Adams, 1610), p. 70.
11 Rich, *New Description*, p. 71.
12 See Judith Bennett, *Ale, Beer, and Brewsters in England: Women's Work in a Changing World 1300–1600* (New York: Oxford University Press, 1996); and Christina Wade, *The Devil's in the Draught Lines: 1,000 Years of Women in Britain's Beer History* (St Albans: CAMRA Books, 2024).
13 John T. Gilbert, *The Calendar of Ancient Records of Dublin in Possession of the Municipal Corporation of That City*, Vol. II (Dublin: J. Dollard, 1891), pp. 166–7.
14 Stephen Hewer, 'Free Gaelic People in English Ireland, c.1250–c.1327,' *History Ireland*, 23/6 (November/December 2015). <https://www.historyireland.com/free-gaelic-people-in-english-ireland-c-1250-c-1327/>
15 Gilbert, *Calendar of Ancient Records of Dublin*, Vol. II, p. 440.
16 Ibid.
17 Hannah Woolley, *The Queen-like Closet or Rich Cabinet stored with all manner of rare receipts for preserving, candying & cookery. Very Pleasant and beneficial to all ingenious persons of the female sex, by Hannah Woolley* (Printed for R. Lowndes at the White Lion in Duck-Lane, Near Smithfield, 1670). Hannah Woolley, *The Compleat Servant-maid; or, the young maidens tutor Directing them how they may fit, and qualifie themselves for any of these employments. Viz. Waiting woman, house-keeper, chamber-maid, cook-maid, under cook-maid, nursery-maid, dairy-maid, laundry-maid, house-maid,*

scullery-maid. Composed for the Great Benefit and advantage of all young maidens (T. Passinger, at the Three Bibles near London Bridge, 1677).

18 See Wade, *The Devil's in the Draught Lines*, Ch. 4.

19 Barnabe Rich, *A true and a kinde excuse written in defence of that booke, intituled A newe description of Irelande Wherein is freely confessed 1 The cause of the writing of that booke. 2 How that booke was brought into obloquy and slander 3 A revocation of all oversightes that through ignorance were published in that booke. 4 A bulwarke or defence of all truthes contayned in that booke. Pleasant and pleasing both to English, and Irish. By Barnabe Rych, Gent. Servant to the Kinges most excellent Maiestie* (London: Thomas Dawson for Thomas Adams, 1612), p. 12.

20 Rich, *New Description*, p. 72.

21 Robert Payne, Aquilla Smith (ed.), *A Briefe Description of Ireland: made in this year 1589, By Robert Payne vnto xxv. of his partners for whom he is undertaker there. Truely published verbatim, according to his letters, by Nich. Gorsan, one of the said partners, for that he would his countrymen should be partakers of the many good Notes therein conteined. With diuers Notes taken out of others the Authoures letters written to his said partners, sithenes the first Impression, well worth the reading.* in *Tracts Relating to Ireland, printed for the Irish Archaeological Society* (Graisberry: University Press and Dublin: Gill, 1841), p. 6.

22 Rich, *New Description*, p. 72.

23 Ibid., p. 74.

24 Ibid.

25 Ibid., p. 70.

26 Ibid., pp. 73–4, p. 72.

27 Ibid.

28 Susan Flavin, *Consumption and Culture in Sixteenth-Century Ireland* (Suffolk: Boydell Press, 2014), p. 228.

29 William Palmer, 'Gender, Violence, and Rebellion in Tudor Early Stuart Ireland', *The Sixteenth Century Journal*, 23 (1992), pp. 699–712, p. 699.

30 Bennett, *Ale, Beer, and Brewsters in England*, pp. 142–3. See also Wade, *The Devil's in the Draught Lines*, Ch. 5.

31 N.J. Byrne, *The Great Parchment Book of Waterford: Liber Antiquissimus Civitatis Waterfordiae* (Dublin: Irish Manuscripts Commission, 2007), p. 211.

32 Ibid., pp. 38–9.

33 Ibid., pp. 186–90.

34 Ibid., p. 190.

35 John T. Gilbert, *Calendar of Ancient Records of Dublin in Possession of the Municipal Corporation of That City,* Vol. III (Dublin: J. Dollard, 1892), p. 69.

36 Ibid., p. 72.

37 Rich, *New Description*, p. 73.

38 Rich, *A True and Kinde Excuse*, p. 14.

39 Ibid., p. 16.

40 Barnabe Rich, *Irish Hubbub or the English Hue and Crie briefly pursuing the base conditions, and most notorious offences of the vile, vaine, and wicked age, no lesse smarting then tickling: a merriment whereby to make the wise to laugh, and fooles to be angry* (London: J. Marriot, 1617), pp. 16–17.

41 Owen Connellan, Esq. (trans. and ed.), (annot.) Philip Mac Dermott, *Annals of Ireland, Translation from the Original Irish of the Four Masters* (Dublin: Bryan Geraghty, 1846), p. 575.

42 Connellan, *Four Masters*, p. 575.

43 John Ainsworth, *The Inchiquin Manuscripts* (Dublin: Stationery Office for the Irish Manuscripts Commission, 1961), p. 47.

44 Ainsworth, *Inchiquin Manuscripts*, p. 47.

45 Ibid., p. 35.

46 Ibid., p. 470.

47 Connellan, *Four Masters*, p. 637.

48 Ibid., p. 637.

49 Ibid.

50 Fynes Moryson, 'The Itinerary of Fynes Moryson', in Caesar Litton Falkiner (ed.), *Illustrations of Irish History and Topography, mainly of the seventeenth century* (London: Longmans, Green and Co., 1904), p. 227.

51 Moryson, 'The Itinerary', p. 227.

52 Ibid., p. 226.

53 William Lithgow, *The Totall Discourse of the Rare Adventures & Painefull Peregrinations* (Glasgow: James MacLehose & Sons, 1906), p. 412.

54 Lithgow, *Rare Adventures*, p. 411.

55 Luke Gernon, 'A Discourse of Ireland, Anno 1620', in C. Litton Falkiner (ed.), *Illustrations of Irish History and Topography, Mainly of the Seventeenth Century* (London: Longmans, Green & Co., 1904), p. 359.

56 Gernon, 'A Discourse', pp. 360–1.

57 William Brereton, 'Travels of William Brereton in Ireland, 1635', in C. Litton Falkiner (ed.), *Illustrations of Irish History and Topography, Mainly of the Seventeenth Century* (London: Longmans, Green & Co., 1904), pp. 388–9.

58 Brereton, 'Travels', p. 397.

59 Ibid.

60 Jonathan Bardon, *The Plantation of Ulster: The Colonisation of the North of Ireland in the 17th Century* (Dublin: Gill & Macmillan, 2011), p. 272.

61 Henry Berry, 'House and Shop Signs in Dublin in the Seventeenth and Eighteenth Centuries', *Journal of the Royal Society of Antiquaries of Ireland*, 40/2 (1910), p. 97.

62 'Examination of Charles Kinsalagh', 2 November 1641, MS 809, fols 075r-076v.

63 Ibid.

64 Aidan Clarke, 'The Genesis of the Ulster Rising', in Peter Roebuck (ed.), *Plantation to Partition: Essays in Honour of J.L. McCracken* (Belfast: Blackstaff Press, 1981).

65 Pádraig Lenihan, *Confederate Catholics at War, 1641–49* (Cork: Cork University Press, 2001), p. 7.

66 Jeremy Black, *Kings, Nobles, & Commoners: States & Societies in Early Modern Europe, a Revisionist History* (New York: I.B. Tauris & Co., 2004), p. 106.

67 M. Perceval-Maxwell, *The Outbreak of the Irish Rebellion of 1641* (Montreal and Kingston: McGill-Queen's University Press, 1994), p. 46.

68 Jane Ohlmeyer, *Making Ireland English: The Irish Aristocracy in the Seventeenth Century* (New Haven: Yale University Press, 2012), pp. 257–9.

69 Bardon, *Plantation of Ulster*, p. 275.

70 Nicholas Canny, *Making Ireland British 1580–1650* (New York and Oxford: Oxford University Press, 2001), p. 476.

71 'Why Are the Depositions Important?', *1641 Depositions*, n.d. <https://1641.tcd.ie/index.php/about-why/ https://www.historyireland.com/the-most-controversial-documents-in-irish-history/>

72 Bardon, *Plantation of Ulster*, p. 277.

73 Ibid.

74 Canny, *Making Ireland British*, p. 468.

75 'Deposition of Reynold and Elizabeth Griffith', 1 January 1642, MS 836, fols 006r-006v.

76 'Examination of Sir Baptist Staples', 18 April 1653, MS 839, fols 074r-075v.

77 Thomas Lee, *The Discovery and Recovery of Ireland with the Author's Apology*, Corpus of Electronic Texts (2009), no page numbers.

78 'Information of Richard Ashbould', 27 May 1642, MS 813, fols 049r-050r.

79 'Letter by William Smyth', 11 March 1645, MS 818, fols 150r-151v.

80 'Examination of George Devenish', 24 March 1642, MS 816, fols 031r-033v.

81 'Deposition of Richard Oburne', 17 August 1642, MS 820, fols 037r-037v.

82   'Deposition of Hugh Madden', 2 February 1642, MS 811, fols 074r-074v.

83 'Deposition of Phillipa Henda', 25 October 1642, MS 811, fols 145r-146v.

84 'Deposition of Helenor Adshed', 20 August 1642, MS 831, fols 033r-033v.

85 'Deposition of Jane Steward', 16 May 1653, MS 831, fols 120r-121v.

86 'Deposition of Margarett Hall', 28 April 1642, MS 811, fols 144r-144v.

87 'Deposition of Maudlin Fisher', 21 January 1642, MS 816, fols 161r-161v.

88 'Deposition of Margery Grey', undated, MS 831, fols 222r-224v.

89 'Examination of Christopher Wolverston', 23 December 1641, MS 811, fol 128r.

90 'Deposition of Robert Boyle', 1 March, 1642, MS 834, fols 098r-099v.

91 'Deposition of Hugh Culme', 25 January 1642, MS 834, fols 112r-112v.

92 Libraries and Archive: Dublin Directory 1647–1706.

93 Christina Wade, 'Reclaiming Their Rightful Place?: An Analysis of the Links between Medieval and Early Modern Female Brewers and Consumers in Ireland with Their Modern Counterparts', *Journal of Franco-Irish Studies*, 6/1 (2019), Article 6.

94 John T. Gilbert, *Calendar of Ancient Records of Dublin, in the Possession of the Municipal Corporation of That City*, Vol. V (Dublin: J. Dollard, 1895), p. 32.

95 'Index', in Gilbert, *Calendar of Ancient Records of Dublin*, Vol. V, p. 114; see also John T. Gilbert, *Calendar of Ancient Records of Dublin, in the Possession of the Municipal Corporation of That City*, Vol. IV (Dublin: J. Dollard, 1894), p. 611.

96 Gilbert, *Calendar of Ancient Records of Dublin*, Vol. V, p. 616.

CHAPTER SEVEN

1 Peg Plunkett, *Memoirs of Mrs Margaret Leeson* (Ex-classics Project, 2016), p. 112. <https://www.exclassics.com/plunkett/peg.pdf>

2 Samuel Morewood, *A philosophical and statistical history of the inventions and customs of ancient and modern nations in the manufacture and use of inebriating liquors. With the present practice of distillation, etc.* 2nd edn. (William Curry, Jun and Company, and William Carson, Dublin, 1838).

3 Morewood, *A philosophical and statistical history*, p. 625.

4 Cormac Ó Gráda, 'The Population of Ireland 1700–1900: A Survey', *Annales de Démographie Historique* (1979), p. 283.

5 K.H. Connell, 'The Population of Ireland in the Eighteenth Century', *Economic History Review*, 16/2 (1946), p. 111.

6 Ó Gráda, 'The Population of Ireland', p. 283.

7 Caen Harris, 'The Irish Brewing Industry, c. 1780–1930: An Archaeology', PhD thesis (University College Cork, 2020), p. 28.

8 Morewood, *A philosophical and statistical history*, pp. 625–6.

9 Andrew Malone, 'A Great Irish Industry: Messrs. Arthur Guinness, Son & Co: I. The History of the Industry', *Studies: An Irish Quarterly Review*, 15/59 (September 1962), pp. 441–53.

10 'The Hell Fire Club', n.d. *Ask About Ireland*. <https://www.askaboutireland.ie/reading-room/life-society/irish-language-legends/myths-and-legends-of-sout/myths-and-legends-in-engl/the-hell-fire-club/>

11 Malone, 'A Great Irish Industry', p. 445.

12 Henry Grattan (ed.) and Daniel Owen Madden (Esq.), *The Speeches of the Right Hon. Henry Grattan: To Which Is Added His Letter on the Union, with a Commentary on His Career and Character*, Vol. 2 (Dublin: James Duffy, 1854), p. 166.

13 Grattan and Madden, *The Speeches of the Right Hon. Henry Grattan*, p. 166.

14 Ibid. pp. 166–7.

15 Ibid., p. 165.

16 Ibid., p. 183.

17 Ibid.

18 Ibid.

19 John T. Gilbert, *Calendar of Ancient Records of Dublin, in the Possession of the Municipal Corporation of That City*, Vol. IV (Dublin: J. Dollard, 1894), pp. 278–9.

20 Gilbert, *Calendar of Ancient Records of Dublin*, Vol. IV, pp. 278–9.

21 Lady Gilbert, *Calendar of Ancient Records of Dublin, in the Possession of the Municipal Corporation of That City*, Vol. XII (Dublin: Dollard Ltd, 1905), p. 204.

22 Lady Gilbert, *Calendar of Ancient Records of Dublin*, Vol. XII, p. 204.

23 Ibid., pp. 372–4.

24 Ibid.

25 Ibid., pp. 373–4.

26 Ibid.

27 Lady Gilbert, *Calendar of Ancient Records of Dublin, in the Possession of the Municipal Corporation of That City*, Vol. XIII (Dublin: Dollard, 1907), pp. 375–6.

28 John T. Gilbert, *Calendar of Ancient Records of Dublin, in the Possession of the Municipal Corporation of That City*, Vol. VI (Dublin: J. Dollard, 1896), p. 318.

29 Lady Gilbert, *Calendar of Ancient Records of Dublin, in the Possession of the Municipal Corporation of That City*, Vol. X (Dublin: J. Dollard, 1903), p. 30.

30 Lady Gilbert, *Calendar of Ancient Records of Dublin*, Vol. XIII, p. 17.

31 Lady Gilbert, *Calendar of Ancient Records of Dublin*, Vol. XII, pp. 488–9.

32 Ibid., p. 433.

33 Ibid.

34 Morewood, *A philosophical and statistical history*, p. 625.

35 'No Title', *Freeman's Journal*, 2 November 1793. <https://archive.irishnewsarchive.com/olive/APA/INA/SharedView.Article.aspx?href=F-MJ%2F1793%2F11%2F02&id=Ar00406&sk=EBACD3CD&viewMode=image>

36 Peter Mathias, *The Brewing Industry in England 1700–1830* (Cambridge: Cambridge University Press, 1959), p. 159.

37 Alfred Barnard, 'Phoenix Porter Brewery Co.', in *The Noted Breweries of Great Britain and Ireland*, Vol. I (London: Sir Joseph Causton & Sons, 1889), p. 71.

38 Barnard, 'Phoenix Porter Brewery Co.', p. 71.

39 Plunkett, *Memoirs of Mrs Margaret Leeson*, p. 112.

40 'Ralph Card', *Volunteers Journal or Irish Herald*, 21 June 1784. <https://archive.irishnewsarchive.com/olive/APA/INA/SharedView.Article.aspx?href=VJIH%2F1784%2F06%2F21&id=Ar00411&sk=F533E5DB&viewMode=image>

41 'Samuel Brown', *Belfast Newsletter*, 18 January 1785. <https://archive.irishnewsarchive.com/olive/APA/INA/SharedView.Article.aspx?href=B-NL%2F1785%2F01%2F18&id=Ar00107&sk=89EE1D06&viewMode=image>

42 'Irish Porter', *Dublin Evening Post*, 15 July 1779. <https://www.british-newspaperarchive.co.uk>

43 'Irish Porter', *Saunders's News-Letter*, 4 November 1776. <https://www.britishnewspaperarchive.co.uk/>

44 'Irish Porter', *Hibernian Journal, or Chronicle of Liberty Friday*, 18 August 1775. <https://www.britishnewspaperarchive.co.uk/>

45 'William Shaw Lurgan', *Belfast Newsletter*, 4 February 1785. <https://archive.irishnewsarchive.com/olive/APA/INA/SharedView.Article.aspx?href=BNL%2F1785%2F02%2F04&id=Ar00104&sk=64334D-3D&viewMode=image>

46 'Irish Porter', *Belfast Newsletter*, 27 September 1785. <https://archive.irishnewsarchive.com/olive/APA/INA/SharedView.Article.aspx?href=BNL%2F1785%2F09%2F27&id=Ar00300&sk=3011417E&viewMode=image>

47 'To the COMMITTEE for conducting the FREE-PRESS', *Freeman's Journal*, 2 September 1779. <https://archive.irishnewsarchive.com/olive/APA/INA/SharedView.Article.aspx?href=FMJ%2F1779%2F09%2F02&id=Ar00400&sk=74011278&viewMode=image>

48 'To the Committee', *Freeman's Journal*, 2 September 1779.

49 'Porter Brewery in Usher-Street', *Saunders's News-Letter*, 7 April 1785. <https://www.britishnewspaperarchive.co.uk/>

50 'James Sweetman', *Cess Records 1647–1648*. Unfortunately, this digital resource is no longer available online.

51 Seán Magee, 'Sweetman Breweries in Eighteenth-century Dublin', *Dublin Historical Record*, 68/1 (Spring/Summer 2015), p. 113.

52 Magee, 'Sweetman Breweries', p. 113.

53 Ibid.

54 Ibid., p.115.

55 'Deed No. 35959', *Transcripts of memorials of deeds, conveyances and wills, 1708–1929*, Registry of Deeds, Book 55, p. 79.

56 'Deed No. 30148', *Transcripts of memorials of deeds, conveyances and wills, 1708–1929*, Registry of Deeds, Book 44, p. 468.

57 'Deed No. 12748', *Transcripts of memorials of deeds, conveyances and wills, 1708–1929*, Registry of Deeds, Book 22, p. 528.

58 'Deed No. 18317', *Transcripts of memorials of deeds, conveyances and wills, 1708–1929*, Registry of Deeds, Book 31, p. 102.

59 Deed No. 21983', *Transcripts of memorials of deeds, conveyances and wills, 1708–1929*, Registry of Deeds, Book, 35, p. 203.

60 *The treble almanack for the year MDCCXCIV. Containing I. Watson's Irish almanack, II. Exshaw's English court registry, III. Wilson's Dublin directory, with a new correct plan of the city. Forming the most complete lists published of the present civil, military, and naval establishments of Great Britain and Ireland* (Dublin: W. Wilson, 1794), p. 82.

61 Peter Wilson, *Wilson's Directory for the YEAR 1768. Containing Alphabetical LISTS of Names, Occupations, and Places of Abode, of the MERCHANTS and TRADERS of the City of DUBLIN, divided under separate and distinct heads* (Dublin: Peter Wilson, 1768), pp. 16–17.

62 'Mary Farrel, Plaintiff. Margaret Plunkett, Defendant. Mary Byrne, Plaintiff. Margaret Plunkett, Defendant', *Saunders's News-Letter*, 26 April 1773. <https://www.britishnewspaperarchive.co.uk/>

63 'Married', *Belfast Newsletter*, 12 January 1768, p. 2. <https://archive.irishnewsarchive.com>

64 *The treble almanack for the year MDCCXCIV*, p. 31.

65 'Married', *Freeman's Journal*, 4 July 1782, p. 4. <https://archive.irishnewsar-chive.com>

66 Peter Wilson, *Wilson's Directory for the YEAR 1780. Containing Alphabeti-cal LISTS of Names, Occupations, and Places of Abode, of the MER-CHANTS and TRADERS of the City of DUBLIN, divided under separate and distinct heads* (Dublin: Peter Wilson, 1780), p. 75.

67 Michael Seery, 'The Eighteenth Century: Crooked Staff', *Wide and Convenient Streets* [website], 25 February 2014. <https://wideandconven-ientstreets.wordpress.com/page/5/#:~:text=The%20Eighteenth%20 Century%3A%20Crooked%20Staff&text=Drawn%20in%20 1749%2C%20it%20is,to%20a%20document%20from%201669>

68 Brewery History Society, 'Joseph Watkins & Co.', *BreweryPedia*. <http:// breweryhistory.com/wiki/index.php?title=Joseph_Watkins_%26_Co>

69 'Private Sources at the National Archives: Pembroke Estate Papers', National Archives. <https://www.nationalarchives.ie/topics/Pembroke/Pembro-keEstatePapers.pdf>

70 'A Brewery', *Saunders's News-Letter*, 8 April 1784. <https://www.britishnewspaperarchive.co.uk/>

71 William Wilson, *Wilson's Dublin Directory for the YEAR 1800* (Dublin: William Wilson, 1800), p. 24.

72 'Ardee Point Student Accommodation and Co-Working Site at Newmarket, Ardee Street and Brabazon Row Dublin, 8', *Conservation Assessment*, 28 August 2019, National Library of Ireland, Longfield Collection, map 21-F-88 no. 124. <https://planningapplication.s3.eu-west-1.amazonaws.com/projects/1003/documents/Conservation%20Assessment.pdf>

73 'No title', *Belfast Newsletter*, 24 March 1761. <https://archive.irishnewsar-chive.com/olive/APA/INA/SharedView.Article.aspx?href=BN-L%2F1761%2F03%2F24&id=Ar00303&sk=BC74DBE2&view-Mode=image>

74 Bishop Edward Synge (ed.), Marie-Louise Legg, *The Synge Letters: Bishop Edward Synge to His Daughter Alicia, Roscommon to Dublin 1746–1752* (Dublin: Lilliput Press, 1997), ebook, p. 292.

75 Synge, *The Synge Letters*, pp. 293–4.

76 Ibid., pp. 472–4.

77 Tara McConnell, '"Brew as much as possible in the proper season": Beer Consumption in Elite Households in Eighteenth Century Ireland', in Máirtín Mac Con Iomaire and Eamon Maher (eds.), *'Tickling the Palate': Gastronomy in Irish Literature and Culture* (Oxford: Peter Lang, 2014), p. 177, p. 180.

78 James Kelly, 'The Consumption and Sociable Use of Alcohol in Eighteenth-Century Ireland', *Proceedings of the Royal Irish Academy: Archaeology, Culture, History, Literature,* 115C (2015), p. 226.

79 Kelly, 'The Consumption', p. 226.

80 McConnell, 'Beer Consumption', p. 182.

81 Madeline Shanahan, "'Whipt with a twig rod": Irish manuscript recipe
    books as sources for the study of culinary material culture, c. 1660 to 1830',
    *Proceedings of the Royal Irish Academy: Archaeology, Culture, History,
    Literature,* 115C (2015), p. 204.
82 Jennifer Nutall née Alexander, 'Introduction', in Hannah Alexander (ed.),
    Deirdre Nutall (intro.), *A Book of Cookery for dressing of Several Dishes of
    Meat and making of Several Sauces and Seasonings for Meat or Fowl*
    (Dundee: Evertype, 2014), pp. xix–xx.
83 Hannah Alexander (ed.), Deirdre Nutall, (intro), *A Book of Cookery for
    dressing of Several Dishes of Meat and making of Several Sauces and
    Seasonings for Meat or Fowl* (Dundee: Evertype, 2014), p. 50.
84 Alexander, *A Book of Cookery*, pp. 47–55.
85 Ibid., p. 159, p. 145, p. 116.
86 Marjorie Quarton, *Mary Cannon's Commonplace Book: An Irish Kitchen in
    the 1700s* (Dublin: Lilliput Press, 2010), p. 84.
87 Dorothy Cashman, 'An Investigation of Irish Culinary History through
    Manuscript Cookbooks, with Particular Reference to the Gentry of County
    Kilkenny (1714–1830)', PhD thesis (Technological University Dublin,
    2016).
88 Monica Nevin, 'A County Kilkenny Georgian Household Notebook',
    Journal of the Royal Society of Antiquaries of Ireland, 109 (1979), p. 9.
89 Melesina Chenevix St George Trench (ed.), Richard Chevenix Trench, *The
    Remains of the Late Mrs. Richard Trench, being Selections from her Journals,
    Letters & Other Papers, Edited by her son, The Dean of Westminster,* 2nd
    edn. (London: Parker, Son, & Bourn, 1862), p. 129.

CHAPTER EIGHT
1 Dorothy Cashman, "'The Cholera Manuscript": A Collection of Recipes
   and Cures from Co Limerick', *The Recipe Project,* 11 October 2018.
   <https://recipes.hypotheses.org/category/networks/page/2#_edn1>
2 Cashman, 'The Cholera Manuscript', *The Recipes Project.*
3 Christina Wade, *The Devil's in the Draught Lines: 1,000 Years of Women in
   Britain's Beer History* (St Albans: CAMRA Books, 2024).
4 Unknown, *Receipt Book* [recipe book], (1811), National Library of Ireland,
   Department of Manuscripts. <https://catalogue.nli.ie/Record/
   vtls000359182>
5 Emphasis mine. Transcription my own.
6 Let's say you need on average 3 litres of water for every kilogram of grain. In
   a 1-litre kettle, a handful of grain is somewhere between 30–60 grams,
   which is still very low – it should be around 330 grams. So this probably
   only made a weak ale.
7 Cashman, 'The Cholera Manuscript', *The Recipes Project.*
8 William Tighe, *Statistical Observations Relative to the County of Kilkenny,
   Made in the Years 1800 & 1801* (Dublin: Graisberry & Campbell, 1802),
   p. 468.

9 Tighe, *Statistical Observations Relative to the County of Kilkenny*, p. 473.
10 Ibid., p. 474.
11 Ibid., p. 494.
12 Ibid., p. 474.
13 Ibid., p. 483.
14 Ibid., p. 504.
15 Hely Dutton, *Statistical Survey of the County of Clare with Observations on the Means of Improvement Drawn up for the Consideration and by Direction of the Dublin Society* (Dublin: Graisberry & Campbell, 1808), p. 177.
16 Dutton, *Statistical Survey of the County of Clare*, p. 205.
17 Ibid., p. 206.
18 Ibid.
19 Ibid.
20 Ibid., p. 207.
21 Hely Dutton, *A Statistical and Agricultural Survey of the County of Galway with Observations on the Means of Improvement; Drawn up for the Consideration, and by the Direction of the Royal Dublin Society* (Dublin: The University Press, 1824), p. 340.
22 Dutton, *A Statistical and Agricultural Survey of the County of Galway*, p. 353.
23 Ibid., p. 366.
24 Ibid.
25 Ibid., p. 367.
26 Ibid.
27 'The O'Connell Brewery', *Waterford Mail*, 23 October 1833. <https://www.britishnewspaperarchive.co.uk>
28 'O'Connell Brewery, Watling Street, Dublin', *Southern Reporter and Cork Commercial Courier*, 26 April 1834. <https://www.britishnewspaperarchive.co.uk>
29 'The O'Connell Brewery', *Waterford Mail*, 23 October 1833. <https://www.britishnewspaperarchive.co.uk>
30 Paul Pry, 'Meeting of the Weeklies', *Newry Telegraph*, 2 January 1829. <https://www.britishnewspaperarchive.co.uk>
31 In contrast to the failed directive of Exclusive Dealings.
32 'Petition of John Alley junior, Dublin, requesting employment in revenue department', 6 June 1819, National Archives of Ireland, *Chief Secretary's Office Registered Papers*, NAI CSO/RP/1819/26.
33 'J Wilkinson, County Limerick: for appointment of husband to post of inspector of stamps in County Galway', 15 August 1820, National Archives of Ireland, *Chief Secretary's Office Registered Papers*, NAI CSO/RP/1820/1362.
34 'Letter from Major Thomas Powell, County Dublin, inspector general of the Leinster constabulary, concerning sectarian divisions in the town of Mountmellick over the presence of orange flags', National Archives of Ireland, *Chief Secretary's Office Registered Papers*, NAI CSO/RP/SC/1825/319.

35 'Letter from Henry Smyth, Mount Henry, Queen's County, reflecting upon efforts to placate divisions between those of the Roman Catholic and orange parties in the town of Mountmellick', 3 September 1824–25, National Archives of Ireland, *Chief Secretary's Office Registered Papers*, CSO/RP/SC/1825/449

36 'Memorial of an Indenture Deasy to Donovan', in *Registry of Deeds, Transcripts of memorial of deeds, conveyances, and wills, 1708–1929*, Book 27, No. 299.

37 'O'Connell Tribute for 1841', *Southern Reporter and Cork Commercial Courier*, 10 September 1842. <https://www.britishnewspaperarchive. co.uk>

38 'Repeal! Repeal! Repeal! Skibbereen. Men of the Baronies of the Carberies, and of the Adjacent Baronies', *Cork Examiner*, 19 June 1843. <https:// www.britishnewspaperarchive.co.uk>

39 Andy Bielenberg, *Ireland and the Industrial Revolution: The Impact of the Industrial Revolution on Irish Industry, 1801–1922* (London: Routledge, 2009), p. 29.

40 Samuel Lewis, 'Newtown-Ardes', in *A Topographical Dictionary of Ireland* (London: S. Lewis, 1837), ebook. <https://www.libraryireland.com/ topog/N/Newtown-Ardes-Ardes-Down.php>

41 Samuel Lewis, 'Donaghmore', 'Templemore', 'Limerick City', 'Strabane', 'Magherafelt', 'Newcastle', 'New Ross', in *A Topographical Dictionary of Ireland* (London: S. Lewis, 1837), ebook. <https://www.libraryireland. com/topog/placeindex.php>

42 J. Lee, 'Money and Beer In Ireland, 1790–1875, Part I', *Economic History Review*, New Series, 19/1 (1966) pp. 187–9; and Patrick Lynch and John Vaizey, 'Money and Beer In Ireland, 1790–1875, Part II', *Economic History Review*, New Series, 19/1 (1966), pp. 190–2.

43 Bielenberg, *Ireland and the Industrial Revolution*, p. 29.

44 Liam Kennedy, Donald M. MacRaild, Lewis Darwen and Brian Gurrin, *The Death Census of Black '47: Eyewitness Accounts of Ireland's Great Famine* (London: Anthem Press, 2023), p. 12.

45 John Crowley, William J. Smyth and Mike Murphy (eds.), *The Atlas of the Great Irish Famine, 1845–52* (Cork: Cork University Press, 2012).

46 William J. Smyth, 'The Longue Durée: Imperial Britain and Colonial Ireland', in Crowley et al., *The Atlas of the Great Irish Famine*, p. 46.

47 Peter Gray, 'British Relief Measures', in Crowley et al., *The Atlas of the Great Irish Famine*, p. 75.

48 Gray, 'British Relief Measures', p. 75.

49 Smyth, 'The Longue Durée', p. 55.

50 Ibid., p. 53, p. 63.

51 David Nally, 'Colonial Dimensions of the Great Irish Famine', in Crowley et al., *The Atlas of the Great Irish Famine*, p. 64.

52 Nally, 'Colonial Dimensions of the Great Irish Famine', p. 65.

53 Ibid., p. 66.

54 Bielenberg, *Ireland and the Industrial Revolution*, p. 32.

55 Patrick Lynch and John Vaizey, *Guinness's Brewery in the Irish Economy, 1759–1876* (Cambridge: Cambridge University Press, 1960), p. 9.

56 Lynch and Vaizey, *Guinness's Brewery in the Irish Economy*, p. 200.

57 Lee, 'Money and Beer in Ireland, Part I', pp. 183–4.

58 Ibid., p. 184.

59 Ibid.

60 Ibid., p. 185.

61 Ibid., p. 186 (citing Lynch and Vaziey, *Guinness's Brewery in the Irish Economy*, p. 80).

62 Lynch and Vaizey, 'Money and Beer in Ireland, Part II', p. 190.

63 'Death of Mr. Thomas Deasy', *Morning Advertiser*, 21 November 1849. <https://www.britishnewspaperarchive.co.uk>

64 'Fatal Accident', *Cork Examiner*, 19 November 1849. <https://www.britishnewspaperarchive.co.uk>

65 'Indenture of Assignment 1876', *Registry of Deeds, transcripts of memorials of deeds, conveyances, and wills, 1708–1929*, Book 52, No. 103; 'Deasy and Co. to Robert Travers 1889', ibid, Book 3 No. 292

66 'Statuable Mortgage, Catherine Fitzgerald to Munster Bank, 1885', in Registry of Deeds, *Transcripts of memorials of deeds, conveyances and wills, 1708–1929*, Book 10, No. 218.

67 'Indenture of Settlement, Johanna Hurley to Francis Hurley, 1870', in Registry of Deeds, *Transcripts of memorials of deeds, conveyances and wills, 1708–1929*, Book 19, No. 114.

68 'Indenture of Settlement, Johanna Hurley to Francis Hurley, 1870'.

69 'Indenture of Rectification, Francis Hurley to Francis MacNamara, 1872', in Registry of Deeds, *Transcripts of memorials of deeds, conveyances and wills, 1708–1929*, Book 43, No. 68.

70 'Brewery, Townsend-Street', *General Advertiser for Dublin and All Ireland*, 11 November 1837. <https://www.britishnewspaperarchive.co.uk>

71 Liam has asked that only his last initial be used in order to maintain his anonymity.

72 Liam K., 'Who Brewed Ireland's First IPA?', *IrishBeerHistory* [website], 30 April 2020. <https://beerfoodtravel.blogspot.com/2020/04/who-brewed-irelands-first-ipa.html>

73 'Boal, Margaret', *1901 Census of Ireland*, National Archives of Ireland; 'Casey, Agnes', *1901 Census*, National Archives of Ireland. <https://census.nationalarchives.ie>

74 'Julia Hogan', *1901 Census of Ireland*, National Archives of Ireland. <https://census.nationalarchives.ie>

75 Alfred Barnard, 'Anchor Brewery', in *The Noted Breweries of Great Britain and Ireland*, Vol. II (London: Sir Joseph Causton & Sons, 1889), p. 378.

76 Alfred Barnard, 'St. James's Gate Brewery', in *The Noted Breweries of Great Britain and Ireland*, Vol. III (London: Sir Joseph Causton & Sons, 1890), p. 27.

77 Barnard, 'St. James's Gate Brewery', Vol. III, p. 6.

78 Ibid., pp. 34–5.

79 Ibid., p. 30.

80 Alfred Barnard, 'J. Arnott and Co. Limited', in *The Noted Breweries of Great Britain and Ireland*, Vol. IV (London: Sir Joseph Causton & Sons, 1891), p. 327.

81 Barnard, 'Cork Porter Brewery', in *Noted Breweries*, Vol. II, p. 353; Barnard, 'Mountjoy Brewery', in *Noted Breweries*, Vol. II, p. 387; Barnard, 'Ardee Street Brewery', in *Noted Breweries*, Vol. II, p. 363.

82 Barnard, 'Anchor Brewery', in *Noted Breweries*, Vol. II, p. 374.

83 Barnard, 'Cork Porter Brewery', in *Noted Breweries*, Vol. II, p. 354.

84 Ibid.

85 Barnard, 'St. James Gate Brewery', in *Noted Breweries*, Vol. III, p. 7.

86 Barnard, 'North Anne Street Brewery', in *Noted Breweries*, Vol. II, p. 402.

87 Barnard, 'Lady's Well Brewery', in *The Noted Breweries of Great Britain and Ireland*, Vol. I (London: Sir Joseph Causton & Sons), p. 547.

88 Barnard, 'North Anne Street Brewery', in *Noted Breweries*, Vol. II, p. 401.

89 Ibid.

90 Barnard, 'Phoenix Porter Brewery Co.', in *Noted Breweries*, Vol. I, p. 75.

91 Barnard, 'Anchor Brewery', in *Noted Breweries*, Vol. II, p. 379.

92 Ibid.

93 Barnard, 'J. Arnott and Co. Limited', in *Noted Breweries*, Vol. IV, p. 327.

94 Barnard, 'Lady's Well Brewery', in *Noted Breweries*, Vol. I, p. 547.

95 Barnard, 'Mountjoy Brewery', in *Noted Breweries*, Vol. II, p. 392.

96 Barnard, 'St James's Gate Brewery', in *Noted Breweries*, Vol. III, p. 36.

97 Barnard, 'Phoenix Brewery', in *Noted Breweries*, Vol. I, p. 78.

98 Barnard, 'St. James Gate Brewery', in *Noted Breweries*, Vol. III, p. 24.

99 Ibid.

100 Barnard, 'Ardee Street Brewery', in *Noted Breweries*, Vol. II, p. 368.

101 Barnard, 'North Anne Street Brewery', in *Noted Breweries*, Vol. II, p. 402.

102 Ibid.

103 Barnard, 'St. James Gate Brewery', in *Noted Breweries*, Vol. III, p. 27.

104 Barnard, 'North Anne Street Brewery', in *Noted Breweries*, Vol. II, p. 404.

105 Barnard, 'Anchor Brewery', in *Noted Breweries*, Vol. II, p. 376.

106 Barnard, 'Plunkett Brothers', in *Noted Breweries*, Vol. I, pp. 553–5.

107 'Committal of a Woman for Firing a Stackyard', *Taunton Courier and Western Advertiser*, 27 September 1865. <https://www.britishnewspaperarchive.co.uk>

108 'St Augustine's Petty Sessions', *Kentish Chronicle*, 16 September 1865. <https://www.britishnewspaperarchive.co.uk>

109 'An Irish Row at Maidstone', *Weekly Dispatch (London)*, 5 October 1862. <https://www.britishnewspaperarchive.co.uk>

110 Wade, *The Devil's in the Draught Lines*.

111 'Bridget Tobin', *1901 Census of Ireland*, National Archives of Ireland. <https://census.nationalarchives.ie>

112 'Mary Tew', *1911 Census of Ireland*, National Archives of Ireland; 'Margaret J. Cousins', *1911 Census of Ireland*, National Archives of Ireland. <https://census.nationalarchives.ie>

113 'Did Any of Your Family Work for Guinness?', *Guinness-Storehouse.com* [website], n.d. <https://www.guinness-storehouse.com/en/whats-hoppening/guinness-employee-family-archives>

INDEX

ACKNOWLEDGEMENTS

I want to begin by acknowledging someone without whom this book would not have been possible: my dog George. Many years ago, long before I put pen to paper, when I was just playing around with ideas, he went on long walks with me while we hammered out the details. He listened patiently as I weighed the pros and cons of including various items and sat by my side as this book came to life. He was the best coworker a woman could ever ask for and dutifully laid by me day in and day out, watching as I worked and always reminding me when it was time to take breaks for walkies or snacks. His untimely passing right as this book was completed will always leave a hole in my heart. And so this entire work is dedicated to him, for without him it simply would not exist. More to the point, he was a beloved member of our family whom we miss every day.

I want to acknowledge the tireless work of my editor and publisher, Kristin Jensen of Nine Bean Rows, whose support was invaluable to this book. I am so incredibly thankful for all her assistance and insight throughout this publication process. Her expertise and kindness have been without equal. I am beyond grateful to have worked with her on this publication.

I also want to thank Emma Marijewycz, whose guidance and expert knowledge have been so important in making this book possible. She has been instrumental in helping me to publicise this work, and for that I am very thankful.

I also want to extend a massive thank you to the designer, Matt Cox, for making this book look so beautiful. You made it all come together in such a fabulous way. Thank you to Tobias Hall for the stunning cover and illustrations, which bring this book to life. This book would not be what it is without your incredible artwork.

I would like to thank everyone at the Beer Culture Center, especially Liz Garibay, for all their support. I want to thank my PhD supervisor, Professor Terry Barry, for his guidance and expert knowledge over the years. I am immensely grateful for his friendship.

I also would like to acknowledge the support from all the wonderful women at Beer Ladies Podcast and the Ladies Craft Beer Society of Ireland. They are the best friends anyone could ever ask for and they have kept me going – I wouldn't have made it this far without them.

From further afield, I would like to thank my dear friend Elicia Gilreath, who has been a source of unwavering support and guidance throughout the years. And to my friend Emily, thank you so much for being such an amazing friend. I am incredibly grateful your advice.

Finally, I want to thank my family. To Paul, my husband, thank you for continuing to be my sounding board throughout this process. You have been my rock in times of stress and for that I am eternally grateful. To my parents, Bill and Bridget, thank you so much for your support ever since I was a little girl and decided I wanted to study medieval history. I want to thank my father for his encouragement and for always believing in me and to thank my mother, my lifelong editor who has been helping me polish my drafts since I was in elementary school. Thank you both so much. To my aunt and uncle, Beth and Bill, thank you for all your love and guidance over the years. It has been instrumental in helping me to finish this book.

NINE
BEAN
ROWS

Nine Bean Rows
23 Mountjoy Square
Dublin D01 E0F8
Ireland
@9beanrowsbooks
ninebeanrowsbooks.com

First published 2025
Text copyright © Dr Christina Wade, 2025
Illustrations copyright © Tobias Hall, 2025

ISBN: 978-1-7384795-2-8

Editor: Kristin Jensen
Cover and illustrations: Tobias Hall tobias-hall.co.uk
Designer: Matthew Cox newmanandeastwood.com
Proofreader: Susan Low susanlow.com
Indexer: Eileen O'Neill
Printed by L&C Printing Group, Poland

The FSC® label means that the paper used in this book has been
responsibly sourced.

ABOUT THE AUTHOR

DR CHRISTINA WADE IS A BEER HISTORIAN specialising in the hidden histories of the brewing trade, especially the role of women. She received her doctorate in History from Trinity College Dublin in 2017 and wrote *The Devil's in the Draught Lines: 1000 Years of Women in Britain's Beer History*, published in 2024 with CAMRA books.

In addition to her monograph, Wade has spent much of her time writing about women and beer history on her website *Braciatrix*, which was shortlisted for an Irish Food Writing Award in 2022, and has recently launched a Substack newsletter of the same name. A BJCP Certified Beer Judge, Wade is also the resident historian, audio editor and co-host of the *Beer Ladies Podcast*, which was recently featured in *Vinepair* and shortlisted in the podcast category for the 2023 Irish Food Writing Awards. Additionally, she founded the Ladies Craft Beer Society of Ireland in 2013, which has grown to over 1,400 members.

Besides her blog and podcast, Wade has written for *BEER Magazine*, *The Medieval Dublin Series*, *The Journal of Franco-Irish Studies*, *TheTaste.ie* and *Beoir Magazine*. She currently sits on the League of Historians at the Beer Culture Center and has spoken about her beer history research at their annual Beer Culture Summit. In addition, Wade has presented her work around the world at events like Electric Picnic, the International Medieval Congress, the Beverage Research Network Conference, the Women's International Beer Summit, Indie Beer Feast, Sheffield Beer Week, Friends of Medieval Dublin Lunchtime Lecture Series, the FemAle Beer Festival, Alltech Brews and Food Fair, BrewCon and the Killarney Beer Festival.